THE FEDERAL OCTOPUS

THE FEDERAL OCTOPUS

A prequel to the rise of an ever expanding federal
bureaucracy and our current constitutional crisis!

By

Sterling E. Edmunds

Edited and New Material by

Philip Espinosa and Mindi Espinosa

WhiteBoardDesign Publishing

Boulder

The Federal Octopus

Published 2010

Printed by Createspace.com in the United States of America

ISBN 1-45-377154-9

In Memory of

My Great-Grandfather

Sterling E. Edmunds

And

My Grand-Mother

Eugenia Edmunds Carver

- Philip Espinosa

Contents

THE FEDERAL OCTOPUS

A survey of the destruction of Constitutional government and of civil and economic liberty in the Unites States of America and the rise of an all-embracing federal bureaucratic despotism.

No political dreamer would ever be wild enough to think of breaking down the lines which separate the States and of compounding the American people into one common mass.

— John Marshall

Preface

My grandmother, Eugenia Edmunds Carver, gave a copy of this book to me when I was entering high school. It was written by her father, Sterling E. Edmunds. Little did I understand then the implications of the author's insights. Little did I connect his arguments to events that either took place or were continuing to take place. In fact, though I did look at the book, and expressed thanks to my grandmother, I did not really read it.

Thank goodness I discovered it later, still on my bookshelf, in the summer of 2009. I shared it with my wife, Mindi, and together we read and were amazed. It was as though we were reading a description of contemporary political events. We shared it with family members, and then were determined to share it with a broader audience.

Preface

I am not a politician, ex-politician, lawyer, community organizer, lobbyist, agitator or a member of any special interest group. I suspect I am much like you: An average American citizen – suddenly much more aware of and more concerned about the state of our great country.

Like so many others, I am conflicted about the promise and power and the peril posed by our federal government: the promise provided by the Constitution and the Bill of Rights protecting our rights and freedoms; the power gradually and consistently assumed by our government, that some claim impinge upon Constitutional promise; and, the peril we face with the erosion of individual liberties.

Like millions of Americans in 2009 / 2010, I am now unemployed. Like millions, I feel betrayed by the company for which I worked - which put company need ahead of many of its employees. A natural tendency is to look for some form of protection. Perhaps the federal government will protect us - where corporations did not. However, I am not willing to give up inalienable individual rights, loss of privacy or bear the burden of ever increasing taxes and long term debt in return for increasing federal powers in broad and sweeping ways.

It is my belief that our Constitution and Bill of Rights provide sufficient separation of powers, and allocation and protection of individual rights, which combine for a natural and balanced approach to the pursuit of life, liberty and happiness, as well as providing the framework for a civilized society. This framework also provides for protections against excesses and abuses without the need for any wholesale shift in the balance of powers or reallocation or minimization of private rights. During the 2009 / 2010 season of political debate, while all of us will most assuredly remember for a long time health care and stimulus debates, the mortgage crisis and the oil disaster in the Gulf, and the rise of independent political voice such as the Tea Party, I believe the cry of the people is demanding this balance be maintained and preserved. Whatever the cost.

In August of 2009, as I read The Federal Octopus, flipping through its pages, its relevancy to current issues astounded me. I was determined to make this work available to others. The author, Sterling E. Edmunds, Esq., is my great-grandfather on my mother's side. The copy of the book I held in my hands contained an inscription to me from my grandmother – daughter of this book's author. I read the book during the following week.

This book is a historical document, and speaks directly to the ever expanding powers and authorities assumed by the federal government, often times, claims the author, in violation of the limitations on federal authority as articulated in the Constitution and intended by its framers. Originally published in 1931, with a Third Edition published in 1933, in The Federal Octopus, I found the themes and concepts which are amazingly significant and relevant to us today. Consider this line from the introduction to the Third Edition –

"The march to federal autocracy has…been greatly accelerated, under the pretext of an 'economic emergency'…"

Are we not debating the role of government, its desire for expanded authorities, and implementation of new and broader programs? Are we not debating the potential loss of some individual rights, personal privacy, expanded public spending and increases in taxes in return for these new programs, and supposed protections, that are for our own good? Are not these dialogs being driven by various national emergencies? Sterling Edmunds, almost 80 years ago speaks to these same themes.

Yes, we want protection, assurances, and predictability; but, we also want to maintain our rights as promised and provided by the U. S. Constitution and the Bill of Rights. I believe the average American citizen is not willing to compromise individual rights, personal privacy, and freedom of choice by granting broader and deeper powers and authorities to the federal government when faced with urgent or emergency situations. The structure of our government and the separation of powers, without the need to further expand federal authorities, are sufficient to govern, and are sufficient to respond to any national internal or external emergency. Consider that the Constitution was drafted during a time of great emergency, and, nonetheless, its framers fully understood and implemented a governmental structure based on "limitations".

I believe the greatest threat to the constitutional promise has been, and continues to be, the expansion of federal power, and the minimization of State and local authority, and limitations of individual rights. While this approach may be acceptable in other parts of the world by other people, it was not the vision or the intended legacy of our forefathers. Our legacy is specifically based on the concept of limitation of federal power.

What struck me was the historical context – the push and pull between federal bureaucracy and constitutionally provided individual rights – both in 1933 and now. Economic emergency is not new. A population seeking certainty is not new. Political maneuvering is not new. Out of control spending, interventional programs, abuse of power, graft, waste, and politics at the expense of the citizen is not new.

Preface

The voices of average American citizens rising spontaneously, demanding balance, is also not new.

This book is provided as a way to help as many Americans as possible understand the balance within a broader historical context. Edmund Burke, British statesman and philosopher (1729 – 1797) said – "Those who don't know history are destined to repeat it."

The words of Sterling E. Edmunds come to us from the early 1900's – his words are simultaneously historical, relevant and prophetic for us almost 80 years later. He does not write about philosophical concepts, abstract forms of governance or archaic political matters. He writes about the federal government of the United States of America, the U. S. Constitution and the Bill of Rights. I may have overused this word, but his writing is "relevant". A broad awareness of our nation's immediate history can do nothing but help the current debate.

As our national debates continue over health care, the economic crisis, federal spending, oil spills and other important topics, let us keep in mind that Sterling E. Edmunds would challenge us to a broader debate – that of the balance between federal power and individual rights.

Sterling Edmunds would be proud to know that his words might have had some small part to play in the current political dialog.

Philip Espinosa
Great Grandson of Sterling E. Edmunds
Boulder, Colorado
August 2010

www.thefederaloctopus.com

Prologue

In the very first of those celebrated lectures, delivered at Oxford nearly two hundred years ago, and preserved in the Commentaries on the Laws of England, Sir William Blackstone tells us that on the continent of Europe no gentleman thinks his education is completed until he has attended a course of lectures on the institutes of Justinian and the local constitutions of his native soil; and that, in the northern part of England, at least, it is difficult to meet with a person of liberal education who has not a competent knowledge in that science which is the guardian of his rights and the rule of his civil conduct.

And it is a significant fact that the Americans, from the period of their first settlement in this country, felt the same necessity for and deep interest in a knowledge of the law. As early as 1682, the first General Assembly of Pennsylvania, held at Chester, enacted as one of the provisions of the Great Law, a requirement that the laws be taught in the schools of the province and territories. But for a widespread knowledge of the laws, and the rights they were instituted to protect, among our ancestors, it is safe to say that their protest against the tyranny practiced upon them by the government of George III, would never have become articulate, and that there would have been no Constitution of the United States.

One who reads Elliot's Debates on the Federal Constitution, which took place in conventions called in the thirteen States, to accept or reject the Constitution, is filled with admiration for the keen analyses and clear expositions of this organic act, made by delegates who were not lawyers, but gentlemen farmers. Thus, no man in the Virginia Constitutional Convention of 1788, not Patrick Henry himself, had a more profound understanding of the fundamentals of free government or indicated more unerringly the points of danger in the new Constitution, than George Mason.

A knowledge of law and government is a knowledge of one's personal and civil rights, in relation to governmental power. Surely, no other can be more important. A citizen without knowledge of the one can have no intelligent appreciation of the other; and when government invades his rights he can only nurture a vague and confused resentment. But when government assaults the rights of a citizen who has a clear conception of what they consist in, it arouses in him one of the purest and most self-sacrificing emotions of which man is capable. This is because right, our rights, in the sense of justice, is the condition of man's moral existence; and as Von Jhering tells us, in The Struggle for Law, any wound inflicted upon it produces a sense of moral pain, akin to physical pain that follows a physical blow. History gives many accounts of the martyrdom of such persons.

Since the closing decades of last century there has been a growing neglect of the study of the law and legal philosophy, in the United States, among the educated classes. In spite of the tremendous sums now expended, publicly and privately, on education, it may be fairly affirmed that there has never been a period in our history when ignorance of an indifference to American fundamentals of government and law have been so widespread.

Though what is termed "civics" is commonly taught in our public schools, it gives to students not the remotest hint that government and liberty are essentially in a relation of antagonism, and that the aim of political science is to seek for the safest methods of reconciliation; the inherent quality in governmental power to expand and the necessity of vigilance in the citizen to check it, before oppressions come upon him, are not so much as intimated. On the contrary, as so-called civics is taught, it glorifies government, inculcates respect and submission, totally unfitting this generation for courageous thinking and a manly defense of the greatest of God's blessings — freedom. And these congenial conditions are not unrelated to the rapid advance of arbitrary power over the American people in recent years.

The long struggle for human liberty is essentially a battle against governmental power to acquire and maintain certain individual rights, for liberty is nothing but the sum of these rights. Among them the most important is the right of acquisition and conservation, against the unlimited claims of governmental power. As Lecky observes, in his Democracy and Liberty, the very essence of despotism is the claim of the supreme power of government over the property of its citizens. From the dawn of civilization this claim has been asserted by Asiatic and Oriental despots, and later, in Europe, by monarchs by divine right; and wherever it was made effective man was degraded to the level of a beast.

Where a government asserts an unlimited power to dispose of the property of its citizens, it equally invades the right of bequest, which rests upon one of the deepest instincts of human nature. The most stimulating factor in human progress is the desire in man to acquire and conserve for the benefit of those who are to follow him. Who will toil without the hope of protection in the rewards of his toil?

Prologue

These rights were first vindicated to mankind on a large scale in the founding of the free republic of the United States of America. The founders of our government, witnessing spoliation of peoples everywhere on the globe, erected in the federal Constitution all of the barriers they could devise out of experience against assault upon the essential rights of liberty. It limited the taxing power and required it, when used, to be applied uniformly; it did not bestow the power to tax inheritances; it required trial by a jury of one's fellow citizens in all criminal prosecutions; it guaranteed free speech and free press; it provided for a Militia in each State to be used, in the last resort, against an oppressive federal government; it forbade search of a citizen's home save upon a warrant issued upon probable cause; it denied to the federal government the right to begin a criminal prosecution save upon an indictment found by a grand jury of one's fellow citizens; it denied the power of government to try a citizen twice for the same offence; it denied the government power to deprive a citizen of his life or liberty without a jury trial, or of his property without just compensation; it required all trials to be public, the accused to be confronted with witnesses against him, with compulsory process for obtaining his own witnesses; it forbade excessive bail and excessive fines and cruel punishments; and finally it declared that all powers not delegated to the federal government in the written enumeration were retained and reserved by the people.

All of these bulwarks against the assaults of tyrannical power are now either breached or completely leveled in the United States, and the once free citizen finds himself in subjection to unlimited power almost as fully as was his victimized ancestor of other centuries.

The form of the old order remains to deceive us, the substance is gone. In the place of our peculiar dual system of free government, founded by the fathers to preserve their newly-won liberty to them and to their posterity forever — with the federal government bound down under strictly limited powers, by the "chains" of the Constitution, and the people in their States retaining in themselves all other powers, and governing themselves as autonomous members of the Union in all domestic concerns — we observe that, through three decades of progressive usurpation, the "chains" of the Constitution have been broken and the powers of the federal government have become practically absolute; that, like a giant octopus at Washington, it has wormed its numberless tentacles around every city and every county, around every hamlet and every home in the land, crushing out civil liberty and self-government, and, through the taxing suckers of its ugly prototype, draining the life from all property, from all trade and from all industry.

This volume is a survey of the steps and processes by which the noblest and most promising experiment in self-government ever attempted by man, has been thus betrayed; and it points to means of possible self-rescue of the American people from impending servitude.

Sterling E. Edmunds
St. Louis, Mo.
March 26, 1932

Third Edition

Well knowing, from the lessons of history, the innate and insatiable greed of governmental power, and its unsleeping purpose to break through the most solemnly-imposed limitations; and understanding the political truism, that as governmental power increases the liberty of the citizen must correspondingly diminish; seeing government clearly, as mere groups of men, like other men, who will violate the rights of other men, when there is a strong incentive, our forefathers founded this government as a constitutional one, of limited and enumerated powers, to insure the blessings of liberty to themselves, and to us, their posterity, and to those who shall come after us.

— Sterling E. Edmunds, 1933

When the first edition of this volume appeared, in the spring of 1932, its author hoped that it might arouse his fellow-citizens to arrest the usurpations of power by their political servants in Washington, before these servants became masters over their lives, their liberty and their property.

That hope has been disappointed.

The march to federal autocracy has not only not been halted, it has been greatly accelerated, under the pretext of an "economic emergency"; and, within three months, from March 9 to June 12, 1933, we find that the 73rd Congress, in special session, has confounded the three co-ordinate and co-equal branches of our government, with their historic checks and balances, and has

Third Edition

assumed to confer upon the Executive vast and irresponsible powers which it did not possess and which it was constitutionally incompetent to bestow.

Let none be deceived by the plea that the exercise of these despotic powers is limited to two or three years. All governments reach out to seize power; no government ever voluntarily relinquished it.

Economic recovery will come, not because of, but in spite of, federal dictatorship; such is the patience and industry of man, even under oppression; and when it comes, our rulers will know how to employ it in an effort to make permanent this autocratic rule set up in contempt of the limitations of the Constitution of the United States.

Sterling E. Edmunds
Baldwin, Mich.
October 15, 1933

"It would be a dangerous delusion were a confidence in the men of our choice to silence our fears for the safety of our rights. Confidence is everywhere the parent of despotism; free government is founded in jealousy, not in confidence. It is jealousy, and not confidence, which prescribes limited constitutions, to bind down those whom we are obliged to trust with power. Our Constitution has accordingly fixed the limits to which, and no further, our confidence may go. In questions of power, then, let no more be heard of confidence in man, but bind him down from mischief by the chains of the Constitution."

— Thomas Jefferson, 1798

Every principle of law which has protected our rights as freemen anywhere had first to be wrung from governmental power that denied it, sometimes in struggles lasting for centuries. We are the heirs of those who manfully strove and won for us these principles that protect the dignity and worth of the individual, but we have permitted a filching of the heritage.

— Sterling E. Edmunds, 1940

To take a single step beyond the boundaries specifically drawn around the powers of Congress is to take possession of a boundless field of power no longer susceptible of any definition.

— Thomas Jefferson, 1791

Introduction

As an average citizen, I found the themes and concepts in this book to be extraordinary. As the author states in his Prologue, this book is a survey of the "steps and processes by which the noblest and most promising experiment in self-government ever attempted by man, has been thus betrayed". A litany of events which transpired in the late 1800's through the early-1930's is chronicled.

Why do we care about this history?

Edmund Burke eloquently stated that "Those who don't know history are destined to repeat it." We might also state that those who don't know history are destined to let others take advantage of them; or, if we don't know history we fail to learn from the lessons of our predecessors. No matter how stated, we run the risk of losing that for which our forefathers fought and died.

Our form of government is based on the U. S. Constitution, and while I am not a constitutional scholar, I do understand that a founding principle is "government of the people, for the people, by the people." It is because of this that I feel qualified to comment. I, like you, am one of the people. Together we are "the government". As a citizen I question, that while the structure of our constitutional system remains, what of the substance? This question is at the core of the history presented in this book.

Consider the following:

Introduction

Long ago the old rule of governmental non-interference was outlived. ...it has been perfectly obvious that the government of every great industrial nation must take notice of the conditions under which men live and work and must control those conditions in the national interest.

Year after year, however, we refused to make the increasingly necessary decision. When times were good we said it was dangerous to interfere. When times were lean we said it was also dangerous to interfere.

All this nonsense was forgotten the day [the President] was inaugurated. ...the new President accepted responsibility for improving conditions then so unsatisfactory to everybody.

Rapidly a great series of revolutionary measures were proposed and as swiftly adopted by Congress. Each law was specifically proposed to deal with some phase of the emergency we confronted. Taken together, these emergency statutes embodied a new philosophy of government. Laissez-faireism was abandoned. Intelligent control was established.

...

Quietly, peacefully, in good temper we have been led. We have had our revolution and we like it.

While the preceding passage is from a 1933 Collier's editorial (Collier's, September 23, 1933; see page 231) it is remarkable in its applicability to current events. It also paraphrases the sentiment which caused Sterling Edmunds such concern; he writes: "...understanding that as governmental power increases the liberty of the citizen must correspondingly diminish..."

Introduction

A similar concern was voiced by former President Ronald Reagan in his 1989 farewell address:

> I hope we once again have reminded people that man is not free unless government is limited. There's a clear cause and effect here that is as neat and predictable as a law of physics: As government expands, liberty contracts.

A short review of the Second Edition, as published in the New York Times (May 16, 1932), reports:

> The alarming growth of bureaucracy in the United States in the past thirty years, described by the author as the "Federal Octopus," the title of the work, is traced in a book by Sterling E. Edmunds, a St. Louis lawyer. Mr. Edmunds declares that while the form of the American system of government, as laid down in the Constitution, remains, "the substance is gone."
>
> He holds the powers of the Federal government have become practically absolute and that "like a giant octopus at Washington, it has wormed its numberless tentacles around every city and county, around every hamlet and every home in the land, crushing out civil liberty and self-government, and, through the taxing suckers of its ugly prototype, draining the life from all property, from all trade and from all industry."
>
> Mr. Edmunds suggests a program of constitutional revision, including repeal of the Eighteenth Amendment, and of governmental readjustment to restore the old balance of the Constitution and curb the growing bureaucracy.

While the author prescribes a program to address his view of constitutional concerns, as it applies today, the specifics of the revision are less important than his overriding themes – preserving constitutional protections; vigorously questioning erosion of those constitutional protections; and, understanding that federal consolidation, even for benign purpose, carries tremendous risk.

Through the chronicling of example after example, this book is a cry for vigilance.

Mr. Edmunds writes about our first President, George Washington:

> When Washington retired from the Presidency, in 1797, his Farewell Address to his fellow citizens reveals plainly enough that he was not over confident that our written limited Constitution would be adequate to restrain the ambition of public men, unless the citizens themselves were vigilant . . .

The original eight chapters of The Federal Octopus are presented, with minor editorial changes; full texts of our U. S. Constitution, Bill of Rights and Declaration of Independence are also presented. These serve as good references, since much of Mr. Edmund's claims are directed to, what in his day were, present day violations of these founding documents. Additional, contextual information is provided which helps add a framework to the narrative – specifically, with respect to cost of living, and the numerous references to dollar amounts.

This book is dedicated to our efforts to keep history alive and to better understand its connection to the current day.

Philip Espinosa
Boulder, Colorado
August 2010

Chapter 1 –
Three Decades of Change

For more than a hundred years our federal government was acknowledged to be one of limited powers, and did not tempt the innate ambition of officials. Today there is constant augmentation of power.

Any American citizen who was living in the closing years of the last century will recall that he was then hardly conscious of the existence of a federal government at Washington, so infrequent were his contacts with its very few local representatives. In the rural sections the postmaster in the neighboring town was the sole federal agent. In the larger cities there were the federal judge, the marshal and a few other officials, who seemed to be immured the day long in the gloomy stone federal building, which also housed the Post Office. These were the only visible symbols of that distant government in Washington, which quietly carried on our circumscribed relations with foreign governments, and unobtrusively but effectively enforced a simple body of general law, to be found in the United States Statutes, enacted in pursuance of the limited, enumerated powers confided to Congress by the Constitution over strictly national concerns.

The federal courts had only a very limited criminal jurisdiction, embracing principally counterfeiting and violations of the postal and national banking laws. Crime in all of its other phases was assumed to be reserved by the Tenth Amendment to the jurisdiction of our State courts. The federal courts were thus comparatively free to devote their time to the consideration of private rights under the great guarantees in our Bill of Rights and to controversies between citizens of different States.

There were no visible federal taxes, save those imposed upon liquor and tobacco; practically the whole of the federal revenue was derived from duties on imports, imposts and excises, which were required by the Constitution to be uniform, throughout the United States, and which the citizen paid indirectly and unknowingly. Congress had the constitutional power to levy direct taxes but from the time of its adoption the Constitution required all such direct taxes to be apportioned to the States according to population; and, as direct taxes would thus touch every citizen, it was not deemed prudent by Congress to impose these taxes save in emergencies. Economy in the federal expenditures was the rule from necessity, rather than risk the displeasure of the great masses of our people by imposing unnecessary burdens upon them.

As the powers of the federal government were limited by the federal Constitution, so, too, were the powers of our State governments limited by like State Constitutions; and State government operated with the same mildness, exacting little from the citizen beyond his general property tax and the licensing of certain lines of business.

Our American system was verifying the argument of Madison in the Federalist, for the adoption of the Constitution, when he wrote:

> The powers delegated by the proposed Constitution to the federal government are few and defined. Those which are to remain in the State governments are numerous and

indefinite. The former will be exercised principally on external objects, as war, peace, negotiation and foreign commerce, with which last the power of taxation will, for the most part, be connected. The powers reserved to the several States will extend to all the objects which, in the ordinary course of affairs, concern the lives, liberties and properties of the people, and the internal order, improvement and prosperity of the State.

Our dual system of government — the federal caring for foreign relations under a restricting Monroe Doctrine and for strictly national concerns, and the States, self-governing, caring for all domestic concerns — functioned with the balance and absence of friction of a piece of perfect mechanism. Each acknowledged the full competence of the other in its constitutional field and each was absorbed in its own proper duties. The best hopes of those who drafted our constitutional system of free government had been fulfilled for more than a century, with the exception of a brief period during the Civil War. It had been and was being demonstrated that man could be governed other than by kings and emperors; that, in fact, he could govern himself, safe even against the oppressions of a majority.

But what a change has come upon us in the brief span of thirty years!

The rural sections no longer have the postmaster as the lone federal official in their midst; they are now overrun with all manner of agents sent out by the ten great executive departments and by scores of bureaus in Washington to instruct, direct and mould the farming population according to certain bureaucratic standards of morals, education, health, agriculture — matters clearly outside of the constitutional delegation of power to the federal government.

These federal agents are not only in the farmer's fields, instructing him in how to grow crops and raise cattle; they are also in his home teaching his wife how to rear her children; and they are teaching the children how to be homemakers and model citizens in federally-directed organizations known as 4-H clubs — the four H's standing for Head, Heart, Health and Hand. The more than 5,000 extension agents of the Department of Agriculture alone engaged in these activities, have thus far enrolled as wards of the federal government more than three quarters of a million rural children in these clubs. If Congress will furnish the money — and that is what the Department of Agriculture is striving for — the ten million or more rural children not yet enrolled will be similarly reduced to federal wardship.

There may be some merit in this governmental direction and entertainment of the children of the countryside, but it is in defiance of the constitutional apportionment of powers, with its design to preserve local self-government in the States.

Not only is the federal government taking over the guidance of the rural child population but, through propaganda and the generous misuse of taxpayers' money, it is seeking to reduce all persons engaged in agricultural marketing, including livestock and dairying, to servitude in socialized, monopolistic groups, known as cooperatives, under governmental tutelage and control.

If the farmer does not care to submit to this governmental control, if he wishes to preserve his independence — as 90 per cent of them do at the present time — he cannot ship his produce, his livestock or his milk into another State save upon a license granted in the good pleasure of the Secretary of Agriculture, which license the Secretary may revoke as he sees fit. Being thus licensed to earn his living the farmer must take care to conform to the great body of regulations and standards which that busy department has established.

In the cities, we find new federal buildings, larger and handsomer than anything existing in that earlier self-reliant period, housing scores of federal boards, bureaus and commissions, the very names of which are unintelligible to the ordinary citizen, who is now summoned in increasing numbers for interrogation. Agents, inspectors, investigators, secret service men, under-cover men, hurry along the corridors to their waiting automobiles — many of them freshly confiscated from offending citizens — to track down some petty violator of some provision of an infinite body of new-fangled federal law. This law, which is ground out daily and may be altered overnight, is not statutory acts of Congress which we may find in the United States Code Annotated; it is made up of rules and regulations promulgated by the Secretaries of the ten great federal departments, and by hundreds of federal boards, bureaus and commissions, to which Congress has delegated its power to legislate, even to the extent of enacting criminal laws.

And, in keeping with an enormously expanded criminal jurisdiction, of which the State courts have been robbed, we have new and larger and more sanitary federal prisons to harbor new thousands of citizens convicted of various newly-created federal crimes.

It is no longer possible in one district for a single judge to handle all of the judicial business, and now there are divisions, with additional judges. All seem to have fallen in with the federal government's zeal to discipline and compel conformity in the citizen to its multifarious new policies of human regimentation. Every morning these courts are filled with the grist ground out by the ceaseless energy of the federal bureaus and their agents. Being charged with crime, these persons are entitled, whether they know it or not, to trial by jury, instead of summary sentence. But it is a physical impossibility, even with our enlarged number of federal district courts, to accord this right to all of them; there are too many — about 70,000 a year. The dockets would never be cleared if all availed themselves of this tedious process. Hence has grown up a practice of offering the accused the alternative of a plea of guilty to a lesser offense, or prosecution before a jury where conviction would mean an excessive fine and long imprisonment. And so thousands of cases are swept from the dockets under plea of "guilty," with the right of trial by jury thus unfairly defeated.

In other days the American citizen accused of crime could be assured of the privileges of "the law of the land," or as it is also termed "due process of law," in his defense. It is inconceivable in that day that crime could have been punished without trial by jury, or under a law enacted, not by the legislature, but by a mere administrative board. Nor would the courts of that earlier day have considered it constitutionally possible for Congress to delegate its legislative power to an administrative agency; for the legislative power was confided by the Constitution to Congress alone as one of the three distinct coordinate branches of government.

Visitorial and inquisitorial powers were unknown to the federal government of three decades ago. The very idea of them was abhorrent to the citizen. They were well-known as the instruments of arbitrary action as practiced upon the peoples of Europe by the old world despotisms. Today they are the settled practices of numerous federal departments, boards and bureaus, backed by a power to intimidate and crush the citizen through capricious civil and criminal prosecution. Investigators of one kind or another now obtrude themselves into the citizen's private office whenever they please and demand, upon penalty for disobedience, his most intimate and personal books and papers. The Fourth Amendment against unreasonable search no longer avails, as it once did, to prevent it. In the Income Tax Bureau the inquisitorial powers of its agents are so extensive and drastic, and the Regulations — bureau-made laws — to which the income taxpayers must conform, are so complex and difficult to ascertain that the less than two per cent of our citizens compelled to pay this tax can safely file a return only after it has been scrutinized by a lawyer. It has been said with truth, that every citizen filing such return thereby initiates a potential civil or criminal suit in which he may be the victim.

Of the Regulations issued by the Income Tax Bureau, with the force of law, it was revealed by the Couzens investigation in 1926, that 17,143 of them were actually secret and unknown outside of the Treasury Department. It can be readily seen that under such law, containing all manners of penalties and lodging in an administrative officer the widest discretionary authority, the power of an unscrupulous official to reward his friends and to destroy his enemies is here complete.

Much of this usurpation of power in the States by the federal government got its footing through the policy of "federal aid," an offer by Congress of public money for certain objects if the States themselves would appropriate like or other sums. Invariably these acts have elevated the federal department or bureau, having authority to allocate the money, to a position of dominance in the particular field. In 1930 taxpayers' money to the amount of $135,256,331.82 was thus spent in the States by the departments of Agriculture, Interior, Labor, Navy, Treasury, the Board of Vocational Education and the Federal Power Commission. Other millions, of course, are squandered on salaries of federal agents, busying themselves with State concerns, and as gifts, such as

$15,490,127 that went to perpetuate the Interior Department's control over the State Agricultural Colleges, the $4,335,000 for the continued control of our State agricultural experiment stations by the Secretary of Agriculture, and the $45,000,000 relief for farmers whose crops were damaged by "drought and hail" in 1930, with $200,000,000 additional in 1932.

Then we have the most generous lending of taxpayers' money to favored classes, which may or may not come back, as in the case of the Federal Farm Loan Board. The loans turn out frequently to be mere gifts. It is of interest to note that on December 23, 1931, the Farm Loan Board Commissioner, in informing a Senate Committee that additional money was needed — and he obtained $125,000,000 — disclosed that the Federal Farm loans in the States then amounted to $1,171,000,000, of which $275,400,000 were in default. In reply to the charge of one of the Senators that the Farm Loan Board had been "harsh" in foreclosures, the commissioner justified his denial by asserting that foreclosures had been proceeded with in only about one-fifth of one per cent of the delinquencies. This is, in effect, a moratorium.

In all of our States one will find swarms of federal officials engaged in the most varied work with which the federal government has not the slightest constitutional concern, such as agricultural education, vocational education, vocational rehabilitation, education in home economics, maintenance of agricultural colleges, military training in high schools and colleges, eradication of tuberculosis in cattle, hog cholera, promotion of forestry, plant diseases, soils, free employment service, study of ground waters, forest fire protection, maternity and child welfare, moving picture entertainment, and hundreds of others, involving expenditures, in some cases, four or five times the State or local outlay. These activities are attaching to the Federal government a vast and growing army of salaried supporters, who are no longer concerned with their highly irregular character and who become interested advocates of this march toward consolidation of the forty-eight States into a single empire ruled by decree from Washington.

Many of these activities are in themselves laudable. But those who approve them forget that, save where they may be justified under the interstate commerce clause or by some other delegated power, they are confided by the constitutional division of powers exclusively to the States; that, in the main, they constitute a wasteful duplication of services, tending always to subordinate the States to federal administrative officials; that they discourage self-reliance, initiative and enterprise, and that in undermining local self-government they are breaking down the safest bulwark in our system against a consolidated federal despotism.

Following this same course of transferring all power to Washington, is the nationalization of our State Militia by the passage of the so-called National Defense Act of 1916. By that act these distinct and constitutionally declared State military units were incorporated into the federal military machine, as the National Guard, placed in federal pay and under a federal oath, under the War Department's own Militia Bureau. The State Militia was designed as essentially State military organizations, reserved to them for the openly admitted purpose, among others, of being used, in the last resort, against the federal government itself. This appears plainly in the arguments of Madison and Hamilton in the Federalist when the Constitution was pending before the State conventions. It was affirmed in the halls of Congress in 1812 when it was proposed to draft certain numbers of the State Militia into the federal service for use in Canada. Cyrus King, of Massachusetts, opposing the proposed draft, declared:

> I again repeat, sir, that the Militia of each State are an independent, organized and armed corps, with an independent commander over each; that you must approach them as such; and I will add that if you attempt to do it in any other manner you will be received at the point of the bayonet. * * * Such arbitrary plans can only be calculated to destroy the Militia System, and, of course, the sovereignty of the States.

In the organization of our constitutional system there was a sharp separation and segregation of the three main divisions, the executive, the legislative and the judicial, in recognition of Alexander Hamilton's truism that the consolidation of these powers in a single body "is the essential definition of despotism." And in this separation our judicial branch, with the Supreme Court at its head, was designedly instituted to guard the boundaries of the powers delegated, and to declare void and of no effect any encroachment of one branch upon another, as well as any encroachment of the federal or State governments beyond their constitutionally limited spheres.

The history of the first century of service of the Supreme Court is one of watchful and zealous guardianship of the Constitution, except for a brief period during the Adams administration. But from the beginning of this century, the Supreme Court has lent its sanction to a vast body of legislation by Congress that has introduced the most far-reaching and revolutionary changes. These include the very ominous practice on the part of Congress to delegate its power to make laws to federal agents, boards, bureaus and commissions, with the power to sit in judgment upon these bureau-made laws. It has upheld the claim of Congress of its right to release itself from the limitations of the Constitution in the rule of alien peoples, and to withhold the protection of constitutional guarantees, as though Congress, a creature of the Constitution, were superior to its creator. It has sanctioned as valid or declined to pass upon many assertions of federal power for which there appears no warrant in the constitutional enumeration, which entail vast expenditures of public money.

The change taking place seems consciously or unconsciously to contemplate the destruction of our dual constitutional system, with its general and uniform law and ordinary courts, and with its self-governing States, and the erection in its stead of a single centralized federal power seated in Washington and subjecting us to clerk-made law and administrative judges, to the complete subversion of what we have come to know and revere as "the law of the land" or "due process of law." These historic terms imply the rule of law as distinguished from arbitrariness or caprice. They embrace a great variety of inhibitions, written and unwritten, limiting the action of executive, legislative and judicial power in the protection of the moral dignity of the free man. They come down to us as accretions of immunities against governmental power in numerous bills and petitions of rights of our English political ancestors, but further developed and elaborated by the founders of our own government.

"The law of the land", among other things, is that general and uniform law, applicable to all, which is found in our statute books, which the citizen is presumed to know and which is enforced in the ordinary courts of the land. Side by side with this, we have recently become aware of the existence of an immense body of rules and regulations promulgated by federal departments and bureaus, with the force of law, which can be found in no statute book and which is enforced, not in a court of law, but before the very department or bureau which created it. The department or bureau thus becomes legislator, judge and executioner, contrary to one of our most fundamental concepts of justice and "the law of the land."

So numerous are these federal administrative agencies, so extensive is their power to vex and even destroy liberty and property, trade and industry, by restrictions and prohibitive requirements, that only an army of lawyers, maintained at great expense in Washington by those engaged in private commerce and industry, now makes it possible for them to carry on. The great railroad industry, in the course of twenty-five years of progressive regulation and restriction, has been brought to the verge of ruin, where the only hope of continued operation may lie in the vicious alternative of federal ownership and operation, with more than a million and a quarter new names added to the federal tax-consuming list.

The great administrative departments and most of the boards, bureaus and commissions — nearly all occupying new huge stone palaces in Washington — have their own tribunals before whom their victims are summoned. Not just any lawyer may appear before them in behalf of the distressed citizen; there is no constitutional right to practice before these administrative courts, according to a recent federal district court decision; it is a privilege which the department or board may grant or withhold. The lawyer who would practice before them must first make formal application for enrollment and submit to scrutiny. Slowly but steadily, with the augmentation of federal administrative power, these administrative courts are absorbing the judicial business of the country.

The excuse for the multiplication of these federal agencies is that the great social and industrial revolution of the last half century and the many demands made upon Congress by the increasing complexity of human activities would overwhelm Congress if it could not create administrative and other agencies and delegate to them powers adequate to their creation. And the Supreme Court, falling in with this supposed justification, declares that such delegations of power to issue rules with the force of law, are not really delegations of legislative power, but are instances of "a mere executive duty to effectuate a legislative policy." Yet Chief Justice Hughes, in a recent address before the Association of Practitioners before the Interstate Commerce Commission, said very frankly:

> The making of regulations is, of course, essentially legislative in character, for they set forth what the citizen may or may not do.

It may be expected that from now on the Supreme Court will cease to deny that the power to make regulations with the force of law is a power to exercise delegated legislative authority, as it has for three decades, in sanctioning the development of our ubiquitous federal bureaucracy.

It was declared by Congressman Joseph T. Deal of Virginia in the House of Representatives, on December 10, 1927, that "by the 85 departments, bureaus, boards and commissions of the federal government, to which Congress has abdicated its power to make rules and regulations", there have been promulgated 100,000 or more laws "all carrying penalties upon American citizens for violations." And, he added, many of them are "unwritten and unpublished, issued by men unknown to the taxpayer, some under civil service, who cannot be reached by the voter." Yet another authority has asserted that between March, 1901 and March, 1929, no less than 492 federal bureaus, boards, commissions and like administrative agencies, were created by Congress to rob the citizen of his ordinary law and his ordinary courts, while eating more voraciously of his taxes.

It is a maxim of our jurisprudence that ignorance of the law excuses no one; but that maxim was evolved over a period of ages when our law was easily discoverable, if not known, in our statute books. The rule becomes preposterous, when law may be ground out in a daily torrent by administrative agencies which may be under no duty even to publish the same. Some years ago Congress authorized the publication of all administrative rules and regulations, but, as new ones are issued daily, the volume speedily became obsolete. Today one may learn what this law consists of, and what his duties are under it, only by employing a Washington lawyer, experienced in departmental practice.

The excuse for the existing disfigurement of our constitutional system, that the great social and industrial revolution of recent times and the growing complexity of human activities have compelled the federal government to rely upon bureaus and boards to effectuate its policies, is no justification for the reintroduction of the despotic practices of the Tudors and the Stuarts, under a rule of departmental clerks. The truth is that the sphere and functions of government have been expanded in response to unchecked ambition and the love of power and its emoluments in our federal rulers. We have been told by government that it possesses wisdom far superior to that among the governed, and that it also possesses the power of magic, the power to cure all ills and to bestow happiness; and we have come to believe it, while indulging government in the most extravagant and dangerous excursions outside of its constitutional enumeration of powers.

The results, which anyone familiar with European history might have foreseen, have not made for our happiness, but for our misery.

Particularly has it weakened our sense of self-reliance, destroyed initiative, strangled commerce and industry by seeking to force them out of normal channels, and left us groaning under taxation, which, though maintained at war-rates, is not yet heavy enough to meet huge deficits.

Actually, government is made up of fallible men, having all of the weaknesses of other men but with greater temptation; and as a rule, they are inferior in character and abilities to the leaders in private life in our various States. The public service, as every one knows, is recruited to a large extent from among men who have either failed or lack the energy to seek to earn a living by private industry and private effort.

Private industry, in whatever period of ruthlessness we may cite, has never been afflicted with the gross frauds and corruption which characterize our public federal service, in such instances as the Teapot Dome Scandal, in the graft in the leasing of the Post Office sites, in the Veterans' Bureau, in the sale of public offices. In attempted Prohibition enforcement corruption was so widespread as to induce a practice of quiet dismissal of bribe-takers, with no prosecution, for fear of bringing the whole policy into the universal contempt that it deserved; and this, in violation of the United States Criminal Code, which requires prosecution.

Government everywhere and at all times is reaching out for power — which means emoluments, prestige, the satisfaction of pride to those who hold the power. The knowledge of this truth was what prompted the founders of our government to bind it down under a limiting written Constitution. Within the last thirty years it has by its own action set aside these limitations and now asserts a power that is unlimited.

It is significant, and not unrelated to the extension of government everywhere that the last half century has been a period of stupendous increase in private wealth. Governments, composed of men possessing authority, have not been insensible to this development, nor have they been idle in their purpose to share in this increase. And various new laws of taxation have been devised to accomplish that purpose, which have repudiated the old and settled principles of equality and uniformity and "no taxation without representation," and substituted "ability to pay." No doctrine could be more congenial to those possessing an unlimited power to tax.

Hence almost everywhere we see wealth being despoiled under what is termed a "graduated income tax", the gradations based upon no criterion save the desires of those wielding the taxing power. It takes on a rising scale, according to the wealth possessed. And a new philosophy — the duty of the citizen to pay in proportion to his wealth — has replaced the only just and intelligible rule heretofore accepted, namely, the taxation of all property of the same class on the same rate of computation. That is the only rule which contains any restraint against the ultimate pillage of the industrious minority by mere exempted numbers.

Progressive taxation is necessarily arbitrary taxation since there is nothing to prevent the most confiscatory rates, save the wishes of the benefiting office-holders themselves, who, in the United States, now have unlimited access to the wealth of the citizens — made possible by the adoption of the Sixteenth Amendment in 1913. And with that power the multiplication of dangerous federal governmental activities, with a constantly expanding office-holding class, became inevitable. Attempting all things in the name of the people and scattering public moneys with a lavish hand among private groups and classes, the federal government has very generally come to be accepted at its own estimate, as a sort of earthly Providence, to whom all who are heavy laden may turn for succor. Not the old wholesome distrust of power which kept us a free people, but confidence and trust in power is our universal weakness, leading us on to destruction.

Evil for evil, a good despotism in a country at all advanced in civilization is more noxious than a bad one, for it is more relaxing and enervating to the thoughts, feelings and energies of the people. There is always hope that a bad one may provoke its own overthrow.

— John Stuart Mill

Chapter 2 –
The Law of the Land

The Law of the Land, or due process of law, is first found in the 29th chapter of Magna Charta. It embodies the general principles of public liberty and private right, which lie at the foundation of all free government.

To understand what is taking place in the structural and doctrinal changes in our dual constitutional system of government, it is necessary to comprehend the significance of that invaluable limiting principle of free government, under which no man may be deprived of life, liberty, property or the pursuit of happiness, or of his privileges and immunities, but "by the law of the land," or, by "due process of law." As we have said, the term means the supremacy, or, as the English phrase it, "the rule of law," as contradistinguished from arbitrary action, in determining the rights of the citizen.

Since "the law of the land" is made up of an accumulation of protective principles and concepts, starting with Magna Charta, in 1215, and added to by all of the bills and petitions of rights enforced by Englishmen for seven centuries, and further enlarged by our own ancestors, to guard against oppression by our federal government, no enumeration of its constituent principles would be safely exhaustive. Yet the more important can be set out.

"The law of the land" means first, that no citizen can be punished or can be made to suffer in his person or in his property, except for a clear breach of the established law, proven before the ordinary courts. It means, further, that no man is above the law, but that every man, whatever his station or condition, is subject, along with the plainest citizen, to the ordinary law and to the jurisdiction of the ordinary courts. As Justice Brandeis said in a dissenting opinion, in Burdeau v. McDowell:

> At the foundation of our civil liberty lies the principle which denies to government officials an exceptional position before the law and which subjects them to the same rules of conduct that are commands to the citizen.

In that case, however, in which an assistant to the Attorney General of the United States had instigated a theft of evidence, it was the victim of the theft who was deprived of his rights and convicted while the assistant to the Attorney General was, in effect, elevated above the law, by a majority of the Supreme Court.

However the Supreme Court may view the matter in particular cases, it is constitutionally impossible in our system to introduce any exemption of government officials from the jurisdiction of the ordinary courts, such as is the practice in Continental Europe, under what is known as droit administratif. In European countries, an official, a policeman or a soldier may not be resisted by a subject in any case where he is acting under pretense of governmental authority; nor may an injured party sue for redress in the ordinary courts. The official is not amenable to the ordinary law, but has his own court and his own peculiar law.

In England and in the Dominions, and in the United States, by "the law of the land," the highest officer may be called to account under the same law and in the same courts as have cognizance of the acts of the humblest citizen, and he may be held accountable there for any trespass upon the rights of another.

It must be regretfully confessed that, while the foregoing is fundamentally and historically true, as an expression of the constitutional rights of citizens, it has been subverted in practice, and particularly with respect to a very large body of federal officials, who, by an act of Congress, which the Supreme Court has upheld, were taken out from under the operation of the ordinary law and from the jurisdiction of the ordinary courts, and were, in fact, placed under the protection of a system peculiarly their own. These were the three or more thousand armed federal Prohibition agents, who were thus able to kill with impunity hundreds of American citizens during the last twelve years. This privileged status was created in an act of Congress denying to State courts the authority to take jurisdiction of their crimes, and transferring their cases to the federal courts, where United States prosecuting officers, instead of prosecuting them, were actually designated as their defenders.

Jurisdiction over common crimes, such as murder and assault, is constitutionally and exclusively in the State courts, save such as are committed on federal reservations or in the District of Columbia; and the fact that the murderer or assailant is a federal official cannot clothe him with any privileges not enjoyed by the ordinary citizen, if the supremacy of law, "the law of the land," still means anything. The federal judiciary have no common law jurisdiction, nor can Congress rightfully confer it upon them. The Supreme Court has many times affirmed this opinion in other days.

A citizen could sue these federal Prohibition agents for trespass upon his rights, but, here again, he could do so only in the agent's special court. Assuming one got judgment, the agents were not under bond, and, in the main, were financially irresponsible.

Attempted redress on the part of the outraged citizen was therefore futile.

"The law of the land" guarantees to us freedom of religious worship, freedom of speech and of the press. Though sixty odd years ago we were told by the Supreme Court and believed that "the Constitution of the United States is a law for rulers and people, equally in war and in peace," that principle was completely swept aside during the Great War, in the development of an obscure despotism called "The war power," under which it appears proper and allowable to suspend any limitation upon governmental action. Hence the Espionage Acts of June 15, 1917, imposing a drastic censorship upon speech and press, under penalties of $10,000 fine and 20 years imprisonment. Only that criticism of the government was allowable, said the courts, which was "favorable to government" and "favorable to its policies." If anyone wishes to measure how far we have been carried from our fundamental anchorage, as to free speech and free press, let him read the Congressional debates and the press during the War of 1812.

Listen to Daniel Webster in the House of Representatives on January 13, 1814:

> It is an ancient and undoubted prerogative of this people to canvass public measures and the merits of public men. * * * This high constitutional privilege I shall defend and exercise within this House, and without this House, and in all places; in time of war, in time of peace and at all times. Living I shall assert it, dying I shall assert it; and should I leave no other inheritance to my children, by the blessings of God, I will still leave them the inheritance of free principles and the example of a manly, independent and constitutional defense of them.

But the Supreme Court would have upheld the imprisonment of Webster for such a defense in 1917-1918.

"The law of the land" comprehends our whole Bill of Rights, including the right of assembly, and the right to a "well regulated Militia, being necessary to the security of a free State," of which mention has already been made. It particularly embraces the Fourth Amendment guaranteeing "the right of the people to be secure in their persons, houses, papers and effects, against all unreasonable searches."

In other days the Supreme Court laid down the rule that —

> A close and literal construction (of this and other guarantees) deprives them of half their efficacy, and leads to a gradual depreciation of the right, as if it consisted more in sound than in substance.

Hence, they were to be "liberally construed", to assure the citizen his full protection against government. And up to three decades ago the court adhered to that noble purpose, frequently thrilling the country with its eloquence and courage in defense of the great guarantees. How tragic, how alarming it is to read some of its more recent decisions, narrowing the scope of these guarantees. Thus, in Carroll v. U. S. Chief Justice Taft, in 1925, in a majority-opinion, upheld the searching of automobiles on the public highways, without a search warrant, if there were "probable cause." The Fourth Amendment does not permit search without a warrant upon "probable cause," but it permits the issuance of a warrant to search upon probable cause, where that warrant is sworn to, particularly describing the place to be searched and the person or things to be seized; and before the warrant is issued upon "probable cause" a judicial officer has tested and weighed its sufficiency. It is not surprising that Justice McReynolds, dissenting, said:

> If an officer, upon mere suspicion of a misdemeanor, may stop one on the public highway, take articles away from him and thereafter use them as evidence to convict him of crime, what becomes of the Fourth and Fifth Amendments?

In other days the sanctity of a man's home was such that he might repel illegal search to the point of killing the intruder. In the case of J. D. Pittman, killed in Beaufort County, South Carolina, in 1925, this doctrine was reversed, and the killing of the resisting home-owner by a federal agent was held to be "justifiable homicide" in self-defense. The case was not even allowed to go to the jury.

In Burdeau v. McDowell there was no search, but merely a theft of evidence. Seven Justices considered this quite proper, and, presumably, in accordance with "the law of the land." Justice Brandeis dissented, saying:

> Respect for law will not be advanced by resort, in its enforcement, to means which shock the common man's sense of decency and fair play.

Again the Supreme Court tells us, in Olmstead v. U. S., that the tapping of telephone wires to obtain evidence, in violation of the criminal laws of a State, is quite consonant with the inhibition against unreasonable searches, and "the law of the land." And again Justice Brandeis dissents, saying:

> As a means of espionage, writs of assistance and general warrants are but puny instruments of tyranny and oppression when compared with wire-tapping.

"The law of the land" comprehends another important body of protections in the Fifth Amendment, which sets out:

> No person shall be held to answer for a capital or otherwise infamous crime, unless on a presentment or indictment of a grand jury, except in cases arising in the land or naval forces, or in the Militia, when in actual service in time of war or public danger; nor shall any person be subject, for the same offense, to be twice put in jeopardy of life or limb; nor shall be compelled, in any criminal case, to be a witness against himself; nor be deprived of life, liberty or property without due process of law; nor shall private property be taken for public use without just compensation.

The first clause requires the interposition of a grand jury — not less than sixteen nor more than twenty-three citizens of the judicial district, not less than twelve of whom must agree before an indictment can be returned — in all cases of capital or infamous crimes. Infamous crimes are crimes for which one may be sentenced to hard labor. The grand jurors, who are private citizens, called in a manner prescribed by law, are not responsible to the court or to the federal government. They sit in secret, as well to hold an inquest upon the action of government as upon the conduct of fellow citizens. They may exclude the District Attorney from their deliberations, but in practice they have quite generally become his facile instrument.

Unless a grand jury indicts for a crime there can be no prosecution. This was intended as a unique institution of protection against overzealous and vindictive prosecution.

The guarantee against twice subjecting a citizen to punishment for the same offense is so firmly fixed in our jurisprudence that a former trial has been successfully pleaded by one who actually procured his acquittal by bribing the prosecuting attorney. Yet Chief Justice Taft, for the Supreme Court, in U. S. v. Lanza, has overthrown this barrier in Prohibition prosecutions, and has upheld convictions in the State and federal courts of the same persons on the same facts.

The clause forbidding compulsory testimony against one's self has been emasculated in a number of recent decisions. Thus evidence stolen at the behest of a federal officer has been held admissible by the Supreme Court. No plainer instance of compulsory self-incrimination can be imagined. So, too, evidence obtained by secretly tapping telephone wires, in violation of the criminal laws of a State, has been upheld. It is doubtful, now, what method, short of torture, is protected by this guarantee.

As to the guarantee against deprivation of life, liberty or property without due process of law, it appears clear to the ordinary mind that trial for crime, by contempt proceedings, without a grand jury or a petit jury, constitutes such a deprivation of liberty. "The law of the land", in addition, accords the accused a "presumption of innocence", placing the burden of proof upon the government. Various recent federal criminal statutes wholly reverse this principle and substitute the "presumption of guilt."

If these devices for "short-cut" justice are allowable in the Prohibition Act, the Narcotics Act and in other recent federal statutes, how much more justified they would be in the prosecution of our increasing crimes of violence. Yet it has not even been suggested that they are permissible in such cases as robbery or murder.

The inhibition in the Fifth Amendment against the taking of private property for public use without just compensation is repeated in the Fourteenth Amendment as a restraint on State action. Yet the rights of property in the United States were never more precarious. They are being invaded in many forms and concealed under many pretexts. Consider first, the Sixteenth Amendment to the Constitution, adopted by Congress and the State legislatures — not by the people — in 1913. It fulfilled the unsleeping purpose of those in power to obtain unlimited access to the whole wealth of the citizens, and threw down the most effective barrier that can be erected to preserve the watchfulness and interest of all the citizens in government, and to restrain extravagance and corruption in the rulers. This amendment removed from the Constitution the requirement that all direct taxes shall be levied under the rule of apportionment among the several States, according to population, and in its place, Congress now assumes unlimited power to take the whole income from every man, woman and child in the United States, and in any discriminatory and unequal manner.

The old limitation of apportionment, as Chief Justice Fuller said for the Supreme Court, in 1894, declaring an income tax law unconstitutional, was intended by the founders of our government "to restrain the exercise of the power of direct taxation to extraordinary emergencies, and to prevent an attack upon accumulated property by mere force of numbers." Judge Story, in his Commentaries on the Constitution, had previously said:

> Indeed, in a free government, almost all other rights would become utterly worthless, if the government possessed an uncontrollable power over the private fortune of every citizen. One of the fundamental objects of every good government must be the due administration of justice; and

how vain it would be to speak of such an administration, when all property is subject to the will or caprice of the legislature or the rulers.

We see this only too plainly today when all industry and commerce are depressed, and when every citizen who possesses any means is under the necessity of the strictest economy. Projects of vast expenditure are contemplated in the name of the welfare of the people — from which the authors hope to reap popular approval in their respective sections — and income tax rates are to be raised on the helplessly insignificant number of payers of this tax to cover any extravagance. It is not to be wondered at if business and industry halt and the incentive to accumulate atrophies, when government may take what proportion it pleases. The wealth and well-being of the people of this country were not built up under any such philosophy, but under the rule of uniformity and the principle recognizing an indissoluble connection between taxation and representation.

It was inevitable, with the adoption of the Sixteenth Amendment, that a graduated or progressive income tax law would make its appearance; for this device is preeminently suited to demagogic policies, permitting the exemption of the overwhelming mass of voters and the realization of great sums from the comparatively few wealthy citizens. It was believed, however, that under the principle of "the equal protection of the laws," which is a part of "the law of the land," the Supreme Court would declare any progressive ratio, based on mere gradations of income, to be an unjust and arbitrary, and therefore, an unconstitutional classification. There was justification for this belief in Justice Brewer's declaration, in Magoun v. Illinois Trust and Savings Bank, in 1897, that —

Equality in right, in protection and in burden is the thought which has run through the life of the nation and its constitutional enactments from the Declaration of Independence to the present hour.

And again, in the same case, involving the question of progressive State taxation of inheritances, he said:

It seems to be conceded that if this were a tax upon property such increase in the rate of taxation could not be sustained, but being a tax upon the succession it is held that a different rule prevails.

Justice Brewer, again speaking of classifications for tax purposes, in Gulf, Colorado and Santa Fe Ry. v. Ellis, said:

Yet it is equally true that such classification cannot be made arbitrarily. The State * * * may not say that all men beyond a certain age shall be alone thus subjected, or all men possessed of certain wealth.

While classifications may be lawfully made for purposes of taxation, they must always rest upon some difference which is reasonable and just, such as particular classes of corporations, particular trades or business, or kinds of property. But no classification that is arbitrary has any sanction in "the law of the land." That a tax based upon classification of wealth alone, a tax intentionally made unequal, violates "the law of the land," would have seemed too elemental to be disputed a few decades ago. In 1915, however, it was settled in an opinion by Chief Justice White, confirming the power in Congress, with no adequate reasoned argument, and dismissing the question with the remark that the court could not inquire into the wisdom or unwisdom of legislation.

From the day of that fateful decision Congress has taken from about four per cent of our citizens the immense sum of $42,000,000,000, and wasted it as political spoils, when it would otherwise have gone back into the reproductive channels of trade and industry to multiply its blessings of employment and opportunity throughout a land now bled white.

To say that Congress has a constitutional power to levy direct taxes, without regard to the "equal protection of the laws," is a contradiction in terms. A constitution is essentially a body of limitations upon governmental power. It has no other excuse or reason. When it ceases to limit that power, as the Supreme Court affirms in respect of the taxing power, it ceases to exist. An unlimited taxing power is not a power of constitutional taxation; it is a simple power of confiscation, which no just government would wish to possess.

According to figures published by the Internal Revenue Bureau November 29, 1931, individual income taxpayers in 1930 numbered 1,946,675, or one and two-thirds per cent of our population. Their combined income was $17,220,753,620. The total income of the American people in 1930 was about $71,000,000,000. Through the federal income tax exemptions the remaining 46,000,000 gainfully employed citizens, with incomes totaling approximately $53,000,000,000, paid no portion of the federal government's expenditures directly. When we consider that the estimated number of federal officeholders and other employees is 1,998,645, who, with their dependent families would number not less than 5,000,000 persons, it will be seen that for every federal income taxpayer there are two and one-half persons sharing in his taxes.

That the federal income tax is unscientifically and arbitrarily enforced may be judged from the fact that in 1929, the Income Tax

Bureau levied additional taxes upon those making returns amounting to $405,855,000, while it returned taxes erroneously collected to the amount of $418,939,000, with a total collection of $2,410,259,230. The cost of the Treasury Department in 1931 was $359,638,676, or more than one-tenth of all federal revenues received in that year.

It should be noted that the Supreme Court, reversing a previous decision, has latterly given Congress carte blanche to impose any confiscatory rate upon income, even up to 100 per cent, in declaring that "due process of law" cannot be invoked against taxation; that "the law of the land" no longer protects one against being plundered of his entire income by government.

It has been asserted, though an accurate estimate is impossible, that the less than 2,000,000 citizens who pay the federal income tax are annually put to an expense for accounting and legal services incident thereto amounting to $300,000,000. Certainly the cost is a huge one, in money, in labor and in anxiety, owing to possible penalties under complex and capricious regulations.

The wealth of the country is now at the mercy of an overwhelming untaxed voting majority. As Lecky says, in his Democracy and Liberty, it has created a state of things "in which one class imposes on another burdens which it is not asked to share, and impels the State into vast schemes of extravagance, under the belief that the whole cost will be thrown upon others."

The vast schemes of extravagance into which the power of unlimited progressive taxation has impelled our federal government may be seen in its constantly rising cost from $7.29 per capita in 1916, when the unlimited direct tax amendment was adopted, to $33.76 in 1930.

With the repudiation by Congress of the just principles of taxation, in 1913, came logically enough a repudiation of the limitations as to the objects upon which it might constitutionally spend the huge sums that could now be extorted.

There are today, in practice, no limits, either to the amount which Congress may take from such citizens as it pleases, or to the objects, individuals or private classes, upon whom it may bestow what it has taken.

William D. Guthrie saw the possibilities of this eventuality and warned against it, in his treatise on the Fourteenth Amendment, in 1898, saying:

> Expediency or prejudice may hereafter prompt attempts at progressive taxes or tax laws exempting those of moderate means; but we shall pay a fearful price if we introduce any such principle into our legislation. Equality of burden, by making every man, according to his means, a contributor to the expenses of the State, is one of the most wholesome things in our civil institutions. It is the contributing citizen who is the watchful citizen. * * * The best assurance of watchful care and interest and vigilance in our institutions — the best assurance of honesty, integrity and economy in public expenditure — is a wide distribution of the burdens of taxation.

That the policy of exempting large masses of voters from taxation was never contemplated by the founders, appears in Chief Justice Marshall's observations in 1829, in McCulloch v. Maryland:

> In imposing a tax the legislature acts upon its constituents. This is, in general, a sufficient security against erroneous and oppressive taxation.

Following close upon the Supreme Court's action in upholding the power of Congress to levy discriminatory, progressive taxes upon income, came a graduated federal Estate Tax Law, for which there is no constitutional warrant, exempting estates up to $50,000. It is justified as an excise, which, according to Section 8, Article 1, of the Constitution, "shall be uniform throughout the United States." The law was not uniform, it was highly discriminatory. But, said the Supreme Court, in upholding its constitutionality, the uniformity referred to in the Constitution has no reference to rates; it requires mere geographical uniformity. Or, we might say, the discrimination must be universal.

We are reminded of some comments of Judge Cooley, in his Constitutional Limitations, on "the law of the land":

> The words "the law of the land", as used in the Constitution, do not mean a statute passed for the purpose of working a wrong. That construction would render the restriction absolutely nugatory and turn this part of the Constitution into nonsense. The people would be made to say to the two houses: "You shall be vested with the legislative power of the State, but no one shall be disfranchised or deprived of any of the rights or privileges of a citizen, unless you pass a statute for that purpose. In other words you shall not do the wrong unless you choose to do it."

By "the law of the land" taxes may be raised, and appropriated, but only for public purposes; or as Justice Bradley said for the Supreme Court in other days:

> In the first place, taxation having for its only legitimate object the raising of money for public purposes and for the

33

proper needs of government, the exaction of moneys from the citizens for other purposes is not a proper exercise of this power, and must therefore be unauthorized.

Yet today heavy discriminatory taxation of the propertied classes is openly advocated in Congress-and applauded by self-appointed leaders of the masses-as a means of "equalizing fortunes." The term is wholly disingenuous; it is a mere policy of public plundering which our federal government has no rightful power to adopt.

Chancellor Kent observed in his Commentaries long ago:

> The legislature has no right to limit the extent of the acquisition of property, as was suggested by some of the regulations in ancient Crete, Lacedaemon and Athens; and has also been recommended in some modern Utopian speculations. A state of equality as to property is impossible to be maintained, for it is against the laws of nature; and if it could be reduced to practice it would place the human race in a state of tasteless enjoyment and stupid inactivity, which would degrade the mind and destroy the happiness of social life.

Such a governmental policy, says Nicholson, in his Historical Progress and Socialism,

> — would be to introduce a creeping paralysis; and, when the time was considered ripe for taking over the land and capital, the land would be a wilderness and the capital old iron.

Under this policy of "equalizing fortunes" Congress has reenacted an oppressive federal tax on gifts, a most vicious and unjust form of taxation. A father may not give to his son for launching that son onto trade or industry, nor to a daughter for her independent support but that a large part is seized by this government. A more tyrannical and stupid tax cannot be easily imagined.

One of the distinctive glories of American civilization has been the creation and maintenance by private individuals of great institutions of learning, foundations for medical research, charitable institutions and funds for the relief of distress. Everywhere else in the world this has been the work of government, closing these fields to the generous impulse of the citizen. If we are now to have heavy inheritance taxes, coupled with gift taxes, it will mean the end of all private endowment and private giving. Every prudent man of property must severely conserve what he possesses if he hopes to transmit anything to heirs. And it must be kept in the most liquid condition in order to meet without penalty the demanded taxes. Capitol for new enterprises or for maintaining old ones will become scarce indeed. No surer road can be found to economic stagnation and paralysis.

The principle that taxes may be levied only for governmental and strictly public purposes pays homage to that other necessary rule for a free people that every citizen is entitled to protection in the rewards of his own labor and self-denial. Once government steps outside that limitation it may take from one and give to another, thus violating the very essence of freedom. It must ultimately result in destroying the industrious and barbarizing the shiftless.

In any free system of government its true functions consist in maintaining peace and order and the guarantees of liberty and security, leaving the free man to do the best that he can by this own endeavors. That inequalities in fortune result in such a society is as it should be, if merit is a virtue to be cultivated. To seek to equalize fortune, as is now the rage of government, is to confound virtue and vice.

Today, though there seems to be no limitation with respect to the objects upon which Congress may lavish public moneys, there appears to be no remedy for the taxpayers since the Supreme Court, in the case of Massachusetts v. Mellon, hereafter to be referred to, declined to pass upon the constitutionality of a federal appropriation for the care of expectant mothers and babies in the States, under the direction of the Children's Bureau, in the Department of Labor.

Returning to the constitutional inhibition against taking private property for public use without just compensation, and descending ID concrete instances, the whole miserable mess of Prohibition may lie traced to the decision of the Supreme Court in Mugler v. Kansas, In 1887, where, after holding for a century that the right of property in liquor is as complete as the right in any other species, it sanctioned; in act of Kansas destroying that right, without a suggestion of compensation, that is, without due process of law. Latterly, the Court has gone on, not only to sanction the destruction of the non-alcoholic near-beer industry of a State, because near-beer looks like the real article, but it has upheld laws declaring the mere possession of this species of property to be criminal.

In the Oklahoma Bank Guaranty case the Supreme Court upheld a law requiring honestly-conducted banks to pay the losses to depositors in dishonestly-conducted banks, whose dishonesty the State itself was bound to detect and prevent.

Finally, in the summary process of "padlocking", under the National Prohibition Act, and forfeiture of so-called "offending" property, including even lands in the States, we have new practices not far removed from bills of attainder.

Embodied in "the law of the land" are also the principles set out in our Sixth Amendment, as follows:

> In all criminal prosecutions, the accused shall enjoy the right to a speedy and public trial, by an impartial jury of the State or district wherein the crime shall have been committed, which district shall have been previously ascertained by law; and to be informed of the nature and cause of the accusation; to be confronted with witnesses against him; to have compulsory process for obtaining witnesses in his favor, and to have the assistance of counsel for his defense.

Liberty can no more exist without trial by jury than without the system of representative government. Its virtues are that it gives the people an opportunity to thwart the excessive and arbitrary demands of government, even to the point of refusing to convict under what they may consider unjust law; it makes the administration of justice a matter of the people and keeps alive public spirit; it teaches law and liberty.

It should be noted, in view of the Wickersham Commission proposals for summary justice, that this amendment guarantees trial by jury "in all criminal prosecutions." The object of public trial is to permit the public to see that the accused is fairly dealt with. This has been withdrawn in recent years from the alien, threatened with deportation on the sole authority of a ministerial decree. And in literally thousands of cases of citizens accused under the Prohibition Act, trial by jury is denied through the physical impossibility of according it to such great numbers as are brought up for trial.

Under the National Prohibition Act, which accounted for about 60,000 federal arrests annually, it appears to have been foreseen that the right of trial by jury was an impediment to effective prosecution, and the authors of that legislation hit upon an extraordinary expedient for speeding up the disposition of cases. That was by a provision adapting the equity processes of injunction and contempt, enforced by the judge alone, without a jury, to Prohibition cases. Thus if liquor were found upon the premises of a citizen, the Prohibition law presumed it was there for illegal purposes and authorized the issuance of an injunction against any future manufacture, sale, storage or transportation. If he was subsequently arrested as an offender he was summarily sentenced for contempt.

When it is recalled that the guarantee in the Sixth Amendment requires that all crimes shall be tried by jury it is clear that the federal government has acted in deliberate bad faith toward the citizen in seeking in this manner to circumvent one of the great guarantees. In addition, it may set a precedent under which an ambitious government might overturn the entire jury system. In fact, the President's Commission of Law Enforcement and Observance, finding trial by jury to be practically impossible under Prohibition enforcement, has actually recommended to Congress, in spite of the Constitution, that it be abolished and that summary trial be instituted as to the most numerous classes of offenders.

In the light of these changes it is interesting to go back to that other happier and quieter period and hear Judge Caldwell, in the United States Circuit Court, in the case of Hopkins v. Oxley Stave Co., on the subject of injunction as a substitute for trial by jury in criminal cases:

> It is said by those who defend the assumption of this (injunctive) jurisdiction by the federal courts, that it is a swifter and speedier mode of dealing with those who

violate or threaten to violate the laws than by the prescribed and customary method of proceeding in courts of law; that it is a "short cut" to the accomplishment of a desired object; that it avoids the delay and uncertainty incident to a jury trial, occasions less expense and insures a speedier punishment. But the logical difficulty with this reasoning is that it confers jurisdiction on the mob equally with the chancellor. * * *

It can make little difference to the victims of short cut and unconstitutional methods, whether it is the mob or the chancellor that deprives them of their constitutional rights. * * * English history is replete with examples showing that the King and his dependent and servile judges would have subverted the rights and liberties of the English people, but for the good sense and patriotism of English juries. * * * The Penn case, and the proceedings that grew out of it, constitute one of the foundation stones in the English bill of rights. With all of their astuteness and eager desire to serve the Crown, it never occurred to the judges in those days to enjoin the Quakers from meeting and Penn from preaching to them. This short-cut would have gotten rid of the jury and placed Penn and his followers completely in the power of the judges; and instead of becoming the founder of a great city and commonwealth in a free republic, he would have languished in an English prison for contempt of court, incurred by preaching to his congregation, for he vowed in court that "all the powers upon earth" could not divert or restrain him from that duty.

Where trial by jury does now take place in the federal courts its full beneficence is not infrequently defeated by the arrogated right of the judges to express their opinions upon the guilt of the accused, thereby concluding the jury. As Judge Cooley truly says:

> A judge who urges his opinion upon the facts to the jury decides the cause while avoiding the responsibility.

The provision of the Sixth Amendment requiring an impartial jury of the State or district wherein the crime is committed, contemplates the historic "jury of the vicinage", where the accused will have the benefit of his known standing among the neighbors, where the jury may have knowledge of the witnesses against him and where he may readily obtain his own witnesses.

Under the Conspiracy statute of the United States, which punishes an aborted offense more severely than a completed crime, this guarantee of a "jury of the vicinage" has been wholly set aside and the accused are usually dragged to some distant jurisdiction in which an alleged overt act took place. In Prohibition cases, it has happened that the accused were transported to some distant court presided over by a judge known for his zeal and severity. In mail fraud cases, "the jury of the vicinage" is likewise non-existent, since prosecution may occur not only where the letter or offending matter was mailed but also where it was delivered.

To be confronted with the witnesses against him and to have the assistance of a counsel, are protections which were not settled in the English common law at the time of our separation.

The Eighth Amendment of our Constitution contains further principles embodied in "the law of the land", in forbidding excessive bail for one arrested or the imposition of cruel and unusual punishments. Certainly summary punishment for crime, without a jury is unusual as well as cruel. And so were the penalties of $10,000 fine and five years imprisonment imposed by a legislative revival of all the old federal laws regulating and taxing a liquor traffic that was prohibited, and with which it was impossible lawfully to comply. Such equivocal legislation has no other object than to multiply the penalties for the same offense.

Can anything be more cruel and unusual as a punishment, under our system of free government, than banishment or exile? Yet it was inflicted upon naturalized citizens of the United States in the fanatical effort to enforce Prohibition. A naturalized citizen who had been convicted of a violation of this act was proceeded against in the federal courts for cancellation of his certificate of naturalization, on the ground that his conduct exhibited a mental reservation in his oath to support the Constitution, and that the certificate was "illegally procured." And the courts now sustain the contention without jury trial. The citizen, having lost his former allegiance, is then sent into exile, without nationality or allegiance, or the protection of any government anywhere.

The invaluable writ of habeas corpus, formerly available to all persons unlawfully detained, is not now open to him, since the courts maintain the fiction that deportation is not a criminal proceeding, nor is it a punishment.

"The law of the land" likewise condemns ex post facto laws, operating to create and punish acts that were not unlawful at the time they were done. It also looks with suspicion upon retroactive laws, yet the Supreme Court lends its approval generally to any retroactive legislation of a non-criminal character which Congress may wish to enact, particularly in tax legislation, where it may work severe hardship.

As an essential element of "the law of the land" is the universality of its application, as well as its uniformity, its destruction may be seen in the development of any exceptions under it, for "the law of the land" plays no favorites. With this in view consider what has happened to the common law rule against conspiracies and monopolies, in the exemption of labor unions, farmers unions, dairymen's unions, cooperative associations, and the like.

Chapter 3 –
Administrative Law-Making

Administrative law is the law of edicts and decrees, issued from above to subjects below, now progressively displacing our constitutional system of general and uniform law, enacted by the legislative branch of government.

Among no people who preserve the rule or supremacy of law, as it has been crystallized in "the law of the land" for all who enjoy the heritage of the Englishman's struggles and those of our own ancestors, against absolutism and in defense of civil liberty, can any system of so-called administrative law, or droit administratif, get a foothold. For they are in irreconcilable antagonism.

Administrative law, as a privileged system for the officials and rulers, is to be found in nearly all European countries. It comes to them logically from the Roman Civil Law, whose influence these peoples of Europe have felt for ages. This Civil Law, unlike the English Common Law, is not founded in custom, it does not rise from among the members of the community themselves in response to social needs, quite independent of any action of the State, but it is essentially rules of action imposed from above, by a supposedly omniscient and omnipotent law-giver. As the legal philosopher, Gareis says:

> Customary law is not formulated by the State, but by the community. It springs from the people in their economic

unity or from a part of the community. It is responsive to social necessity and has its validity for that reason.

Even the Romans lived under the rule of customary law as a free people until the fifth century B. C., when their "ancient customs" were reduced to writing in the Twelve Tables. Thence we see their free customs engulfed in a multiplicity of interpretations by patrician magistrates, and the rise of a polity, adapted from the Greek doctrine, that the State is an earthly god and the giver of every good. The citizen thus disappears and his chief rights and duties become service to and sacrifice for the State. The history of the growth of the Roman system is not without analogy to our own times.

The Roman law developed into an all-pervading written system of such infinite extent, and with such a numerous body of officials, that toward the close of the Republic, it had become "a grievance more intolerable than the vices of the City", as Gibbon informs us. "Three thousand brass plates, the acts of the Senate and the people, were deposited in the Capitol, and some of the acts, as the Julian law against extortion, surpassed the number of a hundred chapters."

The number of statutes, plebiscites, Senatus-Consulta and edicts, decrees, rescripts and mandates of the Emperors, grew to such volume in the time of Hadrian, 117-138 A.D., that simplification of the law was considered the most urgent problem of State. He sought to solve it by a Digest, promulgated as the Edictum Prepetuum, designed as the unalterable code for the future. Yet this expedient was futile where the underlying theory of the State was its omnipotence and its duty to assume all the cares of the people.

The period of Roman law-making ends, significantly enough, with the approaching eclipse of civilization, in the issuance of the Institutes, Digest and Codex of Justinian, in 534 A.D., which were assumed to be so adequate for all time that any future commentary upon them was made a penal offense.

Society was classified, regimented and standardized under the most drastic penalties, which a vast and complicated governmental machine sought in vain to keep in order. As Samuel Dill says in his volume, Roman Society in the Last Century of the Western Empire:

> The system of bureaucratic despotism, elaborated finally under Diocletian and Constantine, produced a tragedy in the truest sense, such as history has seldom exhibited; in which, by an inexorable fate, the claims of fanciful omnipotence ended in a humiliating paralysis of administration; in which determined effort to remedy social evils only aggravated them until they became unendurable; in which the best intentions of the central power, were, generation after generation, mocked and defeated by irresistible laws of human nature and by hopeless perfidy and corruption in the servants of government.

Who, exclaims the same historian, can wonder that a people exposed to such brutality, in the name of civilized government, should welcome the rude justice of the Gothic chief!

But during all this period the insulation of the Anglo-Saxon permitted him to develop doctrines and a system of law that were peculiarly his own. He knew nothing of law as the command of a sovereign or of the omnipotence of the State. His law was the unwritten free customs of the people, evolved from below. His Norman kings were compelled to acknowledge it. His lawyers and judges defended it, and so successfully, that, as Sir William Markby tells us, no one has ever been able to quote a text of Roman law as authority either in the English courts of common law or in those of chancery.

The sharp distinction between these two systems of law appears equally in the theories which underlie legislation. Under the Common Law, government being conceived as having its origin generally in force or fraud, in the passion of a single individual or a few individuals to oppress and live comfortably at the expense of their neighbors, it is a primary essential to limit the powers of government to a point where they can inflict no injury and where government's main object is to give security against internal and external aggression. Legislation is little more than a registration of what society has evolved and adopted as its own rules of conduct, the citizen mean-time being left free to pursue his own happiness and to develop according to the exercise of his own faculties.

Under the Roman Civil Law, which postulates the State as of divine origin, all-wise and all-powerful, it becomes the duty of the State to seek to achieve happiness for all of its subjects, in such manner as it may dictate, and, to that end, its own wisdom must override all private judgment in prescribing regulations for the whole range of human endeavor. Under this latter policy, an extensive system of administrative law, with its particular and varied regulations, enforced by innumerable agents, boards and commissions, becomes necessary and inescapable. For no legislature, however industrious, can itself attend to the details of such an enormous range of duties as is implied in the providential theory upon which government rests. And in the performance of their respective tasks, that the agents of government may not be impeded or thwarted, they must be clothed with certain privileges, not the least necessary of which is exemption from the operation of such local law as is prescribed for the ordinary subject.

Under the Common Law, which denies the divinity, omniscience and omnipotence of the State, which concedes no privileges, which accords to every man the right to work out his own happiness free from intermeddling by government, save where his action may impair the like right of others, and which recognizes but one system of general law for all, rich and poor, high and low, enforced in ordinary courts, there is no function for administrative law to perform and no reason for its existence.

While we may still think ourselves living under the free common law system, there has nevertheless developed in the United States, and in England as well, an ominous body of practice containing the same features, now openly referred to as "administrative law." It has gotten its foothold in very recent years, mainly through the increasing number of boards, bureaus and commissions created by Congress, to which Congress has delegated the authority to make rules and regulations having the force of the law, to sit in judgment under them and to enforce them.

The Supreme Court expounded its views of "administrative law" with what should have been finality, in the early case of U. S. v. Eaton, decided in 1891. That was the case of regulations made in 1886, by the Commissioner of Internal Revenue, with the approval of the Secretary of the Treasury, under an act of that year authorizing regulations, relating to the manufacture of oleomargarine. The regulation in question stretched the law so as to require wholesale dealers to keep books and to make monthly returns. The statute required this only of manufacturers. The defendant, George R. Eaton, a wholesale dealer, did not keep books or make a monthly return, but he was indicted for violation of the oleomargarine act. The government contended that the regulation was needful, was an outgrowth of the statute and acquired and possessed the force of law. But, said the court:

> It is a principle of criminal law that an offense which may be the subject of criminal procedure is an act committed or omitted in violation of a public law, either forbidding or commanding it. It would be a very dangerous principle to hold that a thing prescribed by the Commissioner of Internal Revenue, as a needful regulation under the oleomargarine act, for carrying it into effect, could be considered as a thing "required by law" in the carrying on or conducting of the business of a wholesale dealer in oleomargarine, in such manner as to become a criminal offense punishable under Section 18 of the act; particularly, when the same act, in Section 5, requires a manufacturer of the article to keep such books and to render such returns as the Commissioner of Internal Revenue, with the approval of the Secretary of the Treasury, may, by regulation, require, and does not impose, in that section or elsewhere in the act, the duty of keeping such books and rendering such returns upon a wholesale dealer in the article. * * *

> Regulations prescribed by the President and by the heads of departments, under authority granted by Congress, may be regulations prescribed by law, so as lawfully to support acts done under them and in accordance with them, and may thus have, in a proper sense, the force of law; but it does not follow that a thing required by them is a thing so required by law as to make the neglect to do the thing a criminal offence in a citizen, where a statute does not distinctly make the neglect in question a criminal offence.

The effect of the decision was to confirm the principle of "the law of the land," that no one may be punished under criminal procedure save for an act committed or omitted in violation of a public law, and that a departmental or bureau regulation, not founded on a statute distinctly requiring the conduct set out or making the neglect in question a criminal offence, is not public law, in the sense that it may be invoked to inflict punishment.

But with the progressive creation of federal bureaus by Congress from the opening of this century, the Eaton decision was to be the last of a historic reiteration of that fundamental principle of Anglo-American liberty.

In 1904 the delegation of power to the Tea Board in the Treasury Department to make regulations and to fix standards of imported teas, was upheld as constitutional. In 1906 the open delegation of legislative power by Congress to the Interstate Commerce Commission to fix railroad rates, and to certain administrative agencies in the Philippine Islands, were likewise sustained, Chief Justice White declaring in the latter case that it was "a proposition which is not now open for discussion."

In 1910, came on the case of Grimaud v. U. S. in which a sheep-grazer was convicted of violation of a regulation issued by the Secretary of the Interior by which he had forbidden sheep grazing in the national forests except upon a permit issued by himself. The act authorizing the Secretary of the Interior to administer the national forests nowhere mentioned his right to regulate sheep grazing. The offense had been created by the Secretary's sole decree. Yet, said the Court:

> It is true that there is no act of Congress, which, in express terms, declares that it shall be unlawful to graze sheep in a

forest reserve. * * * But the statutes declare that the privilege of using the reserves for all proper and lawful purposes is subject to the provision that the person so using them shall comply with the rules and regulations covering said forest reservations. The same act makes it an offense to violate these regulations.

Thus the federal departments and bureaus received an accession to their power to make specific laws from any general grant of authority; it was no longer necessary that the act or omission be distinctly prescribed in the statute to make their regulations valid law.

In the case of Thomas E. Brents, and E. E. Van Wert, Interior Department Indian agents, decided in 1913, we learn from Chief Justice, then Justice, Hughes, for the full court, that Indian agents may be punished for accepting money from those convicted of selling liquor to Indians, for "recommending clemency," according to "rules and regulations and the customs, usages and practices" of the Bureau of Indian Affairs, when there was no statutory duty whatever to recommend or to withhold recommendations for clemency. The lower court dismissed the case on a demurrer. But the Supreme Court overruled the lower court, declaring:

> To constitute official action it was not necessary that it should be prescribed by statute. * * * Nor was it necessary that the requirement should be prescribed by a written rule or regulation. It might also be found in an established usage which constituted the common law of the department and fixed the duties of those engaged in its activities. * * * In executing the powers of the Indian Office there is necessarily a wide range for administrative discretion and in determining the scope of official action regard must be had

to the authority conferred; and this, we have seen, embraces every action which may properly constitute an aid in the enforcement of the law.

In this decision the rule that those acts or omissions only are criminal offences under "public law" which Congress distinctly denounces, is abandoned for the amazing affirmation that "public law" may equally embrace administrative rules and regulations, for which no distinct authority was given, as well as unwritten rules or usage and custom, as the "common law of the department." Never before had American citizens heard of the "common law of a department," as a system warranting the imposition of punishment.

With this decision bureaucracy attained full feather in the United States and every rule and regulation "which may properly constitute an aid in the enforcement" of any act confided to a bureau to administer, apparently attains the force of public law, on equality with a statute.

It is a strange fact that the English judges are complaining bitterly today of the practice of Parliament of creating all manner of administrative boards and empowering them to make rules and regulations which "shall be final and not subject to appeal to any court." Parliament has even gone to the extent to authorize a department head to "modify the provisions of this act so far as may appear necessary or expedient for carrying the order into effect;" that is, to make over the law to suit itself.

The English courts have no power to declare an act of Parliament void, since Parliament is supreme and its duty to conform to "the law of the land" is merely a moral one. The most that English courts can do is to declare acts done under a law of Parliament ultra vires, outside the scope of powers conferred, or unreasonable.

Administrative Law-Making

Under our written Constitution, with the federal powers limited, our federal courts may wholly set aside an act of Congress as beyond the powers conferred upon it or as violative of "the law of the land." That is their most vital protective function. Yet in the permitted growth of so-called "administrative law," in this country, in the form of legislative and judicial powers delegated to departments, boards and bureaus, it is now sanctioning the most revolutionary changes affecting the liberty and property of the citizen.

Our new federal administrative courts, which are more and more, absorbing the jurisdiction of our judicial courts, in the regulation of trade and industry, appear in two principal forms. In the one case, judicial power has been delegated by Congress to the office of an "examiner", in the departments and bureaus, who is the appointee and creature of the department or bureau head. When his chief has cited some business institution or person, for a violation of a department or bureau regulation, issued by himself with the force of law, the examiner holds a hearing and sits in judgment. Obviously, the examiner is a partisan; any finding by him against his complaining chief is a challenge of his chief's authority, involving serious consequences in the matter of his own job.

In the second case, judicial power has been delegated by Congress to a host of commissions, which have also been given power to issue regulations with the force of law. These commissions are thus also clothed with the executive power, the legislative power and the judicial power. They summon whom they will under their own regulations and sit in judgment upon their own law.

These administrative tribunals have evolved a hybrid process which has the combined aspects of the equity processes of injunction and mandamus; that is to say, an order to cease doing the thing complained of and to do what the department or commission orders to be done. While violation of this process may involve a fine, these tribunals have not yet assumed to imprison summarily for contempt. This process is termed an order to "Cease and Desist," referring to certain business practices which the examiner or the commission, as the case may be, has found to be in violation of one of the regulations.

And, as has been pointed out, the courts will rarely review the findings of facts, or of mixed fact and law, or of law itself in such cases. These institutions are wholly alien and tyrannical, and unknown to the law of the land.

The culmination of this consolidation of power in the executive branch of our government came in the spring and early summer of 1933, under the pretext of an "economic emergency", when, as temporary measures, the three co-ordinate and co-equal branches of our government were practically merged into the single person of an all-powerful President, authorized to delegate such power to underlings.

In the so-called Emergency Agricultural Relief Act of May 12, 1933, it is arrogantly declared:

> The Secretary of Agriculture is authorized, with the approval of the President, to make such regulations with the force and effect of law, as may be necessary to carry out the powers vested in him by this act.

No legislation of Congress since its first session in March 1789 has embodied such open disregard for the limiting provisions of the Constitution of the United States as is found in the agricultural and industrial acts of the special session of the 73rd Congress, which met in March, 1933.

The so-called Emergency Agricultural Relief Act, to be operative until the President desires to terminate it, is unconstitutional on at least seven grounds, which may be set out here.

First, in its attempt to confer upon an administrative official the power to fix the prices of agricultural and competitive products it flouts a long line of "liberal" decisions of the Supreme Court which have conceded to government the power to fix charges and rates, in business activities "affected with a public interest", first allowed in 1876, in Munn v. Illinois, in respect of public grain elevators and, a few years later, affirmed as to railroad rates, making of the Interstate Commerce Commission our first despotic federal bureau.

But the Supreme Court has not been inclined to extend the field of price and rate control since those decisions, and as recently as 1928, in Williams v. Standard Oil Co., declared a Louisiana statute attempting to fix the price of gasoline, to be unconstitutional. That is to say, the Court declared gasoline to be not affected with a public interest to the extent that a State might fix the price of sale.

In 1927, a decision of the Supreme Court, more in point, in the case of Fairmont Creamery v. Minn., declared a statute seeking to fix the price of milk and cream to be unconstitutional, on the same ground. The principle must be equally applicable to the federal government as to interstate sales, with respect to which the Secretary of Agriculture is now attempting to fix prices under the so-called trade codes.

Second, it is not within the power of Congress or of any State Legislature to tax one citizen in order to give the proceeds to another, as is contemplated in the processing tax which the Secretary of Agriculture is authorized to levy upon processors of agricultural and kindred commodities. Government may lawfully tax only for a governmental or strictly public purpose. This principle was upheld in 1875 in the case of Loan Association v. Topeka, and again in 1882, in Parkersburg v. Brown, where the Court said:

> Taxation to pay the bonds in question is not taxation for a public purpose. It is taxation which takes the private property of one person for the private use of another person.

This principle was again affirmed in Cole v. Lagrange in 1884.

The processing tax which the Secretary of Agriculture is empowered to levy proposes to tax consumers in order to give the tax to the agricultural producers.

Third, the power conferred upon the Secretary of Agriculture – and upon the Dictator under the so-called National Industrial Recovery Act as well – to license processors and others who will not accept their codes, or deny a license and destroy them if they will not submit, has never been conceded to government unless the business were "affected with a public interest". As late as 1932, the Supreme Court said in New State Ice Co. v. Liebmann:

> It may be quite true that in Oklahoma ice is not only an article of prime necessity but indispensable; but certainly not more so than food and clothing or the shelter of a home. And this court has definitely said that the production or sale of food or clothing cannot be subjected to legislative regulation on the basis of a public use. * * * It is a business as essentially private in its nature as the business of the grocer, the dairyman, the butcher, the baker, the shoemaker or the tailor, each of whom performs a service which, to a greater or less extent, the community is

dependent upon and is interested in having maintained, but which bears no such relation to the public as to warrant its inclusion in the category of business charged with a public use.

Fourth, the Emergency Agricultural Relief Act is unconstitutional on the ground that it seeks to transfer from Congress its exclusive power to tax to an administrative official, the Secretary of Agriculture. The power conferred is an uncontrollable discretion to levy upon what products he pleases the amount of tax that he pleases. He may tax the basic agricultural articles named in the act and any commodity competitive with those basic commodities. He may not only fix the tax rate and designate the articles to be taxed but he may fix the time when the tax shall become operative and the time when it ceases, with the vague object of putting the farmer in the favorable position he occupied as to prices from 1909 to 1914, when President Wilson was so deeply concerned to reduce "the high cost of living".

Fifth, the act is unconstitutional in that the undetermined processing taxes, which are covered into the Treasury, are to be withdrawn by the Secretary of Agriculture without an appropriation, in violation of Clause 7, Section 9 of Article I. Not only that, but the act denies to the Comptroller General, the accounting officer of the government, any authority to audit any expenditures under it. The function of the Comptroller General is to refuse the payment of any moneys not contracted to be paid in accordance with law.

The act takes into consideration that the processing taxes may be so heavy that processors may be unable to pay them, and it, therefore, provides that they may borrow the needed sums from the government's own Reconstruction Finance Corporation, with which to pay the taxes.

Sixth, the act is unconstitutional in that it seeks to usurp power over intrastate trade and industry, and subject the local dealer, who does no business outside his own community, to regulations and penalties from Washington.

Seventh, the act is unconstitutional in that it seeks to override Clause 5, Section 9 of Article I, which declares:

> No tax or duty shall be laid on articles exported from any State.

The act directly forbids the export of any articles from one State to another unless the processing tax has been paid.

Onto this act was tacked as a rider, the so-called Thomas Amendment, which has nothing to do with agriculture. It transferred to the President the power confided to Congress alone in Clause 5, Section 8 of Article I, "to coin money, regulate the value thereof and of foreign coin". It authorizes the President, in his sole wisdom, (1) to print $3,000,000,000 of paper money and substitute it for any outstanding interest bearing government bonds, (2) to fix the value of silver in relation to gold and to print silver certificates, and (3) to change the gold content of the dollar by a reduction as much as one-half, in his sole discretion. No more flagrant abdication of its legislative power by Congress can be imagined.

The grand object to be accomplished by the amendment was revealed by Senator Thomas in these words when sponsoring it, on April 24, 1933:

Two hundred billions of dollars of wealth and buying power now rest in the hands of those who own the bank deposits and fixed investments, bonds, and mortgages. * * * If the amendment carries and the powers are exercised in a reasonable degree, it must transfer that $200,000,000,000 in the hands of persons who now have it, who did not buy it, who did not earn it, who do not deserve it, who must not retain it, back to the other side — the debtor class of the Republic, the people who owe the mass of debts of the nation.

The National Recovery Act, of June 16, 1933, has nearly all of the unconstitutional features of its twin, the Emergency Agricultural Relief Act, except those empowering taxation by an administrative official. It is a sort of Two or Three Year Plan for industry, copied after the Russian model, which, if continued, will centralize all power over private trade and industry in the hands of Washington bureaucrats and impose an involuntary servitude in violation of the Thirteenth Amendment.

These new federal autocrats — as well as scores of bureaus – under the power given to make laws, and to grant and revoke licenses to do business, are authorized actually to deprive the offending citizen of his common law right of appeal to his ordinary courts, to defeat their arbitrary action.

This is a wicked denial of the most cherished principle of Anglo-American liberty — the principle of due process of law.

Under the so-called Emergency Agricultural Relief Act, the Secretary of Agriculture has been given irresponsible powers to control crop prices, including that to regulate crop acreage, by distributing the proceeds of processing taxes to those farmers who will hold their lands from cultivation.

Under the so-called National Industrial Recovery Act, the dictator over the industry of the country is given the power to set aside the anti-trust laws and permit combinations in restraint of trade. In reporting this bill to the House, on May 25, 1933, Congressman Edward W. Pou, of North Carolina, said, not in shame, but with a note of rejoicing:

> It is very true that under this bill — and I shall not attempt to discuss its merits — the President of the United States is made a dictator over industry for the time being, but it is a benign dictatorship; it is a dictatorship dedicated to the welfare of all the American people.

All peoples who have ever lost their liberty have been lulled into a false sense of security by such assurances.

Under this measure the powers of the President have necessarily been delegated to underlings, whose orders are final as to hours of labor, wages and prices, as to all manufacturers and dealers in non-agricultural products, engaged in interstate commerce; and all right of appeal to the courts has been denied, however arbitrary and capricious the orders may be.

The right to engage in interstate commerce, to earn a living, in the United States — which is the right "to the pursuit of happiness" — is thus declared to be no longer a natural and inalienable right, but a privilege, conferred or denied in the good pleasure of our federal masters in Washington.

The political spoils afforded in the new agricultural and industrial acts exceed anything heretofore provided by any dozen acts of legislation. Each dictator is empowered to create public jobs without limit, and while the Agricultural Dictator may not fix salaries in excess of $8,500 a year, no provision restrains the Industrial Dictator from creating jobs with any salary he pleases to allow.

While the duration of these unconstitutional and tyrannical powers is limited, none should delude himself with the idea that this mixed Fascist-Communist rule will not be made permanent, if the power holders can bring it to pass.

The old order of freedom, and the protection of life, liberty and property, under a government of limited powers, is gone, and a new order of economic slavery, under a supreme executive government has succeeded. And this has been consummated by the party of the great philosopher and statesman, Jefferson, who wrote to Joseph C. Cabell, in 1816:

> What has destroyed the liberty and rights of man in every government which has ever existed under the sun? The generalizing and concentrating all cares and powers into one body, no matter whether of the autocrats of Russia or France, or of the autocrats of the Venetian Senate.

The assurances which have constantly been given to the country from Washington, that this assumption of despotic powers over our lives and property, is not unconstitutional, serves to recall that the historian Gibbon, referring to the transformation of that other great state, Rome, from Republican to Imperial, remarks:

> Augustus was sensible that mankind are governed by names; nor was he deceived in his expectation that the Senate and people would submit to slavery, provided they were respectfully assured that they still enjoyed their ancient liberties.

It is difficult to understand why the Supreme Court should lend encouragement to this delegation of legislative power and the erection of a huge and complicated administrative machine, whose irresponsible numbers only multiply with its output of law, unless it has been intimidated by various threats made in Congress in recent times to lessen its powers. Yet the next logical step in the magnification of administrative power is to deprive the courts wholly of their judicial power, as is sought to be done in the Emergency Agricultural Relief Act and in the National Industrial Recovery Act, of 1933. There was already a precedent, which the Supreme Court, oddly enough, has upheld, in the authority of the Secretary of Labor to deport certain aliens, and "in every case", "the decision of the Secretary of Labor shall be final." These plenary powers of the Secretary of Labor have very naturally aroused the acquisitive instincts of other federal officials and have emboldened the Postmaster General to contend, and successfully, that his power to forbid the use of the mails to newspapers and other publications — a power to destroy property and rights — is "not subject to be reviewed, reversed, set aside or controlled by a court of law."

This is not law as we understood it to be in other years; it is not the application of known rules and principles and a regular course of procedure, it is the mere exercise of arbitrary power. Judicial and legislative powers cannot be safely confided to an executive department or board. In hearings before the "examiners" of such departments there is little opportunity to test evidence by cross-examination; there is no certainty of having your witnesses summoned or heard; the presiding officer cannot be impartial, since every case is a challenge of his own chief's authority; and such decisions as are arrived at are founded in whole or in part on ex parte statements submitted by his own investigators. The reports in such cases are not unusually secret and give no opportunity for the establishment of precedents, nor is there any obligation to conform to any previous conclusion in like cases. Although the American citizen is still permitted to appeal from the conclusions of some administrative boards to the courts, the right becomes more and more meaningless as the courts refuse to go behind the bureau's judgment "on the facts"; and as a rule, the facts are the only things in dispute. It results therefore, that the citizen is deprived of his common law trial and his common law rights, and subjected to arbitrary power.

Chapter 4 –
Federal Bureaus at Work

Although we elect Representatives to Congress to make the laws Congress has transferred this function to numberless federal bureaus. It is these that are consuming our substance, while promulgating their thousands of penal edicts and decrees.

It has been said of public office-holders that "few die and none resign." Not only is this quality of tenacious life a characteristic of the administrative bureaus that have embedded themselves in our federal system like malignant tumors, but they exhibit also the most fecund capacity for autogenesis; that is to say, a bureau created today becomes two bureaus tomorrow.

By analogy, the bureau is, in the realm of government, what protozoa are in the realm of zoology. Originating as a single cell they immediately begin to reproduce by fission, a self-division of the body into two or more complete cells. The protozoa abound in stagnant waters, as the bureau can flourish only in the stagnation of public spirit. Protozoa are parasites and the cause of certain diseases, as bureaus are parasitic and destructive of the vigor and health of the body politic. Again protozoa are the simplest and lowest form of animal life, as bureau-government is one of the earliest and crudest forms of arbitrary rule. Protozoa are apparently content to remain protozoa, but there the analogy ends; the bureau is ever striving onward and upward, and not only subdivides itself indefinitely, but each subdivision, in turn, seeks to elevate itself ultimately into a mighty department.

Such is the process we witness in the growth and development of the scores of powerful administrative agencies now operating from Washington, consuming hundreds of millions of taxpayers' money, many without any constitutional warrant for their existence, and progressively destroying the independence, initiative and happiness of the American people in an effort to standardize them from birth to death.

It is not possible in a single chapter to present a complete review of all of the hundreds of federal departments, boards, bureaus and commissions, so busily at work undermining the foundations of our free republic. But enough can be presented to exhibit fully the revolutionary process. In order that the reader may judge for himself the absence of constitutional authority in Congress to create most of these bureaus and to endow them with functions outside the federal powers, it will be helpful to set out the limited enumeration of powers delegated to Congress in Section 8, Article 1, of the Constitution, to which he may recur:

> The Congress shall have power to lay and collect taxes, duties, imposts and excises, to pay the debts and provide for the common defense and general welfare of the United States; but all duties, imposts and excises shall be uniform throughout the United States;
>
> To borrow money on the credit of the United States;
>
> To regulate commerce with foreign nations and among the several States, and with the Indian tribes;

To establish a uniform rule of naturalization, and uniform laws on the subject of bankruptcies, throughout the United States;

To coin money, regulate the value thereof, and of foreign coin, and fix the standard of weights and measures;

To provide for the punishment of counterfeiting the securities and current coin of the United States;

To establish post offices and post roads;

To promote the progress of science and useful arts, by securing for limited times to authors and inventors exclusive right to their respective writing's and discoveries;

To constitute tribunals inferior to the Supreme Court;

To define and punish piracies and felonies committed on the high seas, and offences against the law of nations;

To declare war, grant letters of marque and reprisal, and make rules concerning captures on land and water;

To raise and support armies, but no appropriation of money to that use shall be for a longer term than two years;

To provide and maintain a Navy;

To make rules for the government and regulation of the land and naval forces;

To provide for calling forth the Militia, to execute the laws of the Union, to suppress insurrections and repel invasions;

To provide for organizing, arming and disciplining the Militia and for governing such part of them as may be employed in the service of the United States, reserving to the States respectively the appointment of the officers and the authority of training the Militia according to the discipline prescribed by Congress;

To exercise exclusive legislation in all cases whatsoever, over such district (not exceeding ten square miles) as may, by cession of the particular State, and the acceptance of Congress, become the seat of the government of the United States, and to exercise like authority over all places purchased with the consent of the States in which the same shall be for the erection of forts, magazines, arsenals, dockyards, and other needful buildings, and;

To make all laws which shall be necessary and proper for carrying into execution the foregoing powers, and all other powers vested by the Constitution in the Government of the United States, or in any department or officer thereof.

This is a statement of the sum total of the powers which Congress may lawfully exercise. Let us now look at some of the departments and bureaus, which it has recently erected, and the objects of such creations. And first let us take up the Department of Agriculture. Agriculture, the growing of crops by farmers in the States, is essentially a domestic concern of the people of the States, from the superintendence of which the federal government is excluded in the constitutional division of powers. This was clearly understood by the framers of our Constitution, as is evidenced in Elliot's Debates on the Federal Constitution. On August 20, 1787, Gouverneur Morris proposed to the convention a clause to empower the President to appoint a Secretary of Domestic Affairs, "to attend to matters of general police, the state of agriculture and manufactures, the opening of roads and navigation;" and also, "to establish agricultural colleges." These proposals were never reported out of committee; some of the objects were seen to be necessarily within the purview of any system of autonomous and self-governing States, in any federal plan.

After 50 years, however, in 1839, a modest "agricultural section" was authorized by Congress and placed in the Patent Office, with an appropriation of but $1,000, with the duty "to collect agricultural statistics." From this small beginning, this unconstitutional section became, in 1889, a full-fledged executive department, under a Secretary who sits in the Cabinet. Its scores of bureaus dissipated in irregular and dangerous activities, more than $173,000,000 in 1931, and $333,500,000 in 1932. The vast increase in 1933 cannot yet be computed.

This Department, which The Chicago Tribune has aptly said is "lost in its own weeds", is perhaps the most baleful of all of the many meddlesome federal administrative agencies; for Congress has conferred upon it, among other powers, the tyrannical one to enslave or destroy every American citizen engaged independently in agricultural and kindred pursuits, besides reducing to federal wardship the whole of the rural child population. It has acquired the despotic power to forbid tens of thousands of our citizens to earn a living, save with a federal license, which the Secretary may grant or deny, or after granting revoke. The business life of the grain dealer, the livestock dealer, even the potato dealer, are wholly subject to his caprice.

The thousands of agents of this Department, overrunning the land like a plague, are engaged in the most varied unconstitutional activities, which range from licensing a great Board of Trade, and its members to do business, to instructing the rural mother on the best style of rompers for the baby, the pattern turned out, of course, in one of the department's own bureaus.

In October, 1931, the Bureau of Home Economics of the Department of Agriculture, actually advertised under the franking privilege, to the rural mothers of the United States, that approved patterns of rompers for the baby might be had free upon application. Meantime the private manufacturers of such articles and the local store dealing in them will be compelled to continue to support this government competition out of their taxes.

The Agricultural Section's growth is typical of that of all federal administrative agencies, each of which is ever seeking a wider field of action, with larger appropriations and ever-expanding personnel. In 1862, the section became an "agency", under a Commissioner of Agriculture. In 1884 Congress created under it a Bureau of Animal Industry. On becoming a great department in 1889, there was more fission; in 1902, the Bureau of Soils — not the soils of federal reservations, but the soils of the States; the Bureau of Forestry, the Bureau of Chemistry, the Bureau of Plant Industry, all elevated from "divisions", which appropriately describes the embryonic form of a bureau. In this growth it will be seen how one unconstitutional act becomes a precedent upon which new precedents are piled in a never-ending calamitous series.

In 1859 Congress passed what was known as the Morrill Act, granting 6,060,000 acres of the public lands to the States for the establishment of colleges of agriculture and the mechanic arts, setting out that —

> The leading object shall be, without excluding scientific and other classical studies and including military tactics, to teach such branches of learning as are related to agriculture and

the mechanic arts, in such manner as the legislatures of the States may respectively prescribe, in order to promote the liberal and practical education of the industrial classes in the several pursuits and professions of life.

President James Buchanan vetoed the bill, saying:

> The federal government, which makes the donation, has confessedly no constitutional power to follow it into the States and enforce the application of the fund to the intended objects. As donors we shall possess no control over our own gift after it shall have passed from our hands. * * * The federal government has no power, and ought to have no power, to compel the execution of the trust. * * *

> I presume the general proposition is undeniable that Congress does not possess the power to appropriate money in the Treasury, raised by taxes on the people of the United States, for the purpose of educating the people of the respective States. It will not be pretended that any such power is to be found among the specific powers granted to Congress, nor that "it is necessary and proper for carrying into execution" any one of these powers. Should Congress exercise such a power, this would break down the barriers which have been so carefully constructed in the Constitution to separate federal from State authority. We would then not only "lay and collect taxes, duties, imposts and excises" for federal purposes, but for every State purpose which Congress might deem expedient or useful. This would be an actual consolidation of the federal and State governments, so far as the great taxing and money power is concerned, and constitute a sort of partnership

between the two in the Treasury of the United States, equally ruinous to both. * * *

This would be to confer upon Congress a vast and irresponsible authority, utterly at war with the well-known jealousy of federal power which prevailed at the formation of the Constitution.

That should have been conclusive upon any patriotic Congress, that the power to dictate or interfere with education in the States was wholly beyond its enumerated powers; but in 1862, in the midst of the Civil War, the advocates of this measure caused its passage a second time and Lincoln signed it. This was the beginning of one of the most alarming progressive usurpations ever inflicted upon the people of the States, nor are its evils yet fully accomplished, namely, the assumption of power by Congress to control all education in the States.

The history of federal intermeddling with the States' reserved authority over education is the record of a costly scramble on the part of a number of distinct departments and administrative agencies to "muscle in" and dominate this field with the direction of more than 29,000,000 children enrolled in our public and private schools. This is an objective not unworthy of the aims of the most ambitious bureaucrat.

In this rivalry we now find the active participants to be the Department of the Interior, and its own bureau, the U. S. Office of Education; the Department of Agriculture, the Department of Labor, through its Children's Bureau; the War Department, the Navy Department, the Federal Radio Commission and the Federal Board of Vocational Education. This federal intrusion into the field of State education had its beginning in the Morrill Act, which allotted public lands to such States as would establish agricultural colleges, teaching agriculture and the mechanic arts, "including military tactics", in the proportion of 30,000 acres for each Senator and Representative of such State. The Secretary of the Interior was designated to administer the act. In 1866 an amendment to the act required such colleges to report to the Secretary, thus "following the gifts" into the accepting States.

In 1869 the Commissioner of Education, in the Interior Department, was given administration of the subventions of these so-called "land grant" colleges, and he now administers an annual appropriation of $2,550,000 for them with a tightening grip upon their direction.

In 1890 a second Morrill Act launched the federal government upon a policy of annual appropriations, instead of lump-sum subventions, in a provision for $50,000 annually for each such college and forbidding discrimination among the students on account of color, where no separate colored college was established. The powers of the U. S. Commissioner of Education were enlarged so as to include that of prescribing the curricula and withholding funds, according to his discretion. From 1890 to 1930 the federal control of these colleges has been progressively extended with the distribution of funds totaling $74,202,000.

Meantime the U. S. Commissioner of Education has added new prestige to his office in his authority to inspect and require reports from Howard University, a private negro institution in Washington, to which Congress annually gives a large sum, in 1932, $1,500,000; and he is a member of the Federal Board of Vocational Education and of the Children's Bureau board, both engaged in health and educational activities in the States. He is striving to dominate the whole field as the Secretary of a great executive department of education, with a seat in the cabinet, and a bill with that object has already been introduced in Congress. That he is prepared for the day when this will be realized may be seen from the prevision in the organization of his office, in which we find a "Higher Education Division", a "Rural Schools Division" and a "City Schools Division". Meantime he is embarking into general education by radio. The appropriation for his office in 1932 was $510,000.

The Secretary of Agriculture came relatively late upon the scene as the head of a great department — in 1889 — but as Chief of the Bureau of Agriculture, under the Hatch Act of 1887, he was able also to reach out into the States and begin "scientific investigation and experimentation" in agriculture, through the establishment of experiment stations as adjuncts to the agricultural colleges, he to prescribe the research and require reports. The first appropriation was at the annual rate of $15,000 for each station, the beginning of the now universal "federal aid." In 1906, $75,000 was added annually for each station, and in 1925, $60,000 more for the study of production, processing and marketing agricultural products. This was the embryo of the monstrous Agricultural Marketing act, of 1929, with its appropriations of $500,000,000.

The restless bureaus of the Department of Agriculture had long been aware that there were tens of thousands of rural men, women and children, who could not avail themselves of the Interior Department's limited educational facilities in the "land grant" colleges, who ought nevertheless be rescued from ignorance. By 1914, they were able to make a start, through the Smith-Lever Act "for the diffusion of useful and practical information on subjects relating to agriculture and home economics." This, of course, was designed to embrace the education of the whole rural population; all that was necessary was an ample annual supply of taxpayers' money. The first sum appropriated, $4,100,000 annually, was hardly adequate. By the Capper-Ketcham Act of 1928, $980,000 was added for equal division among the States, and $500,000 more to be apportioned according to the proportion that rural population in any State bore to the whole. And, said the act, "at least 80 per centum of all appropriations under this act shall be utilized for the payment of salaries of extension agents in the counties of the several States to further develop the cooperative system in agriculture and home economics, with men, women, boys and girls."

With the $73,145,872 spent by the Secretary of Agriculture in this work from 1915 to 1931, he has been able to establish in more than 2,500 of the 3,000 counties in our forty-eight States definite educational organizations, dealing with multitudes of the rural population on the farms and in the homes, and to organize so-called character-building groups among hundreds of thousands of children, with a constantly enlarging personnel of teachers bearing a federal commission. The staff in 1930, since largely expanded, consisted of 487 State Leaders, State Directors and District Agents, 2,509 County Agents, 1,185 Home Agents, 208 Agents of 4 H Clubs, 1,107 specialists and 300 negro extension workers, not counting radio broadcasters. The federal commission, of course, gives each office-holder the privilege of flooding the mails with franked matter.

These agricultural bureau agents never lose contact with their adult and infant rural wards; if no agent is present in person printed propaganda reaches them almost daily, carried free through the mails. There were 24,150,059 pieces of such literature franked by the department in 1930, which, with other millions of other departments and boards account in part for the Post Office deficit of $165,000,000 in 1931 and $195,000,000 in 1932.

Here is a sample of the franked literature that heralds the approach of the rural speakers from the Bureau of Home Economics:

Who's Boss in your Home?

Are You? Or are your children? Do you know how to meet your child's problems?

And among the problems these are cited:

1. Getting to school on time.
2. Exaggeration and lying.
3. Children who contradict.
4. Carelessness and forgetfulness.
5. Thumb-sucking.
6. Stubbornness and determination.

This literature covers all imaginable subjects. Consider the heretofore undisclosed knowledge which the Department of Agriculture imparts to the farmer in this under the title:

Use and Care of Farm Woods

Fuel wood is in greatest demand in winter. Every stick of wood burned in the stove or in the furnace in winter saves buying its equivalent in other fuel.

Damage can be done by destroying trees prematurely or by cutting up quantities of wood or timber for which there may be no sale.

This presupposes a condition of paternalistic care, in which the farmer need no longer think for himself, a condition not yet here but on the way.

On January 7, 1932 Senator Harrison proposed a two year suspension in the printing of the tons of department bulletins, saying it would save $20,000,000 a year. He cited these titles of some recent ones:

The Love Life of Bullfrogs

How to Dress for Sunbaths

Public Dance Halls

Housing in Family Development

Utilization of Calcium in Spinach

Bringing up Baby

It is not suspension that is called for but total abolishment of this unconstitutional waste.

There is also daily radio instruction given by the Department of Agriculture to what is claimed to be the largest audience that any station reaches. There is likewise moving picture entertainment and instruction provided by the department, 3,000,000 feet of film on 250 subjects having been put out in 1930. Each succeeding year, of course, reveals an increased "service."

In 1911 the Navy Department resolved that it, too, would go in for education in the States, and it procured from Congress money and power to open Marine Schools in States bordering on our lakes and navigable rivers. These schools have the benefit of naval instructors assigned from Washington, with a suitable vessel and the sum of $25,000 annually to be matched by the States.

In 1917 the federal government took up a new branch of education in the States, under the Smith-Hughes Act, namely, vocational education, under a Federal Board of Vocational Education, made up of the Secretaries of Agriculture, Commerce and Labor, the U. S. Commissioner of Education and three civilians. The four political members can, of course, always outvote the three civilians in electing the chairman and otherwise. It receives $200,000 annually for its own use, and other sums to be matched by the States, increasing annually to $9,800,000 in 1934, when it will have disbursed $104,000,000. The States desiring to share must institute like boards and submit to federal direction under the U. S. Commissioner of Education.

It was a short step for the federal government from taking care of the minds and morals of the people of the States, to taking care of their bodies, particularly the curably ill and those injured in civil employments; hence, the enlarged powers and more funds confided in 1920, and extended in 1930, for rehabilitation under the Federal Board, with an annual appropriation of $1,075,000 additional, which, according to the act, is to be used only for salaries.

The War Department, having put over war-time conscription in 1917, lost no time on return of peace in planning for peacetime conscription, and, in order to accustom us to it, launched upon a large program of military education in State educational institutions. The Morrill Act of 1862, made allotment of lands to such State colleges as would teach agriculture and the mechanic arts, "including military tactics." No subsequent allotment or appropriation for these "land grant" colleges mentioned "military tactics", since the Secretary of the Interior had no interest in it. However, the War Department hung its claim upon this slender peg and is now imposing compulsory training on all students in such colleges, with free uniforms, free equipment, and the free use of polo ponies. For the Reserve Officers' Training Corps in these and other institutions, the expenditure in 1930 was over $6,000,000, besides $2,742,158 for the Citizens' Military Training Camps. The total appropriation for 1932 was $483,700,000, an increase of $122,900,000 over 1931.

Since 1927 the Federal Radio Commission has loomed as a formidable rival of all the other federal educational agencies operating in the States. Although by the act of Congress creating it the Commission was empowered to license stations "in the public interest, convenience and necessity", it has construed its authority to be far greater than those terms would imply, even to the point of imposing censorship. It authorizes, inspects and controls radio transmission in all educational institutions, allocating wave-lengths, apportioning time and granting or withholding permission to change equipment. It is giving serious attention to the character of broadcasts that are most conducive to sound education and it is not improbable that before long it will issue and enforce its own regulations concerning the same. Meantime the Secretary of the Interior has set up a rival educational radio section in his department, with the assistance of a very active Advisory Committee on Education by Radio.

Finally the Children's Bureau in the Department of Labor has been striving against obstacles to take over maternal welfare and child hygiene education in the States, but this having been reluctantly authorized for a period ending in 1929, it has been able to survive with only meager appropriations.

No doubt some good may come out of all this costly dabbling in education and uplift by the federal government, but, when it is considered that it is, in the main, usurpation of power, tending to undermine the independence of the people and to destroy the capacity for local self-government, the evil that will result from it appears greatly to surpass any possible good. It is essentially work for the respective States to perform and which they could perform more effectively if the excessive taxes required for it by the federal government were foregone in the interest of the States.

If one wishes to learn more in detail of these widespread, costly and dangerous activities of the various departments, all looking to uniform textbooks throughout our school system, issued from and censored by Washington bureaucrats, let him read the two heavy volumes that comprise the Report of President Hoover's National Advisory Committee on Education. A few at least of this large committee comprehended the menace and declared for its correction.

There are many other bureaus of the Department of Agriculture that are quite as busy in the States, in equally irregular activities, not the least of which is the Bureau of Biological Survey, which not only fights the farmers' battles against destructive animals, but is steadily seeking to regulate every sportsman in the United States, as to his shooting season, through a system of federal hunting licenses and a political army of federal game wardens.

In its big game hunts, at the taxpayers' expense, the Bureau of Biological Survey — "the world's largest organization of its kind" — bagged 45,016 coyotes, 321 mountain lions, 337 bears, 5,070 bobcats and lynx and 1,578 wolves in 1931, all in the protection of the farmer in the western States. This fine sport, for which the bureau sportsmen receive salaries and allowances, consumed $609,950 of our taxes in 1931.

The work of the Bureau of Entomology and the Insecticide and Fungicide Boards must not be overlooked. They can put as many as six thousand federal huntsmen into the field to kill off the farmers' little foes. Incidentally, in their hunt for the Mediterranean fruit fly in Florida in 1929, they destroyed 600,000 crates of citrus fruits and inflicted such damage upon the groves that the fruit farmers appealed to Congress for financial relief.

Although the federal insect hunters have spent and received in salaries more than $7,000,000 of our taxes to destroy the Mediterranean fruit fly, neither they nor any man has seen a living one in the United States, according to Senator Kenneth McKellar. The bureau has found one dead one, however, and it is on exhibition in a fine glass case in the palatial new department building.

Aside from the unconstitutional character of most of these activities, the year 1932, which piled up a deficit for the fiscal year of $2,885,362,299, called urgently for genuine economies in the federal expenditures. In the face of that condition consider these appropriations allowed by Congress:

Cattle tuberculosis service	$6,505,800
Cattle tick service	771,900
Animal husbandry investigations	723,400
Diseases of animals	460,000
Hog cholera service	499,480
Dourine treatments to horses	32,800
Dairy Experiments	727,410
Fungus investigations	59,960
Citrus diseases	40,000
Forest pathology	236,904
Blister rust investigation	456,000
Plant-nutrition investigation	18,050
Cotton diseases and production	233,140
Rubber investigation	140,463
Drug plant inquiry	58,120
Study of worms	58,260

Seed investigations..78,220
Cereal crop diseases... 574,060
Barberry investigation 377,140
Tobacco investigation...91,000
Sugar plant investigation.................................. 413,700
Botany..56,260
Dry-land agriculture 345,740
Irrigation agriculture... 153,940
Horticultural diseases 1,420,360
Phony peach eradication....................................85,000
Gardens and grounds...98,120
Genetics and biophysics....................................36,420
Forest products Laboratory building............. 800,000
Forest products study.. 641,300
Forest survey.. 200,000
Forest economics 75,000
Acquisition of lands for protection of
    watersheds of navigable streams................ 2,000,000
Agricultural chemical investigations................ 501,075
Color investigations 93,460
Insecticide investigations 128,400
Plant dust explosions...36,500
Fertilizer investigations..................................... 370,835
Soil investigations...61,420
Soil microbiology..43,820
Soil fertility investigation 220,080
Fruit and shade tree insects............................. 549,190
Truck garden insects.. 451,690
Forest insects 224,290
Cereal insects 567,220
Grasshopper extermination............................. 1,450,000

Cotton insects 298,820

Insects affecting man 156,900

Household insects 154,920

Classification of insects 238,730

Bee culture 73,920

Rabbit experiment station 12,640

Food habits of birds study 107,660

Biological investigations 128,315

Farm management study 480,760

Home economics investigation 218,700

Pink boll worm control 497,000

Parlatoria date scale 65,460

Thurberia weevil control 34,500

Gypsy moth control 648,580

Corn borer control 950,000

Japanese beetle control 445,000

White pine blister rust 10,200

Phony peach control 12,000

Mexican fruit worm 124,960

Mediterranean fruit fly 30,300

Enforcement Insecticide act 225,458

Livestock production experiments 43,500

Soil erosion investigations 330,000

Forest roads and trails 12,500,000

In the foregoing incomplete list of eighty odd activities, in a single federal department — that of Agriculture — for which $41,463,290 was appropriated, one may get a glimpse of the enormous waste that goes on; nor will the members of Congress put an end to it, because their own political appointees and partisans are its beneficiaries. They have, however, made a general five per cent reduction in the amounts for 1933. This saving is insignificant when it is considered that the federal government will disburse over $10,000,000,000 in 1933-34, and incur another deficit probably exceeding $5,000,000,000 to be concealed by bookkeeping.

Then consider these non-governmental investigations in a single bureau, that of Chemistry and Soils: Carbohydrate work, vegetable by-products, dehydration of fruit, spoilage of food, grapefruit canning, molasses, germinated grain in flour, fish flour, staling bakery products, pigment, ursolic acid in apples, spraying oranges, pin-1 spot molding in eggs, wheat mills, composition of cellophane, tannin, deterioration of leather, paper manufacture, jute manufacture, ramie, utilization of corn stalks, cherry pit oil, sugar cane wax, farm fires, gluten, fish poison plants.

Practically all of this research is going on in private laboratories at private expense, with commercial or scientific objects, and it is unquestionably being carried on more thoroughly. It is not properly a governmental function, but it provides patronage.

After having taken over agriculture, it was inevitable that the dairy interest would not long remain free from federal interference, and it came in 1924, with an act creating the Bureau of Dairying, which has set up experiment stations with the following objects: bacteriology and chemistry of milk; the breeding and feeding of cattle; dairy management; dairy sanitation; manufacture of dairy products and by-products, with an appropriation of $484,340 for a starter. From this entering wedge has evolved a federal power to fix the price of milk at retail sale.

There are some federal bureaus to which Congress has delegated powers under the interstate commerce clause, which have permitted the most serious abuses, notably in the Meat Inspection Act, under which inspectors, located in the various packing houses, have the power of passing or rejecting meats intended for shipment across State lines. An unusually flagrant case was called to the attention of the Senate on March 29, 1928, by Senator Millard E. Tydings of Maryland, during the discussion of a bill to appropriate large sums for the purchase of "migratory game refuges" under the control of the Biological Survey. Senator Tydings said:

> This bill, if enacted into law, would create another bureau, and I want to draw to the Senator's attention an illustration of where the bureaus are leading us. As the Senator knows, we have a Bureau of Animal Industry. Among its various duties is the duty of inspecting meat which is shipped to the people by those killing steers and sheep and other livestock. * * * It so happens that last year in my State four or five small concerns wanted to go into the business of selling meat, and before they could go into that business they had to have certain plans for the building of their plants and certain machinery and certain restrictions surrounding their industry, all approved by the Bureau of Animal Industry. This before they could sell a pound of meat.

> That might be all right in places, but after these gentlemen had built their plants, installed their machinery, and had it all approved by the federal government, the Bureau of Animal Industry served notice upon them that they could not sell any meat anyhow. The question was naturally asked: Why? The Bureau of Animal Industry said that Congress had failed to appropriate sufficient money to permit an inspector to be placed at those points where meats had to be inspected. But these men said: "The big 4 packing establishments have between them upwards of 600 meat

inspectors. We only require one for all our activities. Is it not in the interest of justice that you take one of those inspectors away from the men who now have 500 or 600, because it will not hamper them much, but if we do not get at least one inspector we will be put out of business."

The Bureau said it was powerless to act and could not give them an inspector because they wanted to place inspectors where they could inspect the greatest volume of meat. Therefore after all the plants in question were constructed at a cost of many thousands of dollars, those men were told that they could not actually engage in business, when they had done everything the law required them to do.

Finally, upon my own responsibility, I told the men to go ahead and sell the meat, because the delinquency was that of the government and not theirs; that they had in every way complied with the law, and that, in my judgment, no jury in the world would convict them, when the government, and not they, was at fault. They went ahead and sold the meat. The first carload that went out of the State of Maryland into a neighboring State was seized by the policemen of the federal government, and those men were haled into court charged with the crime of selling meat which was not inspected by the government. I immediately took the matter up again with the proper authorities, and I found that while they did not have money enough to supply an inspector for those meat plants, they did have money enough to have four or five policemen to catch anybody who violated the law. I suggested that they do away with one policeman and appoint one inspector with the money, which was done after a delay of over three months in permitting these small packing establishments to operate.

That is a sample of the way bureaucracy works in this government.

One can see the narrow and vindictive bureaucratic mind at work in almost every step of obstruction narrated by Senator Tydings, and particularly, in the punishment for defiance, inflicted by a three months' delay, after the seizure of the un-inspected meat, before the Bureau permitted an inspector to go to the plants that they might resume business.

These small packers were wholly at the mercy of the Bureau and might have been completely ruined, instead of being merely subjected to bearable financial losses. There is a certain discretion lodged by Congress in these federal agencies which no writ of mandamus can reach. It appears reasonable to suppose that Senator Tydings finally saved their property for them only by the use of his official influence with some superior in the Department, or perhaps with a fellow Senator responsible for the appointment of the Bureau Chief.

The Bureau of Animal Industry has its very proper duty of inspecting meats in interstate commerce — meats put into interstate commerce by farmers doing their own slaughtering are thus far privileged from inspection — but it is under the duty to play no favorites, and to facilitate rather than obstruct the work of the meat industry.

In the Department of Agriculture nothing pertaining to that subject is beyond the Secretary's power of interference, as may be seen from such legislation as the Grain Standards Act, the Cotton Standards Act, the Produce Agency Act, the Apple-Grading Act, the Adulterated Seed Act, the Cotton Futures Act, the Grain

Futures Act, the Warehouse Act, the Perishable Commodities Act, which, with the Agricultural Marketing Act (Farm Board) and numberless others, enforced with an infinite body of clerk-made regulations, are all conspiring to discourage and vex commerce to the point of utter ruin.

The unconstitutional program of the Department of Agriculture in the matter of education, was apprehended in Congress a quarter of a century ago, when Chairman Wadsworth of the House Committee on Agriculture gave warning that the bills to grant "aid" to agricultural schools of the States, would by and by be extended to all State education, and then, he said, "You will have federal control and supervision of your public schools." At the same time Chairman Tawney of the House Appropriations Committee, said, with prophetic vision:

> If we continue this system of paternalism much longer, it will not be long before Congress will be swept off its feet and called upon to account for from $25,000,000 to $50,000,000 annually for the construction and maintenance of good roads.

All this and more has come to pass: a great Bureau of Public Roads has been created in the Department of Agriculture, spending millions of taxpayers' money annually in a fifty-fifty matching system of "federal aid." From 1916 to 1933 this bureau contributed to the States $1,240,375,000, all taken from the people of a few of the States and redistributed unequally. The appropriation for 1931 was $125,000,000. In January, 1932, Congress appropriated $105,000,000 for this bureau, and later $120,000,000 additional as outright "gifts" for road work, allocating it in the most discriminatory manner. What influence particular Congressmen exerted to procure large shares for their States is not disclosed but, upon the announced plan of allotment, some favored States received from one to five times the entire amount of their contributions to the federal Treasury in income tax payments. That is to say the people of certain States are taxed to support the people of other States. Consider the following six States and their allotted shares of these "gifts":

State	Income Taxes Paid 1932	Road Fund Gifts 1932
Idaho	$465,396	$1,508,485
Montana	750,726	2,525,108
Nevada	1,299,099	1,578,025
North Dakota	234,543	1,940,325
South Dakota	414,637	2,002,076
Wyoming	345,616	1,540,811
Totals	$3,510,017	$11,094,830

Thus, by this bill, other States of the Union may be compelled to refund the entire income tax payments made by these six States and to present to them in addition about $7,500,000.

Passed on the pretext of an "economic emergency", the public works relief act of June 16, 1933, contains a gift of $400,000,000 to the States for public road building, which will be allocated to them with some slight changes in the same unequal manner heretofore practiced. The relatively few States which will have to pay it in taxes will receive back only an insignificant proportion.

Alexander Hamilton warned us in The Federalist, that the historic rule of apportioning direct taxes to the States had shut the door to oppression in taxation; that if that door were opened, a majority of the States would combine in Congress to plunder the industrious minority, through unequal and discriminatory taxation; and that is precisely what has happened since 1913, when Congress overthrew the rule of apportionment in the 16th Amendment.

The unconstitutional policy of federal subsidies is the chief vehicle through which Congressmen from the South and West rob the ten or twelve States that pay practically the whole of the federal income taxes. The following Treasury release of what each State paid and what it received in 1932 tells the story vividly:

States	Paid in Internal Taxes	Received in Federal Aid
Alabama	$2,615,750	$3,734,979
Alaska	123,366	88,558
Arizona	918,880	3,712,617
Arkansas	1,034,375	3,989,615
California	76,405,967	10,113,968
Colorado	5,548,218	4,731,502
Connecticut	20,341,705	2,691,201
Delaware	16,368,254	1,160,406
District of Columbia	8,449,637	149,154
Florida	8,478,398	3,137,523
Georgia	4,422,383	6,193,086
Hawaii	3,785,882	952,145
Idaho	485,338	3,265,079
Illinois	106,973,480	11,479,329
Indiana	12,443,758	7,345,362

States	Paid in Internal Taxes	Received in Federal Aid
Iowa	6,455,906	5,047,664
Kansas	7,144,002	5,671,593
Kentucky	26,273,498	4,103,016
Louisiana	6,260,956	3,934,425
Maine	4,345,593	3,006,994
Maryland	23,435,538	2,339,567
Massachusetts	49,160,123	5,628,698
Michigan	59,952,511	8,507,521
Minnesota	14,305,965	6,648,336
Mississippi	844,890	3,376,705
Missouri	34,743,275	6,111,388
Montana	869,792	5,031,202
Nebraska	3,157,412	5,669,262
Nevada	1,346,609	2,722,556
New Hampshire	1,684,239	1,334,031
New Jersey	70,394,221	3,033,776
New Mexico	379,561	2,963,268
New York	395,616,411	19,992,830
North Carolina	231,362,001	5,053,167
North Dakota	247,241	3,526,577
Ohio	61,853,989	9,134,482
Oklahoma	10,178,484	4,965,379
Oregon	2,560,833	4,684,390

States	Paid in Internal Taxes	Received in Federal Aid
Pennsylvania	109,394,468	11,989,944
Rhode Island	6,709,285	1,980,867
South Carolina	1,773,556	2,797,390
South Dakota	448,859	4,161,784
Tennessee	9,253,993	3,331,517
Texas	18,310,533	14,806,670
Utah	1,442,625	2,857,095
Vermont	965,816	1,298,021
Virginia	100,240,343	4,133,301
Washington	5,748,813	4,295,165
West Virginia	7,082,263	3,298,381
Wisconsin	16,508,169	5,805,243
Wyoming	402,389	3,900,555
Philippine Islands		363,829
Porto Rico		289,224
Totals	$1,559,613,345	$250,377,778

The federal gifts scattered about in 1933-34, under the pretext of "an emergency", including $400,000,000 for public roads, may reach $1,000,000,000. Not until it has been spent can any accurate record be made.

Most of these abuses of power gained their foothold in the States during the first decade of this century, under restless energy and driving force of our most reckless and most ambitious President — Theodore Roosevelt. Besides intermeddling in the affairs of other countries, in the promotion of our aggrandizement abroad, he bullied the Congress and scolded the Supreme Court, in the interest of his own aggrandizement at home. His acts conformed always to his public declaration, in 1903, that "we need, through executive action, through legislation and through judicial interpretation, to increase the powers of the federal government." As every one knows, the powers of the federal government can be increased constitutionally only through the amending clause. Any other method is usurpation calling for impeachment. Yet usurpation has been the process most widely used until the States have become little more than geographical areas, under the control of thousands of federal agents.

We pass on now to the great Department of the Interior, better known than some of the others, by reason of its recent ill-renown in connection with the oil scandals in the public lands under its control. Up to almost the middle of last century the federal government managed to get along with three principal departments, those of State, War and Treasury. In 1848 propaganda appeared for the creation of a "Home" department, and a congressional committee promptly recommended it, with the usual idealistic pretense, that —

> War and preparations for war have been practically regarded as the chief duty of this government, while acts of peace and production, whereby nations are subsisted, civilization advanced and happiness secured, have been esteemed unworthy the attention, or foreign to the objects of this government.

The truth is, of course, that "acts of peace and production," are wholly reserved to the people of the States, as domestic concerns, and are, in fact, foreign to the constitutional objects of the federal government. But a bill went through, nevertheless, and a "Home" department, under the name of the Department of the Interior, came into being in 1849. As to its functions, Congress looked about and found a number of independent offices that could be transferred to it, such as the General Land Office and its Commissioner, the Patent Office with its agricultural section, Indian Affairs, public buildings in Washington, the Census and the District of Columbia penitentiary.

In his very first annual report the Secretary recommended raising the agricultural section of the Patent Office, into a full Bureau of Agriculture and also asked authority and funds for the building of highways. In 1867, there was created in the Interior Department a Bureau of Education. Then came the bureaus of National Parks, Geological Survey and Labor.

In 1903, in response to Roosevelt's policy of increasing the federal powers by legislation, and to attach to himself the farmers of the West, Congress passed an act establishing in the Department of the Interior, a Reclamation and Irrigation Service, to undertake the building of reservoirs, the formation of water-users associations and the sale of water for irrigation purposes. In 1906 the constitutionality of this act was challenged in a case brought by the State of Kansas against the State of Colorado to enjoin the diversion of water from the Arkansas River into Colorado. Justice Brewer for the Supreme Court said:

> The government of the United States is one of delegated, limited and enumerated powers. Turning to the enumeration of the powers granted to Congress by the eighth section of the first article of the Constitution, it is enough to say that no one of them, by any implication refers to reclamation of arid lands.

But did the Reclamation and Irrigation Service close up shop with this decision declaring the act null and void? Not at all; at least twenty great and costly projects of the kind have been carried through since that day, and in some, only an unlimited taxing power has been able to conceal the financial losses. That it has been a policy of waste is to be seen in the wide-spread default in the payment of rentals, and in recent acts of Congress, empowering the Secretary of the Interior to suspend these payments, write off the losses and pass the burdens on to the federal taxpayers, to the extent of $27,000,000.

The Bureau of Reclamation reports that 2,718,130 acres of private lands were being irrigated by water from a score or more of federal works in 1930, an increase of 41,030 acres over 1929; this at a time when there is a surfeit of agricultural lands on the market.

At a hearing before the Appropriations Committee of the House in December, 1931, it was revealed that on all of the projects, except a number that were paying all debts from the proceeds of the sale of power, in competition with private industry, there was a universal demand for a moratorium on reclamation payments and other obligations on the part of the settlers. On October 27, 1931, reclamation farmers from twenty Western projects, representing 880,000 acres, met in convention in Boise, Idaho, and demanded a three year moratorium, without interest, as to "construction and other payments."

Of the 880,000 acres represented at this meeting, water users of 200,000 acres make no construction payments to the government, since the government kindly makes these payments for them out of the sale of power from plants erected on the projects; and half the construction charges are paid from the sale of power on 200,000 additional acres. Where annual construction charges are made at all they amount to five per cent of the annual crop income, the total to be paid within forty years.

It was further disclosed that the loss from "interest-free subsidies" on these projects for 1931, calculating interest at six per cent, was $9,000,000; that is to say, the total subsidies amounted to $150,000,000.

The Commissioner of Reclamation reported to a Senate Committee under date of December 10, 1931, that in one of the projects where the settlers were suffering "economic and financial distress", a Federal Land Bank has loaned $80 to $90 an acre on 62 per cent of all the lands in the district, and, he says "the loans are more than the land is worth." And, added the Commissioner "that is not an isolated instance."

In 1929, certain Western Congressmen put over one of the most costly irrigation raids which the Treasury has ever had to meet, in the Boulder Dam project, on the Colorado River, twenty-five miles southeast of Las Vegas, Nevada, where the river forms the Arizona-Nevada boundary. The appropriation for this enterprise was $165,000,000. Of this sum $38,000,000 is being used to build an "All-American canal," to carry water eighty miles to the Imperial Valley, and one hundred and thirty miles into the Coachella Valley, in Southeastern California, to irrigate 2,000,000 acres of now worthless privately-owned lands; and to provide an adequate supply of drinking water for Los Angeles and other California towns.

Incidentally, there will be generated at Boulder Dam 1,200,000 horse-power of electrical energy, to be sold in competition with privately-owned plants "at 1.63 mills per kilowatt-hour for firms and ½ mill per kilowatt-hour for secondary energy", according to a bureau bulletin.

Since the close of the Great War there has been a group in Congress working steadily to enlarge the federal government's competition with privately-owned power plants, through the governmental operation of Muscle Shoals; this in spite of repeated offers from private power groups to lease the plant at Wilson Dam and pay a rental as high as $2,200,000 a year, and submit to governmental regulation as to the price of electrical energy sold.

In 1933, under the leadership of Senator Norris, legislation was passed, not only for governmental operation at Wilson Dam, but for the building of a second clam, to cost $6,000,000 three hundred miles upstream, all placed under a new bureau, entitled the Tennessee Valley Authority, which is to be given millions of our taxes to create a model valley in parts of Tennessee and Alabama, embracing the Tennessee River basin.

This Act, of May 18, 1933, provides that even though Muscle Shoals is operated at a loss — as federal enterprises universally are — the States of Tennessee and Alabama shall each receive annually five per cent of the gross proceeds from the sale of power or steam, and each an additional two and one-half per cent from the gross proceeds from the sale of power from the new proposed dam, at Cove Creek.

This is a fine specimen of the log-rolling methods through which the Western and Southern States are constantly raiding the Federal Treasury of the taxes extorted from the people of the relatively few industrious States.

It is interesting to learn from Thomas F. Woodlock, former member of the Interstate Commerce Commission, how these vast projects adapt and readapt themselves for the sake of long life. In the Wall Street Journal on November 5, 1931, he said:

There are three important instances where government competition with its citizens in the power industry is plainly threatened. They are Muscle Shoals, Boulder Dam and St. Lawrence. We all know the history of Muscle Shoals. It originally was intended as a war measure for the production of nitrate as a base for explosives. The war being ended, we were next told that it was a great help to the farmer in the production of fertilizers, and we still hear a great deal of talk about that. All this is pure humbug.

The real purpose of those advocating development by the government of the Muscle Shoals situation is the production and sale of electric current in competition with private plants.

Boulder Dam started out first as a measure of flood control, and next as an irrigation measure. As in the case of Muscle Shoals, however, the real pressure which has been successful in this case, is development of power to be supplied in competition with private and public power industries in the territory to be served.

All this building of dams is justified under the so-called power of Congress "to improve navigation", where, in fact, on the Colorado River, navigation will be effectively obstructed; and the Supreme Court has just decided that, whether the particular structures authorized by Congress on the Colorado River for the purpose of improving navigation are reasonably necessary, is not for the court to determine.

With the court thus closing its eyes, it is not surprising to learn that the Secretary of the Interior has gone on to construct near the Dam a model city, in which he is the only landlord. The literature proclaiming this tells us that $2,000,000 will be expended for streets, sewage and water systems, lighting and dwellings, including a $35,000 swimming pool, for a population of about 5,000, including federal employees. In this literature is the following, in question and answer form:

Q: Who owns the lands in the town site?

A: The government owns the land, which is public vacant land under first form withdrawal.

Q: How can one obtain a town lot for business purposes?

A: The land is leased for a ten-year term ending June 30, 1941, to those awarded business permits, the government to retain ownership and supervisory control. Continuation of the lease is contingent upon compliance with the terms of the contract. A model town is the objective.

And another bulletin says:

One of the features of these leases is that they will continue only during the period of good behavior of the tenant.

There is not the vaguest constitutional authority for this building of a second federal town and the incidental usurpation of State jurisdiction therein, as there is none for the building of Boulder Dam itself; but if there were, what citizen not lost to all sense of moral dignity and forgetful of his heritage of freedom, would voluntarily seek a permit to place himself and his conduct under the detestable surveillance of federal bureaucratic censors, as is here contemplated?

One need only read the enumerated powers of Congress to see that the manufacture of electrical energy for sale, the furnishing of water to farms in the States, and to our towns and cities for drinking purposes, are wholly outside that grant of authority.

There is yet a vaster and more costly enterprise in the making whereby federal taxpayers are to be made to contribute $400,000,000 in order that certain constituents of the Senators and Representatives from Washington, Oregon, Montana and Idaho may bring under cultivation 1,200,000 acres of now un-tillable soil. This is the Columbia River Basin project, for which Congress authorized surveys by army engineers in an act of January 21, 1927.

The fact that it will entail an expenditure of $333.33 per acre for all the land to be irrigated — when good farm lands may be had in any of these States for not to exceed $57 — and the further fact that, according to the Department of Agriculture, our farm acreage should be reduced 30,000,000 to 40,000,000 acres, if the farmer is to obtain fair prices — these facts in no way restrain the ardor of Western Congressmen, or of the Department of the Interior to make privately-owned sections of the Western desert bloom at public expense.

The irrigation of private lands is properly a work for private cooperation among land-owners or for private companies. Ninety per cent of all irrigated lands in the United States are watered in this manner and pay their way or fail. This is as it should be, if initiative and enterprise are traits to be encouraged. We may be certain that private irrigation can stand no such financial waste as characterizes the federal government schemes.

In order to justify its reclamation service, and the bringing in of more lands for cultivation, the Department of the Interior has undertaken the publication of its own monthly magazine, entitled The New Reclamation Era. It is a handsome and well illustrated periodical, discussing subjects from "The Benefits of Irrigation" to "Raising Rabbits for Pets and Market", franked through the mails to anyone who will pay 75 cents a year for it.

The generosity of the Interior Department with American taxpayers' money may be further seen in its government of the Virgin Islands, purchased from Denmark in 1917 for $25,000,000. Under Denmark the islands were practically self-supporting. The annual average contribution from the Danish treasury from 1910 to 1917 was only $22,750.39. The contributions of American taxpayers for the support of the islands has risen from $100,000 in 1918 to $322,410.76 in 1931, or about $10 for each of the 32,000 inhabitants, largely consumed by American office-holders. The principal source of the former revenue of the islands, liquor taxes, was abolished with Prohibition, but other taxes yielding about $200,000 annually, or $6.00 per capita, are in force. Among new projects in the islands is a $58,356.83 government hotel.

Another tax-eating bureau of ravenous capacity, that of Pensions, operated in the Interior Department until 1930, when it was consolidated with the Veterans' Administration. The demands for pensions never cease and are never denied by members of Congress hoping for re-election. That is why there are now 1,300,000 persons in the United States who receive a monthly check from the federal Treasury, of whom 683,110 are veterans of the World War. Our total casualties in that war, including wounded, missing and dead from all causes, were 350,000. That is why the estimate for 1933 for pensions is $1,072,064,527, an increase of nearly $300,000,000 over 1932. That is why the Veterans' Administration has been able to disburse over $15,000,000,000 up to June 30, 1932. By an act of 1930 those disabled by any malady — even an automobile accident due to one's own negligence —

were granted pensions of from $20 to $40 per month, just because they were drafted in 1917. In 1933 Congress empowered the President to end these abuses in the interest of economy but the organized veterans are a formidable power.

The Bureau of Indian Affairs, in the Interior Department, whose cost to taxpayers has increased from $15,000,000 in 1927 to $25,000,000 in 1930, could be abolished with great resulting benefit to taxpayers and Indians as well. Its only public excuse for existence is "to educate" the 250,000 Indians remaining in twenty-four of our States. None of the uneducated of any other race that has come to the United States has been subjected to special government care. The schools of the States are open to all.

The undisclosed reason for this bureau, however, is that these Indians own about one and one-half billion dollars worth of property, of which the bureau has induced Congress to make it trustee, and of this sum about $100,000,000 is in cash or its equivalent. It is the bureau, not the Indian owner, which may lease his vast acreages, his water power rights, and oil rights; sell his timber, irrigate his land, raise cattle, and do as it pleases with his property generally. And this in spite of the fact that an act of Congress of 1924 granted him presumably unqualified citizenship.

If the Indian is dissatisfied with his trustee or the trustee's stewardship, he cannot apply to the Courts of the country, nor can he employ an attorney to represent him before Congress or the bureau, unless that attorney is previously approved by the bureau — the bureau has final say as to what fees shall be paid to the "approved" attorney. If, however, the bureau approves of a particular attorney, he may present the Indian's case, not to the courts, but to the bureau, the trustee itself.

Could any system better suited to exploitation have been devised?

It is of interest, in this connection, to point out that Congress has been induced to permit the filing in the United States Court of Claims of 86 separate suits by various Indian tribes asking for approximately two billion dollars from the federal government to cover past mis-administration of their affairs by this bureau. If they get judgment the result will be that the bureau will have three and one-half billions to play with in place of only one and one-half. All the attorneys in the cases have been "approved" and need have no worry about collecting their fees.

Nothing can be done to end this monstrous condition since most of the Congressmen from the twenty-four States find it personally advantageous to themselves and to their friends at home. The irrigation of Indian lands at the Indians' expense is rapidly transferring these farms to white purchasers at bargain prices. The irrigation costs are a first lien, and when an Indian dies his land must be sold to discharge it. Then, too, there is one Indian school job-holder for every 8.2 Indian school children, and that is fine patronage right at home.

One may find the full exposure of this gigantic racket in the serial leaflets of Joseph W. Lattimer, a member of the Peoria, Illinois, bar.

The Bureau of Education, which came into existence in 1867, and became an Office of Education in 1869, is of very great concern to the States, since its field of possible usurpation embraces the control of every public school child and every student of the State colleges of all of the forty-eight States.

A bill to raise the Office of Education to a full department was introduced in the Senate in 1918 by Senator Hoke Smith of Georgia, known as the Smith-Towner bill, and later as the Sterling-

Towner bill. It seems to have gotten sidetracked, but it may make its reappearance any day.

If the Child Labor Amendment is ever ratified the "Office of Education" will become a great Department of Education, under a Secretary in the Cabinet, directing the education of 45,000,000 children under 18, with the backing of a greedy federalized teachers' union, 850,000 strong.

The only reference to education in the enumerated powers of Congress is in its authority "to promote the progress of science and useful arts", by authorizing the granting of copyrights and patents. By no stretch of the imagination can anyone deduce from this a power to launch the federal government into the field of general or special education.

The Interior Department's budget for 1933 is $58,190,929, but the Secretary, as public works administrator was given an additional sum of $3,300,000,000 of easy money to disburse.

The Post Office Department, which in the past has provided the largest amount of patronage for Congressmen, is a department of annual deficits. While the postal services of nearly all other countries in the world produce revenue to meet the costs of government, ours had a loss of nearly $200,000,000 in 1932.

An indication of its lack of business organization may be seen in the 46,000 fourth class postmasters, whose compensation consists of the proceeds from the sale of stamps. Not a penny comes to the government from these post offices, while these postmasters, all rural, have free parcel post service for such chickens, eggs and other products as they care to send to market. They put the cost of postage into the till, and on canceling the stamps, take it out again and replace it in their own pockets.

They can, of course, extend the same free parcel post service to their friends.

The Department of Commerce and Labor was created by an act of 1903, but it became necessary to placate the labor politicians by splitting off and creating a distinct executive Department of Labor in 1913. The functions of the Department of Commerce, in the Bureaus of Census, Navigation, Lighthouses, Steamboat Inspection, Coast and Geodetic Survey, Standards and Patent Office, fall fairly clearly within the federal sphere. The Bureau of Fisheries, however, has felt the lure of the inland streams of the States and is promoting "cooperation" with its 37 hatcheries and 34 substations; and it is reaching out to control the sockeye salmon industry of Puget Sound, a natural resource of the State of Washington.

As the Biological Survey is seeking to license and regulate all game bird shooting in the States, so an entering wedge has been driven for the Bureau of Fisheries to regulate all inland fishermen through the Hawes act, which forbids the interstate shipment of black bass. This net appropriates $19,000, which is consumed by one chief at $6,400 a year, one assistant at $5,400, one stenographer at $1,800 and two "enforcement" officers at $2,600 each. One officer is allocated to Kentucky and the other to Vermont, while the chief's headquarters are in Baltimore. Soon, of course, there will be hundreds of federal fish policemen snooping along the banks of our streams, destroying that quiet sport as well as the fresh water fish industry.

Among the wholly incongruous new services of the Department of Commerce is that of public consulting interior decorator for the American home. In January, 1932, the Department sent out this franked notice to thousands, perhaps hundreds of thousands of home-owners, no doubt compiled from the last census:

Department of Commerce
Office of the Secretary
Washington

National Committee on
Wood Utilization.

Furniture. Its Selection and Use, is a new government booklet which should help you to solve your home furnishing problems

It's crammed full of interesting facts about styles, designs and construction, and shows you how to get the best values for your money — as well as how to make your home attractive.

It's beautifully illustrated.

Axel H. Oxholm, Director.

Price 20 cents a copy.

P. S. Sold by Superintendent of Documents, Washington, or by district officers of Bureau of Foreign and Domestic Commerce in principal cities.

When the federal departments can spend public moneys in such private services as this, and in making surveys for private business groups, high taxes and deficits are logical consequences.

This department, which has just moved into its new $17,000,000 stone palace in Washington, dissipated only $30,900,000 of our taxes in 1927, but its 20,971 job holders required $54,700,000, an increase of 77 per cent, in 1932.

The Department of Labor first appeared as a bureau in the Department of the Interior in 1884, and in 1903 it was transferred as a bureau to the newly created Department of Commerce and Labor. It was created an executive department in 1913. In the five year period from 1927 to 1932 this department has increased its expenditures of taxpayers' money from $9,900,000 to $14,994,200, or more than 50 per cent. It furnishes only 5,931 jobs.

The Bureau of Immigration made its appearance in embryonic form, in 1829, in an act seeking to secure some degree of comfort for steerage passengers and to ameliorate the conditions of immigrants, then welcomed to this land of the free. In 1864, a Commissioner of Immigration, under the department of State, was authorized. In 1891, a Bureau of Immigration was created and placed under the Treasury Department, with medical and other inspection service provided for at various ports of entry. Thence follows much legislation, excluding large classes of aliens and lodging in the immigration authorities the widest discretion. Among other powers conferred was that to prevent admission of and to deport aliens, without judicial hearing, though with a right of appeal to the Secretary of Commerce and Labor, and, later, to the Secretary of Labor; which was no appeal at all, in any true sense.

During the "radical" scare in this country following the war, the Attorney General instigated a round-up of aliens on a given night in January, 1920, in which 3,000 persons, including hundreds of American citizens, were arrested on "alien warrants" for summary deportation and exile. Only the interposition of Assistant Secretary of Labor, Louis F. Post, from whom the plan is said to have been concealed, saved the Americans from possible banishment.

The Bureau of Naturalization had its beginning in an act of 1790, under the constitutional power of Congress "to establish a uniform rule of naturalization." The right of expatriation — the right of a man to live where he pleases — was early incorporated into our political theory, as supplementary to the doctrine of naturalization elsewhere. But it was not until after the middle of the last century that European governments acknowledged any right of expatriation in their subjects. Even now it is qualified by what is held to be the right of the State to conscript the citizen for war. The federal government itself now claims this power, since its right to conscript American citizens was for the first time in our history upheld by the Supreme Court, in the Selective Draft Cases, in 1918.

Naturalization in the United States today is subjected to a much more interested scrutiny by federal officials than ever before. Our imperial position in the world and the widening influence of the War Department upon our civil institutions, have made it impossible, for example, for a woman to become a naturalized citizen, if she will not take an oath "to bear arms" in defense of the country. And the Supreme Court has upheld this view. Whether the War Department is really looking to the time when it will conscript our women as well as the men — it has many girls' rifle teams in co-educational colleges — or whether this is a mere device to promote "patriotism", is difficult to say.

The Children's Bureau in the Labor Department was created in 1912 by the Borah-Peters act, with an appropriation of $21,936. Its declared object was to gather statistics on infant mortality and child welfare.

Before the bill was passed the Director of the Census appeared before Congress to ask why a branch of his work should be duplicated in a new bureau, but there was no explanation.

The bureau started off, not collecting statistics on infant mortality, but studying child welfare legislation in European countries, including the nationalization schemes of Russia. Every year but one its appropriation was increased — $25,640 in 1914; $161,285 in 1915; $164,640 in 1916; the same in 1917; $280,581 in 1918 and $283,610 in 1919. A definite program for the regimentation of American children was being formulated; they were to be molded as this bureau thought they should be. In the words of the bureau chief:

> None of the studies made by the bureau attempt to approach infant mortality as a medical question. They are concerned with the economic, social, civic and family conditions surrounding young babies.

While studying and issuing bulletins on foreign methods, including doles, the bureau was also sending its agents into the States to violate the sanctity of the homes of the poor — they didn't molest the well-to-do — to subject the young mother to inquisition as to her husband's salary, his habits, his health; and these agents even entered the factories to consult payrolls in checking up on the mother and wife. As the bureau chief naively explained in 1919:

> The surroundings of each child were traced through the first year of life. * * * by women agents of the bureau who called upon each mother. * * * While it was plainly necessary to accept the mother's statement with reference to matters directly pertaining to the daily life of the baby, it was thought that she might not always know about her husband's earnings, and that other sources of information might be more important. Payrolls were consulted and employers and fathers were interviewed.

The results of these intrusive inquiries were embodied in a report which said:

> The logic of the evidence adduced seemed to indicate that a very large ratio of the families of the United States obtain incomes too small to make possible the rearing of children in the manner in which scientific and humane considerations, as well as the prosperity of the nation, demand.

And the conclusion was:

> The cost of living must come down or there must be a nationalization of financial responsibility which will relieve the individual family of a portion of the cost which they now bear, or wages must rise to cover the cost of living.

This sounds like the bureau was advocating a "maternal dole", but it had another plan, announced in the "Minimum Standard for the Public Protection of the Health of Children and Mothers." It was that there should be a public health nurse for each 2,000 of our population, and although this was a labor, and not a health, bureau, it nevertheless visualized itself as the potential dispenser of nurse jobs to 100,000 women. The Office of Education was intending to take over the 850,000 teaching jobs; why shouldn't this bureau take over all the nursing jobs in the States?

The act of 1912 gave this bureau no authority to invade the homes and factories in the States; that was not at all incident to the authority to gather statistics on infant mortality. Yet in 1921 the bureau determined to clarify its right to intrude itself into the States in an act to promote "the welfare and hygiene of maternity and infancy", in what is known as the Sheppard-Towner act, appropriating $1,240,000 annually until June 30, 1927, when the act and appropriations would cease. Discussing this measure Senator Moses said:

> The so-called maternity bill is designed to create jobs and to procure the circulation of literature, accompanied by unwelcome and unwise intrusion into the most intimate private affairs. If the real desire of the proponents of this measure is to give real help to expectant mothers, they should realize that provision should be made for doctors and not documents, for medical men instead of meddlesome Matties.

The bill was adopted and, in 1926, a year before its expiration, the bureau was back again asking Congress for two years more of life, which was granted. Though this bureau has remained very much alive the recent tendency of appropriations for its activities has been downward.

While this bureau was intruding itself officiously into the homes of the poor, it had other plans for the young of America; it was determined to prevent the employment of children in the States. In 1916 it put through Congress an act excluding from interstate transportation articles that were the product of child labor. By a five to four decision the Supreme Court declared this act unconstitutional in 1918, as an unwarranted effort of the federal government to usurp control over the police powers of the States.

Next, in 1919, the Children's Bureau put through Congress an act levying a ten per cent tax on the net profits of any factory in which children under 14 years of age are employed, or in which children between the ages of 14 and 16 are permitted to work more than eight hours a day. The Supreme Court again in 1926 declared this act not a bona fide taxing measure but one seeking to regulate contracts of employment in the States.

The Children's Bureau now determined to circumvent these truly laudable decisions of the Supreme Court by one of the most astounding proposals ever brought forward in our legislative history, namely, an amendment to the Constitution, which it put through Congress for submission to the State Legislatures, which would give to Congress — that is, to the Children's Bureau — "power to limit, regulate and prohibit the labor of persons under 18 years of age" This amendment was drafted by a woman in the Children's Bureau who had spent much of her life in Europe, in collaboration with Frederich Engels, the financial backer of Karl Marx, and who was, herself, a translator of the works of Engels and Marx.

Marx and Engels, it is pertinent to recall, were the authors of the Communist Manifesto of 1847, which declared, among other things, that when the proletariat attained power, they must take a number of measures in the most advanced countries to pave the way for socialism; that these measures must include the abolishment of the right of inheritance, a progressive income tax, state control of credit and the means of communication, obligatory labor and free communal education of all children.

The proposed amendment, submitted in 1924, was in these words:

> Section 1. The Congress shall have power to limit, regulate and prohibit the labor of persons under 18 years of age.

> Section 2. The power of the several states is unimpaired by this article, except that the operation of State laws shall be suspended to the extent necessary to give effect to legislation enacted by the Congress.

The Children's Bureau christened this tyrannous proposal a "Child Labor" amendment. That was disingenuous; a "child", in legal definition, is one under 14 years of age. Its design was to enslave about 45,000,000 persons under 18 years of age in the United States and subject them to such standards of conduct as the bureau wished to impose.

The second section of the proposal is dishonest, in that it gives a false assurance that the States may not be completely deprived of such jurisdiction as they have over the subject. Acts of Congress are supreme within the scope of their constitutional powers, and all State laws must yield.

During the pendency of this proposed amendment, from 1924 to 1931, the legislatures of twenty-six States rejected it. But six ratified it.

Being thus decisively defeated, the proposal was considered to be dead, but, as there is no time limit within which it must be acted upon, or within which a State may reverse its previous action, the Children's Bureau did not give up hope. On the contrary, their well-organized campaign, recently launched with the approval, if not with the active assistance of the national administration, has influenced the legislatures of nine States, two of which had previously rejected the proposal, to ratify it. Thus there are fifteen States, of the necessary number, that have ratified.

The States that have thus far ratified the amendment are: Arkansas, Arizona, Wisconsin, California, Montana, Colorado, Michigan, New Hampshire, Washington, Ohio, New Jersey, Oregon, Oklahoma, North Dakota and Illinois.

The alarming character of this proposed amendment prompted Clarence E. Martin, President of the American Bar Association, to denounce it in a leading article in the August 1933 issue of that association's Journal. In the first place Mr. Martin reveals, from census statistics, that out of the 45,000,000 children under 18 years of age in the United States, who would be regimented from Washington, only 667,118 were gainfully employed in 1930, of whom 469,497 were children on the farms, 89 per cent of whom were unpaid family workers. Of the 197,621 in non-agricultural pursuits, only 28,592 were engaged in cotton mills and similar condemnable employment. To correct abuses from Washington, which the States themselves can and have corrected, 45,000,000 are to have substituted for the natural protection of their parents a federal bureaucrat directing a mighty army of inspectors, invading every home in the land.

Under this amendment, as Mr. Martin points out, Congress or the bureau could impose peace-time conscription; it could destroy our State school systems and direct them all from Washington. And he adds:

> The Children's Bureau in 1924, seriously advocated a law providing for compulsory registration of pregnancy, through local health offices. Recalling the wire-tapping and automobile searching decisions under the Eighteenth Amendment, does anyone doubt the power of Congress, which will have jurisdiction over the physical and mental exertions from the time of birth forward, to enact such a law, if this amendment is ratified? * * * Adopt it and other amendments, nationalizing and socializing our governmental structure, will follow. And their adoption will be more or less a matter of form. Given jurisdiction of the activities of children, certainly the national government should have the regulation of marriage and divorce. In its

train comes the settlement of personal and property rights.
If these, why not other domestic relations?

In addition to the Children's Bureau the Department of Labor has another called the Women's Bureau. It started off as an "emergency" section in 1918 as the "Women in Industry Service," but like all temporary federal offices, it became permanent in 1920. Its declared objects were "to formulate standards and policies to promote the welfare of wage-earning women, to improve their working conditions, increase their efficiency and to advance their opportunity for profitable employment," objects also wholly beyond the purview of federal constitutional power, save in the District of Columbia. This bureau has become essentially a propaganda center, through bulletins, moving pictures, radio talks, exhibits and addresses in churches and schools, to make over the whole body of legislation in the States, according to the bureau's ideas of the needs of the women of the United States.

The Women's Bureau, taking a lesson from the Children's Bureau, also tried its hand at legislation. They put through Congress in 1918 what they conceived to be a model minimum wage law for women and children in the District of Columbia, under a wage board empowered to fix wages for women "adequate to supply the cost of living, to protect their morals and maintain their health"; and also to determine reasonable wages for minors. They had no better luck than the Children's Bureau; the Supreme Court rightly declared the act void as interfering with the freedom of contract, guaranteed by due process of law. Chief Justice Taft was one of three to dissent.

No one will question the worthiness of many of these objects, but, if we are to remain a free people, they must be accomplished by the people themselves in their own States, and not commanded by a distant and irresponsible master.

The United States Employment Service, also a Labor Department agency, was authorized in 1923, under an act "to foster, promote and develop the welfare of the wage-earners of the United States, by so conserving and distributing their industrial activities as to improve their working conditions and advance their opportunities for profitable employment, in harmony with the general good, with the necessities of war, with the just interest of employers, and with the development in practice of the recognized principle of a common responsibility for production and a common interest in distribution," whatever all that may mean.

The simple facts are, however, that this agency started off in 1915 as a seaman's recruiting service, but has now intruded itself into the States, under "cooperative arrangements," as a general employment agency, with State officials on the federal payroll, permitted under an allotment of funds to each State for that purpose. The work is carried on under regulations prescribed by a Director General, who sits with his staff in Washington, directing his Field Organizations, his Local Placement Offices, his Junior Guidance and Placement Offices, and his Farm Labor Divisions to the number of 155, located throughout the land. This service is to be greatly expanded. It is a pet activity of Senator Wagner of New York.

Will the reader kindly turn to the enumeration of the powers delegated to Congress and point out the authority whereby it created the Women's Bureau, the Children's Bureau, the United States Employment Service, or the Department of Labor itself? There is none, and yet they are made up of thousands of men and women on the public payroll spending millions of public money in all manner of irregular activities in the States. And no citizen can now challenge their constitutionality before the Supreme Court.

As the Departments of Agriculture and Interior and other federal agencies are seeking to federalize education, and thus take from the States this reserved field, so is the Public Health Service, in the Treasury Department, reaching out to absorb and dominate the whole field of health, essentially the function of the States under their exclusive police powers. Its ambition is to become a great executive department with a Medical Secretary seated in the Cabinet. This service was instituted in 1798 to care for "sick and disabled seamen," later extending its activities to the ports of the country, in connection with the inspection of vessels and questions of quarantine, all proper and necessary federal functions.

Today it has forced its way into the States, in the administration of the infant and maternity act, jointly with the Children's Bureau, and it has introduced a policy of "cooperation" with State and local health boards in all manner of local work, with the prospect of attaining control as soon as the funds are voted by Congress in sufficient proportions. It duplicates some of the work of the Department of Agriculture, in its milk investigations, its rural sanitation surveys and the like. It maintains in the States twenty-seven marine hospitals and over one hundred so-called relief stations, forming the tentacles for the approaching embrace.

The varied and costly activities of federal agencies in concerns almost wholly reserved to the State governments by the constitutional division of powers, possess, in the Government Printing Office, their most effective instrument of propaganda. This federal establishment is the largest printing office in the world. It has more than 5,000 personnel on its payroll in its mechanical departments. Every board, bureau and department in Washington keeps it busy turning out "educational" literature, in the form of books, pamphlets, documents and bulletins, which floods the mails as franked matter. The propaganda of the Department of Agriculture alone thus put out in 1931 consisted of 29,866,506 pieces, including 400,000 copies of the Agricultural Yearbook, costing $273,320. There were also 12,225,000 farmers' bulletins, four-fifths of which are allotted by law to members of Congress for free distribution to their rural constituents. The total number of books, pamphlets and other matter printed in this federal shop in 1931 was 3,400,447,250. While some of it is for sale, the amount purchased is negligible; all that is left over is sold for waste paper.

One ignorant of our traditions and of our dual system of government might find something commendable in such a vast "educational" program directed from Washington; actually, it is usurpation of power, conspiring to erase all State lines and to consolidate us under a single bureaucratic empire.

> *As we cannot, without the risk of evils from which the imagination recoils, employ physical force as a check on misgovernment, it is evidently our wisdom to keep all the constitutional checks on misgovernment in the highest state of efficiency, to watch with jealousy the first beginnings of encroachment, and never to suffer irregularities, even when harmless in themselves, to pass unchallenged, lest they acquire the force of precedents.*

— Thomas Babington Macaulay

Chapter 5 –
Congress Expands Its Powers

Congress, no longer acknowledging its powers to be limited has become a universal almoner, with other people's money and is attempting to usurp the benign mission of Providence.

When George Washington retired from the Presidency in 1797, his Farewell Address to his fellow citizens reveals plainly enough that he was not over confident that our written limited Constitution would be adequate to restrain the ambition of public men, unless the citizens themselves were vigilant, and, as if foreseeing that it would be particularly difficult to hold Congress within its constitutional sphere, he said:

> If, in the opinion of the people, the distribution or modification of the constitutional powers be in any particular wrong, let it be corrected by an amendment in the way in which the Constitution designates. But let there be no change in usurpation; for though this, in one instance, may be the instrument of good, it is the customary weapon by which free governments are destroyed. The precedent must always greatly overbalance in permanent evil any partial or transient benefit which the use can at any time yield.

John Adams was hardly inaugurated before Congress enacted two penal measures of the most tyrannous character, not only without constitutional authority but in the teeth of specific inhibitions in our Bill of Rights. These were the Alien law and the Sedition law of 1798. Under the former the President was empowered to banish any alien, without accusation or trial, in his own good pleasure; and under the latter act, to "write, print, utter or publish, or cause to be written, printed, uttered or published", anything with intent to defame the government, or either House of Congress or the President, was made punishable by a fine not exceeding $2,000 and by imprisonment not exceeding two years. The first amendment in our Bill of Rights declares that Congress shall have no power to pass any law "abridging the freedom of speech or of the press".

When Jefferson came into office in 1801 he ordered the release of all persons in prison or under prosecution for violation of the Sedition law, declaring "that law to be a nullity, as absolute and as palpable as if Congress had ordered us to fall down and worship a golden image." Its permanent evil, as a precedent, reappeared, however, in the Espionage Acts of 1917 and 1918, with much severer penalties for criticism of the government.

In those early years up to the middle of last century, Congressional usurpation manifests itself mainly in the passage of acts appropriating money or allocating public lands to the States, for what was called "internal improvements" — the building of roads, canals and harbors, the deepening of river channels, and grants in aid of education in the States. Jefferson, Madison, Monroe, Jackson, Pierce and Buchanan uniformly opposed this legislation as beyond the legislative grants of power, but Congress wore them down and ultimately found executive approval, not only for the exercise of these powers but of a host of others, progressively reaching into the reserved field of the States.

To the mass of citizens this contest was more or less academic; it did not touch them, because the federal government was forced to rely for its revenue upon duties and excises, which the people did not feel, refraining from imposing direct taxes by the necessary rule of apportionment, which the people would unquestionably feel and resent, if unnecessarily imposed.

As early as the Washington administration Congress had asserted, under the power "to establish post offices and post roads", a power to build roads in the States. In 1796, Jefferson had written to Madison:

> Have you considered all the consequences of your proposition respecting post roads? I view it as a source of boundless patronage to the executive, jobbing to members of Congress and their friends, and a bottomless abyss of public money. You will begin by only appropriating the surplus of the post office revenues; but the other revenues will soon be called to their aid, and it will be a scene of eternal scramble among the members, who can get the most money wasted in their State; and they will always get the most who are the meanest.

When Jefferson was inaugurated in 1801, he procured from Congress acts abolishing the whole internal taxation, yet there was still a tempting surplus being piled up. In a message of December 2, 1802, he recommended that if Congress wished to embark upon internal improvements in the States, such as "public education, roads, rivers, canals and such other objects", a constitutional amendment should be submitted to the people of the States to grant the necessary powers. This was not done, however. The easier way seemed to be to infer the existence of such new powers as it might be considered desirable to exercise, from those seventeen powers specifically enumerated in section 8, article 1.

In 1817, Madison discussed the constitutional powers of Congress comprehensively in a message vetoing "an act to set apart and pledge certain funds for constructing roads and canals and for improving the navigation of water courses, in order to facilitate, promote and give security to internal commerce among the several States, and to render more easy and less expensive the means and provisions for the common defense." Here was an attempt to justify road and canal construction and river improvements under the first and third of the enumerated powers — the power "to lay and collect taxes * * * to pay the debts and provide for the common defense and general welfare," and the power "to regulate commerce with foreign nations and among the several States." Madison said:

> The legislative powers vested in Congress are specified and enumerated in the eighth section of the first article of the Constitution, and it does not appear that the power proposed to be exercised by the bill is among the enumerated powers, or that it falls by any just interpretation within the power to make laws "necessary and proper" for carrying into execution those or other powers vested by the Constitution in the government of the United States. * * *

> To refer the power in question to the clause "to provide for the common defense and general welfare" would be contrary to the established and consistent rules of interpretation, as rendering the special and careful enumeration of powers which follow the clause nugatory and improper. Such a view of the Constitution would have the effect of giving to Congress a general power of legislation instead of the defined and limited one hitherto

understood to belong to them, the terms "common defense and general welfare" embracing every object and act within the purview of a legislative trust."

Nor, said Madison, does a power "to regulate commerce" embrace a power to construct internal improvements, even with the consent of the States. The States can give such power only in the way the Constitution prescribes. This elucidation of the powers of Congress by the "Father of the Constitution" was entitled to the greatest weight and respect, yet it received neither.

On succeeding Madison, in 1817, President Monroe's first message discussed the subject of federal construction of roads and canals, and asserted that authority for them "is not contained in any of the specific powers granted to Congress, nor can I consider it incidental to or a necessary means, viewed on the most liberal scale, for carrying into effect any of the powers which are specifically granted." And, as Jefferson had done, he suggested that an amendment be submitted to the States to add those powers, if Congress wished to exercise them. No amendment was proposed. In 1822, a bill reached Monroe, "for the repair and preservation of the Cumberland road", which he seized upon as the occasion for an exhaustive analysis of the seventeen distinct powers of Congress, in Section 8, Article 1, and of the eighteenth, the power to "make all laws necessary and proper" to carry the seventeen into execution. It is a State paper of great power and perspicacity, but today has a mere antiquarian value.

Certainly, said Monroe, if the people of the several States had thought proper to incorporate themselves into one community, under one government, they might have done it. But they wisely stopped after creating a national government for specified national purposes, leaving the State governments, without that limit, perfectly sovereign and independent. If Congress has power to build roads in the States, it must embrace the power to condemn land and extend complete civil and criminal jurisdiction. Then he said:

> A power to provide for the common defense would give to Congress the command of the whole force and all the resources of the Union; but a right to provide for the general welfare would, in effect, break down all the barriers between the States and the general government and consolidate the whole under the latter.

In his Constitutional History of the United States, George Ticknor Curtis elaborates Monroe's argument in these words:

> We hear much nowadays about the so-called "general welfare clause" of the Constitution. * * * Now, look at the stupendous communism that is wrapped up in the taxing power on the supposition that it includes a power to tax for the promotion of the welfare of individuals. There is no limit to the taxing power excepting that duties, imposts and excises must be uniform throughout the United States. All the property of the country may be taxed for the legitimate objects of taxation. If one of those legitimate objects is the welfare of individuals or masses or classes or the whole people, the two Houses of Congress and any President acting together can divide up all the property in the country upon the plea that a general division will promote welfare. By this process this government could devour itself and there would be nothing left for it to subsist upon.

While the Supreme Court has never particularly construed the scope of the "welfare clause," Chief Justice Marshall did so, indirectly, in Gibbons v. Ogden, in 1824, when he said:

> Congress is not empowered to tax for those purposes which are within the exclusive province of the States.

The old struggle in Congress to assume the power to build roads in the States — a power of patronage of no mean proportions to a perennial candidate — continued into the administration of Andrew Jackson, who, in 1830, vetoed the "Marysville, Washington, Paris and Lexington turn-pike bill", reinforcing his own arguments against its constitutionality, with those of Madison and Monroe.

In 1833, education in the States made its appearance for the first time as an object of federal solicitude, in a bill allotting certain public lands to seven western States, to be applied to the "objects of internal improvements or education within said States under the direction of their several legislatures." It might appear unobjectionable to make such a donation and leave its disposition to the State legislatures, free from federal "cooperation", but President Jackson saw the camel's head under the tent, and he vetoed the bill in a vigorous message, saying:

> The leading principle then (in his previous message) asserted was that Congress possesses no constitutional power to appropriate any part of the moneys of the United States for objects of a local character within the States. That principle I cannot be mistaken in supposing has received the unequivocal sanction of the American people, and all subsequent reflection has but satisfied me more thoroughly that the interests of our people and the purity of our

government, if not its existence, depend on its observance.
* * *

It appears to me a more direct road to consolidation can not be devised. Money is power, and in that government which pays all the public officers of the States will all political power be substantially concentrated. The State governments, if governments they might be called, would lose all their independence and dignity; the economy which now distinguishes them would be converted into a profusion, limited only by the extent of the supply. Being dependents of the general government, and looking to its Treasury, as the source of all their emoluments, the State officers, under whatever name they might pass and by whatever forms their duties might be prescribed, would, in effect, be the mere stipendiaries and instruments of the central power.

In 1854, President Pierce, discussing a bill for certain river and harbor improvements, reviewed all the preceding measures of the kind and pointed out that up to 1824, Congress had made no claim to appropriate public moneys for river improvement, beyond the erection of "light-houses, beacons, buoys and public piers." He urged great caution in asserting a power over internal improvements, saying that, if it existed, it could be extended to an infinite range of objects and involve a dangerous augmentation of political functions and patronage.

In 1856, President Pierce vetoed "an act to remove obstructions to navigation at the mouth of the Mississippi River, at the Southwest Pass", on the ground that "the Constitution does not confer on the general government any express power to make such appropriations; that they are not a necessary and proper incident to any of the express powers, and that the assumption of the authority on the part of the federal government" is prejudicial to the several States and inconsistent with their true relations.

Through perseverance Congress has constantly gained its point in every new assertion of power, and in the exercise of this power, to build levees and deepen channels and harbors, it has lavished, and continues to lavish, hundreds of millions of public moneys, with little or nothing to show for the constant outlay.

The penetration of federal power into the States has the marked characteristic of progression, which is an attribute of all power. As Lieber says, power imposes; it receives everywhere respect and homage, however illegally acquired. Hence, usurpation itself becomes a facility for further usurpation. It is not surprising, then, that the bill of 1833, allotting public lands to certain States for "internal improvements or education," should have led to the Morrill bill of 1862, donating vast acreages to such States as should establish "colleges for the benefit of agriculture and mechanic arts", to which reference was made in a previous chapter; and that this act, in turn, should have been succeeded by others contemplating the ultimate absorption of the whole educational system of the States into federal control.

In 1860, President Buchanan made the last stand against the assumed power over river improvements, in vetoing an act to deepen the channel in the St. Clair flats in Michigan. This power, if it exists at all, said President Buchanan, can only flow from the power to regulate commerce. Yet Chief Justice Marshall had said that the power to regulate commerce, "is the power to prescribe rules by which commerce is to be governed"; to say that the power to prescribe rules for commerce embraces a power to deepen channels, would be to adopt a latitude of construction under which all political power might be usurped by the federal government.

With the coming of Lincoln, and the beginning of the Civil War, we hear little more of the Constitution and its limitations upon the powers, either of Congress or of the President himself. There is no quibbling over the relatively small irregularity of the Morrill Act, which is now revived, reenacted and signed. Agriculture becomes of national concern, under an active commissioner. Yet the chief object at that time appeared to be the mere gathering of statistics. It is to be noted that nearly all of the federal bureaus are launched with the harmless object of "gathering statistics". But the power "to issue rules and regulations", for the discipline of the citizens, in their respective fields, invariably follows. The statistics, of course, have revealed the supposed need of regulation. Statistics are now being gathered by the federal government in dozens of new fallow fields, which we will hear from in time.

The arbitrary conduct of the federal government during the Civil War, under the plea of necessity, its long indulgence in power without restraint under a suspension of the writ of habeas corpus, and its dominant position at the end, with the South under military rule, destroyed for the time the old concepts of a dual system of sovereign States and a national government of limited and enumerated powers. Such is the effect of all wars upon government, in justifying the exercise of any power thought to be needed by the rulers, and in accustoming the citizen to it, until its novelty and unusual character no longer excite protest or surprise. Thus censorship and the conscription of all wealth and all persons, which proposals the Great War made familiar to us, no longer impress our minds as measures of intolerable domestic despotism beyond even that to which a foreign conqueror would pretend. Not long ago the

Supreme Court itself said that "a country preserved at the sacrifice of all the cardinal principles of liberty, is not worth the cost of preservation."

Thus the Civil War, the Spanish-American War and the Great War have prepared government and people for those tremendous accessions of power which Congress has seized, as it wished, usually justifying it, if at all, as warranted under the power to tax "to provide for the common defense and general welfare." Nor is it usual for any member of Congress now to challenge the constitutionality of any act brought before it, on any ground. If Congress possess a substantive power "to provide for the common defense and general welfare", there can no longer be any question of the constitutionality of any of its acts, since that power is bound only by its own discretion.

On March 3, 1926, however, Henry St. George Tucker, of Virginia, had the courage to rise in the House to oppose an appropriation for the Children's Bureau, in the execution of the Welfare and Hygiene of Maternity and Infancy Act, which excursion into the States is justified by its apologists under the "general welfare clause." Taking Madison's Journal of the Constitutional Convention, Mr. Tucker traced the "general welfare clause" from its first appearance to its final inclusion in the Morris revision, demonstrating unanswerably that it was never considered a substantive power, but was always intended to be qualified by the seventeen powers that immediately follow it.

The interruptions of Mr. Tucker during the course of this argument actually show surprise on the part of his colleagues that anyone should question the right of Congress to appropriate public money for what Congress may consider the general welfare. Said Mr. Oliver of Alabama:

Do I understand the gentleman to take the position that the power vested in Congress to tax is limited to certain declared purposes or powers set out in the Constitution, and these same declared powers or purposes likewise define and fix the limits on the power of Congress to appropriate money?

Mr. Tucker:

I certainly do hold, as every Judge on the Supreme Court discussing this subject has held, that taxes can be levied only for public purposes, and those purposes are limited by the power of government.

Mr. Tydings of Maryland was an exception; he knows his constitutional history. He asked:

What would be the use of the other seventeen powers if the general welfare clause gave power to Congress to do everything anyway?

Although the "general welfare clause" has never come squarely before the Supreme Court for consideration, in U. S. v. Boyer, decided in 1898, the District Court for the western district of Missouri, discussed it exhaustively. That was a case involving the constitutionality of an act of Congress of 1890, empowering the Secretary of Agriculture to place inspectors in all plants slaughtering and packaging cattle, sheep and hogs, which were to be transported in interstate commerce. Said the Court:

Under what clause or provision of the Constitution did Congress enact the legislation authorizing the inspection of meats, or cattle, hogs and sheep, or their carcasses, while or before being slaughtered, in the slaughter houses within a State? The learned counsel for the United States suggests, in argument, that the power may be found under what is commonly called the "general welfare clause."

Then, quoting from Justice Story's work on the Constitution, that if the power to tax, "to provide for the common defense and general welfare", is a substantive power, "the government of the United States is, in reality, a government of general and unlimited powers," the Court continued:

> After a most elaborate and historical discussion of the subject, presenting the different views of the different political schools or parties, he (Story) concludes that the "general welfare clause" contains no grant of power whatsoever, but it is a mere expression of the ends and purposes to be effected by the preceding power of taxation. I content myself with the fact that the former construction has never been sustained by any court, and the reverse has been held so often as not to require citations to support it.

Not only did Congress possess no power under the "general welfare clause" to authorize the placing of inspectors in packing plants in the States, said the Court, but no such power could be inferred from the commerce clause of the Constitution. But that was before the Spanish-American War brought its accretion of federal power.

An act of 1907, to accomplish the identical objects as that of 1890, declared unconstitutional in the above decision, was, however, upheld by the Supreme Court in 1918, in the case of Pittsburg Melting Co. v. Totten, though the Supreme Court did not attempt to point out whence the power came. It merely declared the enactment as "within the power of Congress in order to prevent interstate and foreign shipment of impure or adulterated meat food products." Since the decision in the Totten case, the Supreme Court has not infrequently sustained new stretches of power, on the general ground that the act "was not prohibited" by the Constitution, from which the inference may be fairly drawn that, not only may Congress exercise all powers conferred upon it in the enumeration, but all powers not denied. Such a doctrine falls only a little short of a "general welfare" power.

From this point federal penetration into the States has gone steadily on until it has embraced agriculture, education, health, maternity, child welfare, vocational training, nursing the injured, employment, food, drugs, rural sanitation, narcotics, automobile thefts, dairying, apple marketing, agricultural marketing, industrial marketing, destruction of predatory animals and insects, chemistry of soils, mining, regulation of duck shooting, farm relief and loans, flood relief, farm mortgage relief, home mortgage relief, State doles, drought relief and scores of other activities, costing the taxpayers hundreds of millions of dollars annually, with, in most cases, no constitutional authority for such acts of power. And multiplication of such activities to an indefinite extent, with rising taxes, is inevitable for the future in such a policy.

So completely has precedent destroyed the constitutional restraint against the application of federal taxes to objects of exclusive State concern that, on March 21, 1933, the President, in a message to Congress, asked for a grant to him of $225,000,000 to use in his own discretion, in the formation of a great civilian conservation army to work in the State, as well as the national, parks. Nearly every State is now harboring so-call Civilian Conservation Camps.

Almost the first expenditure was $280,000 for toilet kits at $1.40 each, purchased without competitive bids, when the army supply officers testified before a Senate Committee that a top price should have been 80 cents. Since then about $500,000 has been spent for radios, libraries and athletic equipment, to add to the delights of camp life.

The members of this civilian army draw from $30 to $45 a month, with free clothing, board and lodging, laundry and medical care, and the widow of every man dying in camp will receive a monthly pension of $45 for life.

It is interesting to note that an enlisted man in the regular army receives $18.75, minus laundry, per month; and that the widow of a Brigadier General receives a pension of $15 per month.

By an act of December 19, 1930, the sum of $45,000,000 was placed in the hands of the Secretary of Agriculture to lend to farmers who had suffered damage from "drought or hail". The sum was loaned to 371,012 persons in seventeen Southern and Western States. In January 1932 an additional $200,000,000 was given to him to lend in any sort of "farm relief". The absence of any adequate safeguards in the act has aroused Secretary Hyde's humor and prompted him to tell the National Cooperative Council in Washington, on January 27, 1932, that he is "the world's first prize boob" as a lending agent. He explained that he "has lent more money on less security, on thinner margins and with more losses than any other agent ever has;" that Congress had merely told him to lend the money "wherever we find an emergency, on whatever security we think proper and through any agency we see fit."

By the summer of 1933 the urge to lend and give federal taxes to certain farm groups in favored States had produced seven distinct federal lending and donating agencies.

By an act of June 16, 1933, these were all consolidated into what is styled the Farm Credit Administration, with more the $2,000,000,000 at its disposal. It stands ready not only to make seed or "production" loans — which may or may not be repaid — to the tune of $120,000,000, but it will refinance at public expense all private farm mortgages, given or held by those who have guessed wrong in farm land speculation in recent years.

Not to discriminate against the city dweller with a mortgage on his home, the federal Home Loan Bank, through the Home Owners' Loan Corporation, with another $2,000,000,000 will take over his burden of he doesn't care to exert himself to discharge it.

These successive irregular appropriations of federal taxes, beginning in small abuses, led on logically to the La Follette Bill to appropriate $250,000,000 and the Costigan Bill to appropriate $350,000,000, introduced in the Senate in December, 1931, for "unemployment relief" in the States.

The politicians in the States have been taxing and bonding and spending with quite as much profligacy as the federal politicians, and, facing the prospect of exhausted local credit, they eagerly rallied behind these measures to tap the federal Treasury. Though stoutly opposed for a time, as ushering in the dole, the policy was adopted in 1932, and, to October 12, 1933, $300,000,000 had been disbursed as loans by the Reconstruction Finance Corporation.

By an act of May 12, 1933, the huge sum of $500,000,000 was made available for doles in the States.

The Federal Emergency Relief Administrator had expended $175,736,885 by October 12, 1933, in direct allocations to relief agencies in the states, and in the purchase of a large amount of hog crop, which, appropriately, was converted into pork for distribution to those on the relief rolls. On October 1, the President announced plans for a Relief Corporation which would supply not only food, but fuel and clothing to all who needed it, thus going far beyond the dreaded dole of the British.

Of the new spending and lending and donating United States Corporations and Administrations, now multiplying with a rapidity that suggests a purpose to dissipate all private wealth, the more important are:

Reconstruction Finance Corporation, with $4,500,000,000 to refinance banks, railroads, etc.

Industrial Recovery Loan Corporation, a subsidiary of the R.F.C., to provide loans for business firms unable to meet the increased cost of doing business imposed by the National Recovery Administrator's Codes of wages and prices.

Farm Credit Administration, with $2,000,000,000 for refinancing farm mortgages in default.

Public Works Administration, under Secretary of the Interior, with $3,300,000,000 of easy money for public works in the States.

Home Owner's Loan Corporation, with $2,200,000,000 to refinance urban mortgages in default.

Agricultural Adjustment Administration, to pay farmers for ploughing under crops and for withholding land from cultivation. On Oct. 12, 1933, it had paid $80,000,000 to cotton farmers, and owed $30,000,000 more, while it was committed to pay $100,000,000 to wheat farmers.

Subsistence Homestead Administration, with $25,000,000 for the launching of a model federal agricultural community of farmless farmers on 1100 acres of land in Preston County, West Virginia.

When it is considered that, on June 1, 1933, the borrowing power of 4,000 municipalities in 41 states was destroyed through defaults in interest payments on the bonds, the pressure behind these raids may be better understood.

As a result of these widespread defaults, a bill has been introduced in Congress to permit municipalities to go through bankruptcy and thus rob the bondholder of the money he lent. If such a bill passes no private investor will again purchase a municipal bond, and the alternative will be new confiscatory local taxes, or direct support of our cities out of new confiscatory federal taxes.

Not only did the 73rd Congress, in special session, provide all of the billions mentioned — though the Treasury was empty — but, by an act of June 16, 1933, it made the largest peace time relief appropriation known to history, in authorizing the expenditure, in the President's sole discretion, of $3,300,000,000 for public works, nearly all of which will find its way into the hands of greedy interested groups in the forty eight States. Of this huge sum, $400,000,000 will go into the pockets of the public roads contractors, and to the cement companies.

This far reaching program would appear to some as heralding a new Eden in the United States, but what the realist sees is endless graft and scandal, tens of thousands of new public jobs, the demoralization of millions of men, and, finally a tax burden so great that it will tempt Congress into a capitol tax levy to meet it.

Private cooperation is the only safe means of dealing with local distress. Even if that is not wholly adequate it is better that some go unrelieved in the present than that the whole of our posterity shall suffer spoliation and bondage under federal absolutism, to which these policies necessarily lead.

Only one President has had the disinterested courage to oppose these irregular uses of public money — the object of which is primarily to popularize the generous Congressman — and that man was Grover Cleveland, who, in 1887, vetoed a bill for the purchase of seed for some "drought suffers" in Texas, saying:

> I can find no warrant for such an appropriation in the Constitution and I do not believe that the power and the duty of the general government ought to be extended to the relief of individual suffering, which is in no manner related to the public service or benefit. A prevalent tendency to disregard the limited mission of this power and duty should, I think, be steadfastly resisted, to the end that the lesson should be constantly enforced, that though the people support the government the government should not support the people.

Since that day, however, free seeds for the farmer voter, at the public expense, have become a fixed form of beneficence, bestowed annually by the rural members of Congress.

All of our Presidents of the last three decades have talked economy in their public addresses, all have given us warnings against the tendencies toward consolidation under federal bureaucrats, but rarely has a President actually vetoed a measure abetting that process or invoked those arguments against it when the bill was before him. President Hoover even believes that the present progressive federal inheritance tax, and the graduated income and excess profits taxes, are desirable, because they "tend to a better distribution of wealth". Can it be imagined how this would have sounded in the Constitutional Convention of 1787? High progressive taxation does not accomplish a "better distribution of wealth". The poor citizen gets none of it, unless it may be said to come through his supposed exemption from taxes, which, far from being a benefit, is a positive injury. No sophistry can conceal the fact that the public officeholder and his political partisans are the main distributees.

It is not generally known that members of Congress have voted themselves so many and such varied perquisites and gratuities, that the average member receives the equivalent compensation of $20,000 a year; and a perfectly conscienceless member can draw down the equivalent of $38,000 a year.

When it is considered that the man in public life, usually lost to habits of industry, is animated by one overwhelming desire — to hold his job, and perhaps scramble higher — the manufactured pressure in behalf of unwise and irregular measures, exerted by those who will benefit most, is given the semblance of genuine public demand, and opposition becomes a serious personal problem. The exempted masses are not interested in economy or regularity, against the assurance of new benefits, while a protest on the part of the numerically insignificant taxpayer might even recoil upon his own head as the miserliness of a shirker in a noble cause.

It is this that explains the usually noiseless manner in which improper bills find their way into and out of the White House, with presidential approval, ever imposing new burdens and fresh regulations and restrictions upon the lives and conduct of the citizens. One would suppose that in his second, and traditionally last, term of office, the President would reassert his independence, but having yielded so constantly to expediency during his first term, there is no argument left upon which to justify an altered position, without self stultification.

If the reader will compare that simple list of eighteen powers, delegated to Congress in section 8 of Article I, of the Constitution, with the boundless new powers which Congress has assumed over our lives and our property, he will readily learn the extent of his betrayal.

He will find there no authority whatever for its attempt to create, under the Department of Agriculture, a national monopoly in our food supplies, with the power to fix prices, authorized in the Agricultural Relief Act, assuming to confer upon the Secretary of Agriculture the power, not only to make laws and impose penalties, freed from judicial review, but the power actually to levy taxes upon all of us for the enrichment of a private class.

He will find no authority to make loans and gifts of hundreds of millions of our taxes to favored rural and urban groups, to promote their private fortunes and to make good their private losses in the purchase of lands; nor for like loans and gifts to favored States, municipalities and private corporations.

He will find no warrant in the Constitution for the recent waste of $400,000,000 and the proposed waste of probably a billion more in irrigation schemes, designed primarily to enrich certain favored private land owners.

In the Tenth Amendment he will discover an explicit denial to Congress of any power to meddle with the reserved rights of the States over agriculture, education, public health, and scores of other objects, upon which Congress is annually squandering still other hundreds of millions.

He will find a like denial of any power to authorize the fixing of prices, wages and hours of labor, or to license, regulate and control any trade or industry, in the states, save as to such of their products alone as have actually entered into and become interstate commerce.

Within the limited range of the constitutional powers of Congress, there is no room for socialistic experiments; yet much of its recent legislation is founded squarely on the doctrines of Karl Marx.

The calamitous result has been that every forced construction of the Constitution, adopted to permit a desired experiment, has destroyed the constitutional safeguard involved.

If the experiment fails, as in the Federal Farm Board, the precedent remains, but your constitutional safeguard that was construed away to permit it, is gone; and you cannot put it back.

This we witness, rising upon the Farm Board precedent, a more colossal experiment in crop and crop price control, in the so-called Emergency Agricultural Act, of 1933.

We Americans once possessed a constitutional safeguard against taxation by executive fiat, which came down to us with the glorious fame of John Hampden.

But that also has been construed away, first in executive customs taxation; and now it fails to protect us against the new executive processing tax, authorized in the latest agricultural act.

As Judge George Stewart Brown, of the U. S. Customs Court, recently said in the case of Dutchess Hat Works v. U. S., no charter designed to limit the powers of government, so as to preserve ordered human liberty, can long survive this process of construing those limits away. It is a piece meal tearing down of the

Constitution, which destroys its continuity and symmetry and leaves no political philosophy in its place.

There results a hodge-podge of conflicting tendencies and theories, impossible of any logical reconciliation, leading on to a capricious absolutism.

In 1814, Gouverneur Morris, whose pen phrased the Constitution as one of the Committee of Style and Arrangement, sent to Timothy Pickering, then in Congress, this cynical commentary on the constitutional legislator, which, in the light of our Congressional history, was a remarkable prophecy:

> But, after all, what does it signify that men should have a written Constitution, containing unequivocal provisions and limitations? The legislative lion will not be entangled in the meshes of a logical net. Legislation will always make power which it wishes to exercise, unless it be so arranged as to contain within itself the sufficient check. Attempts to restrain it from outrage will only render it the more outrageous. The idea of binding legislators by oath is puerile. Having sworn to exercise the powers granted, according to their true intent and meaning, they will avoid the shame, if not the guilt, of perjury, by swearing the true intent and meaning to be, in their comprehension, that which suits their purpose.

Chapter 6 –
The Supreme Court and the Constitution

"To what purpose are powers limited, and to what purpose is that limitation committed to writing, if these limits may, at any time, be passed by those intended to be restrained."
– John Marshall

The Supreme Court, placed beyond the reach of clamor and faction, with its members appointed for life, is the body designedly instituted to guard the Constitution, by declaring void and of no effect, all governmental acts beyond its distribution of powers. In such a radical transformation as is, and has been, taking place in our free system of government, it is well to consider what the Supreme Court has done in the discharge of its peculiarly solemn mission.

It is not possible to say how many laws have been enacted by Congress since its first session, but we know that in the fifty-six volumes of the United States Code Annotated today there are more than 45,000 laws. In addition, there are tens of thousands of rules, regulations, instructions, general orders, circulars, bulletins, notices and memoranda, issued by the federal executive departments and commissions, as supplementary legislation.

In the 143 years since the founding of our government the Supreme Court has heard and disposed of more than 30,000 cases, to be found in the 285 volumes of its Reports. And of this very large number of contests, involving the constitutionality of

141

thousands of federal laws, the Supreme Court has declared just fifty-four acts, or parts of acts, unconstitutional.

In view of these facts, it would appear obvious that the Supreme Court has not been an effective instrument in combating congressional usurpations. And the explanation is to be found in a number of limitations, some self-imposed, progressively restricting its power to review the acts of government. In the first place, the Court has no power, of its own motion, to inquire into the validity of any action taken by the executive or legislative branches; it can consider only actual cases, involving the rights of litigants, properly brought before it. Its power to declare an act of legislation void does not result from any inherent supremacy, but only from the fact that, being required to declare what the law is in a given case, it must enforce the Constitution as the paramount law, whenever an act of the legislature is in conflict with it.

Again, it is a principle, and the practice, of the Court "that every possible presumption stands in favor of an act of Congress until overcome beyond rational doubt"; and, that the exercise of a power by the federal government for a long period of time tends to confirm it as a proper one. Thus usurpation, if practiced unchallenged for a sufficient period, may, and has, acquired validity.

A further restriction upon the effectiveness of the Court to halt the irregular exercise of power is to be found in its narrowing jurisdiction. Since the passage of the Judiciary Act, of February 13, 1925, it is now no simple matter to get a case before the Supreme Court. Up to that time, the litigant had a right of appeal or to a writ of error, which took his case up from an inferior court. But by the Judiciary Act in question, these means have been restricted and, in their place, the Supreme Court has been given discretion to review or refuse to review a case, on its own writ of certiorari; that is to say, if a litigant, who feels he has been denied his rights in a lower court, wishes a review by the Supreme Court, he must, within a fixed time, petition the Court to bring the case on, which it may do or refuse to do, in its own good pleasure.

This change, while working a hardship upon the citizen, as a litigant, has accomplished its main object, in greatly lightening the work of the members of the Supreme Court. It is a remarkable fact, however, that the private litigant appears to have only a relatively slim chance to obtain a writ of certiorari, while the federal government seems to be on a much more favorable footing, when it wishes the decision of a lower court reversed. In the year from February 1929 to February 1930, applications for writs of certiorari were made to the Supreme Court by one hundred and fifty-one private litigants, of which twenty-six were granted. At the same time the United States government applied for writs forty-one times, with thirty-two granted. That continues to be about the proportion.

The field of inquiry into unconstitutional acts of other branches of the federal government has been further narrowed as the result of the extension of an early doctrine of Chief Justice Marshall, in the case of Marbury v. Madison, in which he said:

> By the Constitution of the United States the President is vested with certain important political powers in the exercise of which he is to use his own discretion and is accountable only to his country and to his own conscience. * * * The subjects are political. They respect the nation, not individual rights; and being entrusted to the executive, the decision of the executive is conclusive. * * * Questions in their nature political can never be made in this Court.

It would be manifestly improper for the Court to meddle in the political policies of the President in foreign affairs, but this decision has now been stretched to exclude the review of certain questions of "domestic policy" as well, which are necessarily within the scope of constitutional control. It was applied in the case of Massachusetts v. Mellon, and appears to make it impossible ever to test the constitutionality of the new policy of "federal aid", the chief instrument by which the federal government is insinuating itself into the control of State concerns. In that case the State of Massachusetts sought to enjoin the expenditure of public moneys in the States by the Children's Bureau, in the administration of the Maternity and Child Welfare Act. The complaint pointed out that the powers given in the Act were so undefined that they would permit enforced federal registration of expectant mothers, physical examination of those contemplating marriage, insurance of mothers and other measures wholly beyond the constitutional power of the federal government to undertake; that the Act was invalid, in assuming powers not granted to Congress; that it usurps the police powers of the States, and that it imposes an illegal option on the States, either to yield a part of their reserved powers or to give up their share of the appropriations.

The Supreme Court refused to review the case, saying:

> In the last analysis, the complaint of the plaintiff State is brought to the naked contention that Congress has usurped the reserved powers of the several States by mere enactment of a statute, though nothing has been done and nothing is being done, without their consent; and it is plain that that question, as thus presented, is political and not judicial in character, and, therefore, is not a matter which admits of the exercise of the judicial power.

States, as such appear to be foreclosed by this decision, as possible plaintiffs in the future, in any contest against the legality of "fifty-fifty" appropriations, for any purpose. Yet it cannot be contended that the defects of an unconstitutional act can be cured by the assent of one or even all of the States, otherwise than by amendment, under Article V.

At the same time that the Massachusetts case was disposed of the Court also rejected a like petition brought by a taxpayer, Mrs. Frothingham, to enjoin the expenditure of this appropriation, saying:

> The right of a taxpayer to enjoin the execution of a federal appropriation act, on the ground that it is invalid and will result in taxation for illegal purposes, has never been passed upon by this Court. * * * The administration of any statute likely to produce additional taxation to be imposed upon a vast number of taxpayers, the extent of whose several liability is indefinite and constantly changing, is essentially a matter of public and not of individual concern. If one taxpayer may champion and litigate such a cause, then every other taxpayer may do the same, not only in respect of the statute here under review, but also in respect of every other appropriation act and statute whose administration requires the outlay of public money, and whose validity may be questioned. The bare suggestion of such a result, with its attendant inconveniences, goes far to sustain the conclusion which we have reached, that a suit of this character cannot be maintained.

The Court said that a taxpayer's interest in municipal revenue is direct and immediate, but the relation to revenues of the United States is very different and very minute.

The declaration, that no taxpayer can enjoin expenditures under an unconstitutional federal appropriation, comes as a shock to those who thought public moneys may be appropriated only for public purposes; and that the pronouncement should be sustained on the ground that it might entail "inconveniences", is equally as remarkable. Any inconvenience that the government might be put to, by enjoining the execution of an unconstitutional appropriation, would be the consequence of its own misconduct. If the court means, that to allow such suits would be inconvenient to itself, it is enough to say that inconvenience has never before been set up by an American court as a decisive influence on whether or not the rights of a citizen may be vindicated.

It is just such an obstacle as this — introducing the doctrine of a domestic political question — placed in the way of inquiry into irregular appropriations by Congress, that encourages that body in the feeling that there are no limits to the objects to which it may apply public moneys. In like spirit, the Supreme Court has refused to permit a judicial inquiry into appropriations for so-called "claims", under which practice millions of dollars are annually disbursed by Congressmen to their constituents.

The complacency of the Supreme Court toward expanding federal power, manifested in legislation, may be seen more readily by a comparison of earlier decisions with the more recent decisions of the Court in concrete cases.

In 1824, in the case of Gibbons v. Ogden, Chief Justice Marshall, in pointing out the constitutional divisions of power, said:

> Congress is not empowered to tax for those purposes which are within the exclusive province of the States.

This is now being done to the extent of hundreds of millions of dollars annually, and there appears to be no way in which one of the States or a taxpayer can move the Court today to pronounce upon the practice. Health, education, agricultural marketing and scores of other matters of governmental "policy", on which the federal government is now spending millions of public moneys, are plainly "within the exclusive province of the States", by the Supreme Court's own heretofore settled decisions.

In 1874, in the case of Loan Association v. Topeka, the Supreme Court laid down this further principle in respect of taxation:

> It was said by Chief Justice Marshall, in McCulloch v. The State of Maryland, that the power to tax is the power to destroy. * * * This power can as readily be employed against one class of individuals and in favor of another, so as to ruin the one and give unlimited wealth and prosperity to the other, if there is no implied limitation of the uses for which the power may be exercised.

> To lay with one hand the power of government on the property of the citizen, and, with the other, to bestow it upon favored individuals, to aid private enterprises and build up private fortunes, is none the less a robbery because it is done under the forms of law and is called taxation. * * * We have established, we think, beyond cavil [quibble], that there can be no lawful tax which is not laid for a public purpose.

In the days of Chief Justice Marshall, the Supreme Court seemed less inclined to narrow its own jurisdiction. In the case of Cohens v. Virginia, decided in 1821, the Chief Justice discussed the principles underlying our dual system of government and declared:

The maintenance of these principles in their purity is certainly among the great duties of the government. One of the instruments by which this duty may be peaceably performed is the judicial department. It is authorized to decide all cases, of every description, arising under the Constitution or laws of the United States. * * * We have no more right to decline the exercise of jurisdiction which is given, than to usurp that which is not given. The one or the other would be treason to the Constitution. Questions may occur which we would gladly avoid; but we cannot avoid them.

And again, in 1858, in the case of Abelman v. Booth, the Supreme Court said:

The judicial power covers every legislative act of Congress whether it be made within the limits of its delegated powers or be an assumption of power beyond the grants of the Constitution.

The now common practice of Congress to delegate its legislative power, culminating in the so-called Emergency Agricultural Relief Act and the Industrial Recovery Act of 1933, consolidating the most plenary legislative power in the President, was denounced by the Supreme Court in an unbroken line of decisions for a hundred years. As late as 1890, in Field v. Clark, the court declared categorically:

Congress cannot delegate legislative powers to the President.

The principle had always been recognized, as Cooley expressed it, in his Constitutional Limitations:

* * * the power to whose judgment, wisdom and patriotism this high prerogative has been entrusted cannot relieve itself of the responsibility by choosing other agencies upon whom the power shall be devolved, nor can it substitute the judgment, wisdom and patriotism of any other body for those to which alone the people have seen fit to confide this sovereign trust.

The Supreme Court has as consistently denied the existence in the federal government of any police powers, such as Congress assumed to confer upon the President in the agricultural and industrial acts, of 1933. In 1891, Chief Justice Fuller declared for the Supreme Court, in Rahrer's Case:

The power of the State to impose restraints and burdens upon persons and property in conservation and promotion of the public health, good order and prosperity, is a power originally and always belonging to the States, not surrendered by them to the general government nor directly restrained by the Constitution of the United States, and essentially exclusive.

Let us now consider the power of Congress to regulate interstate commerce, as it was interpreted in earlier days and as it is now sanctioned. Before the adoption of the Constitution the thirteen original States laid such restrictions and duties upon commerce as they pleased. These impositions created great bitterness and plainly pointed to the necessity of surrendering that power to the federal government, in the interest of free commerce among all. In the opinion of Washington's Attorney General, Edmund Randolph, this power to regulate interstate commerce was declared to be —

little more than to establish the forms of commercial intercourse between the States, and to keep the prohibitions which the Constitution imposed upon that intercourse undiminished in their operation; that is, to prevent taxes on imports or exports, preference to one part over another by any regulation of commerce or revenue, and duties upon the entering or clearing of the vessels of one State in the ports of another.

Yet from this power, conceived primarily as one to prevent the placing of impediments upon commerce among the States, Congress has assumed and delegated a vast range of restrictive powers, including that even to prohibit commerce altogether, in such articles as it pleases, and to attach to its own prohibitions an ever-growing federal police power. It has regulated the hours and wages of those employed by interstate carriers; it has set aside intrastate railroad rates and substituted those prescribed by its own regulatory body, the Interstate Commerce Commission. It has assumed to regulate hours, wages and prices in trade and industry in the States, drawing its supposed authority from the fact that the articles are designed to enter interstate commerce at some future time. It has usurped the police powers of the States in the control of food, drugs, liquors, automobile thefts, and many other matters, including private morals.

From the power to regulate commerce among the States there has been deduced a power to set up various commissions to investigate and regulate the corporations of the States; and the Attorney General of the United States has even assumed the power to grant or to withhold bills of immunity, under the anti-trust laws, in cases of corporate consolidations. The rights of private corporations and their stockholders are thus no longer protected under any general body of laws, but are dependent upon the irregular decisions of administrative officials.

Since usurpation never retreats, it is not surprising to find a succession of acts following the second and successful Meat Inspection Act of 1907, all extending federal power over intrastate commerce or invading the police powers of the States. A typical one is the Harrison Narcotics Act, of 1914, ostensibly a revenue measure levying a tax of one cent an ounce upon opium and its derivatives. Actually its purpose is not revenue, but to control all sales of narcotics in the States. Hundreds of agents, their pockets bulging with entrapment funds, are operating with stool pigeons throughout the country, doing a work that is essentially one of local police. Occasionally, the temptation of the magnificent entrapment allowances are too great and the agent decamps, as an agent at Buffalo did in December, 1931, with $13,000 given to him to make a purchase. Yet the Supreme Court has upheld this act as a valid revenue measure when the revenue derived is less than the entrapment funds appropriated to enforce it. The expenditures in 1931 exceeded the receipts by more than $1,000,000. No one can question the worthiness of the object — the suppression of the drug habit — but it is a matter of local police and four Justices of the Supreme Court denied the act's constitutionality when the matter was decided.

Federal inspection laws now enforced in the States would have had no chance of being held valid in the earlier days of the Supreme Court. Of them, Chief Justice Marshall said, in Gibbons v. Ogden, in 1824:

> The object of inspection laws is to improve the quality of articles produced by the labor of a country, to fit them for exportation, or, it may be, for domestic use. They act upon

the subject before it becomes an article of commerce, or of commerce among the States, and prepare it for that purpose. They form a portion of that immense mass of legislation which embraces everything within the territory of a State not surrendered to a general government; all which can be most advantageously exercised by the States themselves. Inspection laws, quarantine laws, health laws of every description, as well as laws for regulating the internal commerce of a State, and those which respect turnpike roads, ferries, etc., are component parts of this mass.

Today, the federal inspector is on every farm and in every factory, enforcing a multitude of regulations issued by some autocrat in Washington, who knows little or nothing about the business, but whose powers in the matter have been confirmed by recent decisions of the Supreme Court. The commerce and industry of the country every day find it more difficult to carry on in the face of this increasing harassment.

There was a period in our history when the Supreme Court denied that the interstate commerce power extended to the regulation of everything that was transported across State lines. Thus in 1865 federal control of the insurance business was prevented by the Supreme Court on the ground that —

> Issuing a policy of insurance is not a transaction of commerce. The policies are simple contracts of indemnity against loss by fire, entered into between corporations and the assured, for a consideration paid by the latter. These contracts are not articles of commerce in any proper meaning of the word. They are not subjects of trade and barter offered in the market as something having an existence and value independent of the parties to them.

* * * Such contracts are not interstate transactions, though the parties may be domiciled in different States.

It had for many years been held that the power of Congress to regulate interstate commerce "applies to the subjects of commerce and not to matters of internal police". Yet in 1902, the Supreme Court, in a five to four decision, upheld an act of Congress forbidding the interstate carriage of lottery tickets, which was the assertion of a police power not within the competence of Congress. The majority opinion held that the power to regulate commerce embraced the power to prohibit interstate carriage that was injurious to the public generally. The dissenting opinion, written by Chief Justice Fuller, denied that lottery tickets were articles of commerce, citing a previous decision by the court, and declared that the mere transportation of a noncommercial article did not thereby transform its character into a commercial one, adding:

> An invitation to dine, or to take a drive, or a note of introduction, all become articles of commerce under the ruling in this case, by being deposited with an express company for transportation. This, in effect, breaks down all the differences between that which is, and that which is not, an article of commerce, and the necessary consequence is to take from the States all jurisdiction over the subject so far as interstate communication is concerned. It is a long step in the direction of wiping out all traces of State lines, and the creation of a centralized government.

It is not to be wondered at that the Supreme Court, in 1909, by a six to three decision, declared the papers of correspondence schools to be articles of commerce, under the unlimited control of Congress. In the normal application of the doctrine that everything that crosses a State line becomes an object liable to regulation by Congress, there is an infinite opportunity for the creation of new federal boards of control; nor is it beyond the probabilities that the ordinary citizen, desiring to go by train or bus or airplane, from one State to another, may soon be required to undergo various interrogations and examinations by federal inspectors, who have discretion as to granting or withholding from him a permit to travel.

Although the power of Congress over interstate commerce is now declared to be unlimited, and although, being lodged in Congress by the Constitution, it cannot be delegated, it has nevertheless been delegated to the Interstate Commerce Commission, respecting the regulation of railways; and it has likewise been abdicated to the States in the Webb-Kenyon and other acts, which suspend the power in favor of State regulation as to incoming shipments of alcoholic liquors. It may next be applied to cigarettes or lipsticks.

Let us now consider the power of Congress "to establish a uniform rule of naturalization" throughout the United States. In 1824, Chief Justice Marshall said of this power, in Osborn v. U. S. Bank:

> He (the naturalized citizen) becomes a member of the society possessing all the rights of the native citizen, and standing, in the view of the Constitution, on the footing of a native. The Constitution does not authorize Congress to enlarge or abridge those rights. The simple power of the national legislature is to prescribe a uniform rule of naturalization and the exercise of this power exhausts it, so far as respects the individual.

This view of the power was consistently followed until 1906, when Congress arrogated to itself a power to establish a rule of de-naturalization. Yet as late as 1897, the Supreme Court had declared, in the case of U. S. v. Wong Kim Ark, that "the power of naturalization vested in Congress by the Constitution is a power to confer citizenship and not a power to take it away."

And in 1908, when the Act of 1906 was challenged as unconstitutional, in the case of U. S. v. Mansour, in the District Court, for the Southern District of New York, Judge Hough not only upheld the law as valid and cancelled the certificate of naturalization, but denied the right of a jury trial in such case. From that beginning, the punishment of exile, without trial by jury, has become fixed in federal criminal practice. It is usually invoked as a superadded penalty when a naturalized citizen has been previously convicted of violating some federal statute. It is considered to be peculiarly well adapted, in its severity, as an added punishment of violations of the enforcement acts of the Eighteenth Amendment.

From the foundation of our government until the Great War, it was supposed that the Constitution fixed the limits to federal power in war as well as in peace. It had been so declared by the Supreme Court in 1866, in ex parte Milligan, in these words:

> The Constitution of the United States is a law for rulers and people, equally in war and in peace, and covers with the shield of its protection all classes of men, at all times and under all circumstances. No doctrine involving more pernicious consequences was ever invented by the wit of man than that any of its provisions can be suspended during any of the great exigencies of government. Such a doctrine leads directly to anarchy or despotism, but the theory on which it is based is false; for government, within the Constitution, has all the powers granted to it which are necessary to preserve its existence; as has been happily

proved by the result of the great effort to throw off its just authority.

With the coming of the Great War we discovered that there exists in the federal government a "war power" of undefined limits, and, though no federal court declared definitely that the "war power" might override the Constitution, they constantly upheld as valid acts of Congress which did, in fact, set the Constitution aside.

The Espionage Acts, imposing heavy penalties upon anyone who criticized the President, or Congress or any policy of the government, was plainly violative of the First Amendment, which forbids Congress to pass any law "abridging the freedom of speech or of press." Yet the Espionage Acts were upheld by the Supreme Court in 1919, in this language of Justice Holmes:

> When a nation is at war many things that might be said in time of peace are such a hindrance to its efforts that their utterance will not be endured so long as men fight and that no court could regard them as protected by any constitutional right.

Under what was known as the Federal Control Act of 1918, Congress assumed to authorize the President to take over and operate all of the railroads of the United States, thus completely extending federal power over all internal commerce within the States carried on by the railroads. In the test of the constitutionality of this act before the Supreme Court, in 1918, we first hear of the "war power", in these words:

> The complete and undivided character of the war power of the United States is not disputable. On the face of the statutes it is manifest that they were in terms based upon the war power, since the authority they gave arose only

because of the existence of war, and the right to assert such authority was to cease upon the war's termination. * * * The elementary principle that under the Constitution the authority of the government of the United States is paramount, when exerted as to subjects concerning which it has the power to control, is indisputable. This being true, it results that, although authority to regulate within a given sphere may exist in both the United States and in the States, when the former calls into play constitutional authority within such general sphere, the necessary effect of doing so is, that to the extent that any conflict arises the State power is limited, since in case of conflict that which is paramount necessarily controls that which is subordinate.

This statement of Chief Justice White might have been put in much clearer and more concise language. Frankly, it might be restated to mean that, though the power to regulate internal commerce is constitutionally reserved to the States, if Congress wishes to usurp that power, any conflict must be resolved in favor of the federal government.

The Lever Food Control Act was another sweeping assumption of power over all internal trade and manufactures in the States, seeking to punish the making of "any unjust or unreasonable rate or charge in handling or dealing in or with any necessaries". The act was declared unconstitutional, not because it was a usurpation of the power to regulate internal commerce, but because, as a penal statute, it failed to define with certainty what constituted an offense.

The war-time Prohibition Act, of 1918, is another piece of federal legislation which reached into the States to control their commerce and limit their reserved police powers, in the clearest defiance of the constitutional division of authority. And this act was upheld as a proper assertion of the "war power."

What this "war power" is and what its limits, no one knows. It may be deduced from Supreme Court decisions, upholding acts under it, however, as a power in Congress to pass any law it sees fit that is alleged to contribute toward the successful prosecution of war, and extending into the period of completed demobilization. Incidentally, all the reserved powers of the States may be swallowed up in unified control from Washington. This may, indeed, be wise, from the standpoint of the War Office, but it certainly repudiates the earlier contention of the Supreme Court that the Constitution is a "law for rulers and people, in war as in peace", and that none of "its provisions may be suspended during any of the great exigencies of government".

The seventy-third Congress, which met in March, 1933, has given us a peace-time counterpart of the "war power", which may be styled the "emergency power". Judging from the amazing bills enacted, without debate and without permitting amendment from the floor, and justified as "emergency" legislation, this strange new power may be described as that to consolidate the legislative and judicial functions of the federal government in the President and constitute him our supreme ruler, whenever economic conditions become hard and trying for a considerable proportion of our people.

This may be wise, it may make for efficiency, but it is certainly not constitutional, whatever the Supreme Court may ultimately say about it.

Under the power delegated "to make all laws which shall be necessary and proper for carrying into execution" the seventeen specifically enumerated powers of Congress, there is always ground for controversy as to what means are "necessary and proper". In 1819, Chief Justice Marshall said of this clause:

> We admit, as all must admit, that the powers of the government are limited, and its limits are not to be transcended. But we think the sound construction of the Constitution must allow to the national legislature that discretion, with respect to the means by which the powers it confers are to be carried into execution, which will enable that body to perform the high duties assigned to it, in the manner most beneficial to the people. Let the end be legitimate, let it be within the scope of the Constitution, and all means which are appropriate, which are plainly adapted to that end, which are not prohibited, but consistent with the letter and spirit of the Constitution, are constitutional.

Yet in recent years the Supreme Court has upheld some very questionable federal legislation by imputing to Congress a much wider discretion. Thus, in Dooley v. United States and in Downes v. Bidwell, decided in 1901, involving the question of withholding from the Filipinos and Porto Ricans the benefits of the great guarantees of liberty under the Constitution, the Supreme Court said:

> If those possessions are inhabited by alien races, differing from us in religion, customs, laws, methods of taxation and modes of thought, the administration of government and justice, according to Anglo-Saxon principles, may for a time be impossible; and the question at once arises whether large concessions ought not to be made for a time, that, ultimately, our own theories may be carried out, and the blessings of a free government under the Constitution

extended to them. We decline to hold that there is anything in the Constitution to forbid such action.

Here, of course, is laid down, inferentially, the doctrine that Congress may do anything not forbidden by the Constitution. Actually, Congress had suspended the operation of the Constitution itself in these dependencies. Being the creature of the Constitution it was wholly incompetent to do such a thing.

In a case arising in 1919, challenging the authority of Congress to extend the power of the federal government into the States, in pursuance of a treaty, to control the shooting of migratory birds, when an identical act not founded upon a treaty had been declared unconstitutional, the Supreme Court said:

> No doubt the great body of private relations usually fall within the control of the State, but a treaty may override its power. * * * We see nothing in the Constitution that compels the government to sit by while a food supply is cut off and the protectors of our forests and our crops are destroyed. It is not sufficient to rely upon the States. * * * The reliance is vain.

In this decision, the idea of any fixed division of power between the States and the federal government, confirmed in a solemn and permanent constitutional act, is arrogantly ignored, and supposed utility becomes the measure of the power of Congress. Incidentally, the contemptuous rebuke of the States in this public utterance, further stripping them of their powers, reveals the depth to which they have sunk in submission to federal aggrandizement.

The Supreme Court was instituted as the special guardian of the Constitution, and it was a valiant defender of that great charter in other times.

Today it usually refuses to take jurisdiction in suits challenging the constitutionality of such experimental legislation or of the appropriations to enforce it, on the ground that the questions involved are of a political nature, and are not judiciable.

But, if the Supreme Court should assume jurisdiction, and sustain as constitutional the recent consolidation of legislative power in the executive, in the Agricultural and Industrial Control Acts of 1933, on that day our free republic will have vanished. On the other hand, if that Court should declare such consolidation of power unconstitutional, we shall then witness in response the Federal Octopus sending forth its evil tentacles to destroy the Supreme Court of the United States, as the last obstacle to its absolute control over the lives and property of the 122,000,000 of our people. We shall witness an inspired campaign to take from that court all power to declare any action of Congress unconstitutional, by modifying its appellate jurisdiction.

There are some well-worn verbal devices used by the Supreme Court to avoid open self-stultification, when it wishes to uphold some new stretch of federal power that is under the condemnation of its earlier decisions. Thus we find the Court saying:

> The rule as laid down in the earlier case and the language there used must be accepted only in connection with the facts and issues there presented, and, if stated too broadly, was, at the most, dictum, and cannot be extended to the new situation here presented;

> or,

> Counsel did not in the earlier case call to the attention of the Court certain facts which are now brought to its attention;

or,

The doctrine earlier enunciated can have no application to the facts here presented which are radically different and do not come within the rule;

or,

Argument to the contrary is not convincing, for "the mere statement of the proposition carries its own condemnation with it."

Thus the American doctrine of stare decisis (to stand by decisions and not disturb settled matters) has almost ceased to have any validity in our federal jurisprudence, with the consequence that our system of constitutional law is in chaos. No lawyer can foresee how the Supreme Court will decide any question of constitutional law presented to it. The old landmarks of fixed principles have been undermined and toppled over, and decisions may now be found on both sides of all questions. This is tragically true with respect to the rights of life, liberty and property of American citizens under the great guarantees embodied in the first ten Amendments.

If the three powers of our government maintain their mutual independence of each other, it may last long, but not so if either can assume the authority of the other.

— Thomas Jefferson, 1820

Chapter 7 –
The Strangulation of Trade

Why do governments continue to try over and over again, in the name of progress, to impose upon peoples those forms of wrong and oppression which history teaches us promote only misery and degradation?

The vast augmentation of power in the federal government is menacing not only all of the spiritual values of civil liberty — self-reliance, manliness, dignity — which we have enjoyed as a free people and without which man descends to the level of the brute, but it is also destroying those marvelous material values of our economic system, which the heretofore unrepressed and unfettered energies of our people have built up.

Through unhampered trade and industry the material well-being of the American citizen has been advanced beyond that of any people ever known to history. During these years — up to the end of last century — the Americans were practically the only people anywhere who were not cursed with a meddlesome government of unlimited power, and their energies had free play. Everywhere else on the globe a paternal government, ostensibly to promote the well-being of the people, was imposing upon commerce and industry all manner of restrictive laws, which only worked to their injury.

Today, with the characteristic arrogance and stupidity of these old world governments of unlimited power, the federal government, in the name of progress, is pursuing that ancient policy of repression of trade and industry, oblivious to the fact that its ultimate effect would be to turn this country again into a wilderness. This policy is effectuated through the multiplying federal boards, bureaus and departments, to which are given power to impose any senseless regulation or requirement upon the private business of the country. It is a power of life and death over commerce and industry, placed in the hands of men largely without knowledge, experience or ability.

The periodic meetings of Congress have become occasions of genuine alarm to all engaged in trade or industry, to all possessed of any property, since every session brings forth its new laws narrowing the rights of private property and the free field of private industry and expanding the scope of federal regulation, and even of federal competition. This process, going steadily forward, gives rise to many evils. It discourages capital from entering new enterprises, it intimidates those at the head of our business institutions whose very existence may depend upon the whim of some federal bureaucrat, and it transfers thousands of citizens annually from the private responsibility for earning a living to the spiritless comfort of public support.

Excessive regulation of private and quasi-public enterprises is an evil of such magnitude as already to have halted the progressive creation of wealth in this country; but, not content with that, the federal government is using the taxpayer's money to destroy him a competitor.

According to the Shannon Committee report, of February 8, 1933, (House Report No. 1985, 72nd Congress, 2nd session) the federal government is in unfair or destructive competition in at least 225 articles of trade, manufacture, and personal and professional service, with those engaged in:

> Agriculture, amusements, architecture, baking, banking, live stock, ship chandlery, brick making, printing and binding, canning, brush and broom manufacture, canvas products, cement dealers, chemicals, clothing, coal, coffee, contracting, cotton industry, creameries, animal and fowl feeds, fruit and vegetable shippers, furs, the grain trade, ice manufacture, laundries, mechanical shop and marine work, shoe factories, wool industry, dairy farming, engraving, envelopes and stationery, explosives, express industry, fertilizer products, furniture dealers and manufacturers, gasoline and oils, electrical energy, hotels and restaurants, insurance, lumber, saddlery and harness manufacture, shipping.

Consider the federal government's shipping business, on the oceans and on our rivers, in competition with private ship owners; it is under no necessity of economical management, its bookkeeping takes no account of items that must necessarily appear in the statements of private owners who value their liberty in making income tax returns; yet this federal business has passed on to taxpayers deficits as high as $41,000,000 in a single year.

The U. S. Shipping Board was created by an act of Congress of September 17, 1916, to develop a merchant marine in contemplation of the possibility of war. It was given power to form a $50,000,000 corporation under the laws of the District of Columbia for the purchase, construction and operation of merchant vessels. The corporation was "to be dissolved at the expiration of five years from the conclusion of the present European war", that is, in 1924. It has not only not dissolved but it is competing with private shipping with 1,341 vessels, having 2,200,000 gross tonnage, and it has 56 new vessels in process of construction.

Since its creation, up to June 30, 1933, this tax-free federal agency consumed $3,652,991,915 of taxpayers' money. In nine years, from 1924, when it should have dissolved, to 1933, its admitted deficits have been: $41,000,000 in 1924; $30,000,000 in 1925; $20,000,000 in 1926; $16,000,000 in 1927; $14,435,000 in 1928; $11,000,000 in 1929; $9,336,000 in 1930; $9,330,000 in 1931; $8,430,000 in 1932, or $159,531,000.

The federal government's Inland Waterways Corporation, operated by the War Department on the Mississippi, Warrior and Tombigbee rivers affords a splendid example of how government-in-business conducts itself. It also got its start as a war measure, in 1917, with $3,860,000 set aside by the U. S. Shipping Board for the building of barges and towboats, to be privately leased and operated, though under the supervision of the War Department. A little later the contract with the private lessee was arbitrarily cancelled and all equipment seized, the lessee suffering a very heavy financial loss which has never been made good.

With a War Department General in command the service survived the war and the assumed emergency, and by an act of Congress of June 3, 1924, it passed formally under the federally-incorporated Inland Waterways Corporation, with the same General at its head. In addition to assets of about $12,000,000, Congress granted another $12,000,000, the total of which is its capital. However, owing to some objection in Congress to extending the field of government competition with private business, the life of the corporation was limited to five years to demonstrate the feasibility or impracticability of such operation by private enterprise; and it was required that the test be made "in the same manner and to the same extent as if such facilities were privately owned and operated". That the operation has not been conducted in such manner may be seen from a study of its annual statements wherein it appears that it earned $213,197 in 1926; lost $21,808 in 1927; earned $327,712 in 1928; lost $109,729 in 1929, and earned $46,767 in 1930. Its annual deficits continue.

The bookkeeping takes no account of interest on its $24,000,000 capital advanced, which at four per cent would amount to $960,000 annually; nor of its river terminals, built at the expense of the cities interested, at a cost of $24,000,000. No account is taken of the cost of channel maintenance, nor is there included even general office expense in Washington and salary of the chairman, amounting to $57,617, which was charged to profit and loss. With this last mentioned correction alone the statement would show a deficit of $10,850 for 1930.

It has been fairly calculated, on a basis of accounting specifically required by the act, and which would be required of any private operator under federal income tax regulations, that the corporation lost $928,193 in 1926; $1,384,365 in 1927; $1,105,798 in 1928; $1,334,624 in 1929, and $1,146,861 in 1930, or a total of about $6,000,000 in the five year period. And this with no taxes of any kind to be paid by the corporation.

Before the end of the five year experimental period, the test as to the feasibility of private operation was forgotten about, and by the Denison Act of May 29, 1928, the corporation was permanently fixed in the federal system, closing these rivers to private enterprise and perpetuating serious competition with the railroads in the Mississippi Valley. These barges take tons of cotton and other freight from the railroads, and they are enabled to do it by establishing any rate, secret or public, that they wish. Their maximum rate in 1931 was 20 per cent lower than the minimum rate which the Interstate Commerce Commission prescribed for the railroads, and in joint rail and water traffic the railroad must absorb the lower rate. Incidentally shippers located on the rivers are enabled to undersell others not so favorably situated.

The report of the House Committee, March 26, 1924, recommending passage of the original act, declared:

> If the government, after making these rivers navigable, cannot profitably operate a transportation system on them, then it is hopeless to expect private capital to do so, and Congress should no longer appropriate money from the public treasury for a useless purpose. Therefore, the Committee was of the opinion that this bill should pass in order that this pioneering demonstration might be conducted by the Secretary of War until such time as its success or failure may be made apparent.

Its failure is already apparent to anyone who will carefully analyze its annual statements; even its own statements give no warrant for calling it successful, with an apparent profit of only $456,149 for a five year period, on an invested capital of $24,000,000, or less than two per cent, with no taxes to pay.

The navigable mileage on the Mississippi river, over which the Inland Waterways Corporation is competing with and destroying private lines, is 6578, and on the Missouri, 2562. The Inland Waterways program calls for new outlays of $508,000,000, with universal government lines on our rivers and on the Great Lakes.

The War Department is operating yet another tax-free shipping system in competition with private industry, in its Panama Railroad

Steamship line, from the Canal Zone to New York City, with two passenger and two freight vessels. Though instituted incident to the building of the Panama Canal it has flowered into a sort of private junketing or vacationing facility for federal office-holders, in its passenger service. Congressmen may journey back and forth free of charge, whether on "official business" or on pleasure bent. This privilege, of course, assures appropriations to meet deficits, which in 1931, amounted to $244,695, according to the annual report. But no doubt this line's accounting methods are equally as favorable to itself as are those of the Inland Waterways Corporation.

Congressmen's wives and others of the family may have an outing to Panama for $60. Rates for other federal office-holders range from $60 to $150. Similar courtesies are enjoyed on the Panama Railroad.

The Interior Department has like tax-free facilities in Alaska, with 801 miles of railroad, a steamship line and hotels. The annual deficits of this railroad alone were $1,673,997.36 in 1925; $1,169,202.04 in 1926; $900,174.67 in 1927; $840,890.93 in 1928; $954,294.65 in 1929; $1,237,120.12 in 1930, and $589,750.55 in 1931. The river boats on the Yukon are operated at a loss averaging about $10,000 a year.

The power delegated to Congress to regulate interstate commerce was essentially one to keep the channels of trade open and free to private enterprise. No fact of our history is better known than the injury inflicted upon the people of the thirteen independent States, under the Confederation, through their discriminatory duties and burdens upon commerce. To take this power from the States and place it where it could not be abused, was the principal moving cause of the meeting of delegates of the thirteen original States in Philadelphia, in 1787, to form our federal union. But it was never for a moment supposed that, in confiding to Congress the power "to regulate commerce among the States", that power would be used by the federal government to suppress commerce by competition and to bedevil it with restrictions more numerous and ruinous than those from which it was freed. Yet that is precisely what has resulted, and is going on progressively, under the pretext of promoting our moral and material welfare.

The American people, who began their career as a nation under the conviction that government is best which governs least; that the proper functions of any government of a free people are essentially negative in character; that all energetic governments are oppressive and destructive of self-development, have recently abandoned those salutary convictions. Yet all experience shows that the share of government in the progress of civilization, insofar as its positive acts of legislation are concerned, is almost invariably a record of mischief and impediment to progress; that progress has generally gone on, not because of the legislative acts of government, but in spite of them. But there are degrees of repression under which even virile peoples will not continue to persevere; and that degree is now being reached in some of our overburdened private activities.

A review of the acts of Congress and of the innumerable administrative regulations imposed upon the business activities of the people from Washington, in recent years, leaves one amazed that any intelligent legislator could have devised them without the knowledge that they must result in a general commercial paralysis.

The history of government reveals that whenever it has successfully over-ridden the rights of a people, relating to the security of life and liberty, it has invariably gone on to overthrow all protection to the right of property; that it sets itself up as the arbiter of all trade and industry, and through the imposition of senseless burdens, usually succeeds in destroying rather than promoting progress.

All the peoples of Europe have been required to submit to these governmental crimes and follies. Our independence as a people is founded in a revolt against them. Our government of limited and enumerated powers was instituted with the purpose forever to escape them. And so long as the American people held the federal government within its limited powers, so long as the Supreme Court was alert to restrain its unconstitutional acts, we prospered as no other people in all time.

But the old European doctrines of an all-wise and all-powerful government have taken possession of our system, and we shall experience the misery which has been the lot of those peoples. What these doctrines lead to was vividly set out by H. T. Buckle, in his celebrated work, The History of Civilization in England, published about the middle of last century. No more ghastly indictment of governmental stupidity was ever drawn, yet there is hardly a count in that indictment upon which the federal government at Washington does not today stand convicted.

Consider this:

> But every European government that has legislated much respecting trade has acted as if its main object were to suppress the trade and ruin the traders. Instead of leaving the national industry to take its own course, it has been troubled by an interminable series of regulations, all intended for its good, and all inflicting serious harm. To such heights has this been carried, that the commercial reforms which have distinguished England during the last twenty years have solely consisted in undoing this

mischievous and intrusive legislation. The laws formerly enacted on this subject, and too many of which are still in force, are marvelous to contemplate. It is no exaggeration to say that the history of the commercial legislation in Europe presents every possible contrivance for hampering the energies of commerce. Indeed a very high authority, who has maturely studied the subject, has recently declared that if it had not been for smuggling, trade could not have been conducted, and must have perished, in consequence of this incessant interference. In every quarter and at every moment the hand of government was felt. Duties on importation, duties on exportation; bounties to raise up a losing trade, and taxes to pull down a remunerative one; this branch of industry forbidden, and that branch of industry encouraged; one article of commerce must not be grown, because it was grown in the colonies, another article might be grown and bought, but not sold again, while a third article might be bought and sold, but not leave the country. Then too, we find laws to regulate wages; laws to regulate prices; laws to regulate profits; laws to regulate interest on money; customhouse arrangements of the most vexatious kind, aided by a complicated scheme, which was well called the Sliding scale — a scheme of such perverse ingenuity that duties constantly varied on the same article, and no man could calculate beforehand what he would have to pay. To this uncertainty, itself the bane of all commerce, there was added a severity of exaction felt by every class of consumers and producers. The tolls were so onerous, as to double and often quadruple the cost of production. A system was organized and strictly enforced, of interference with markets, interference with manufactories, interference with machinery, and interference even with shops. The towns were guarded by excise men and the ports swarmed with tidewaiters, whose sole business was to inspect nearly every process of domestic industry, peer into every package and tax every article; while, that absurdity might be carried to its extreme height, a large part of all this was by way of protection; that is to say, the money was avowedly raised and the inconveniences suffered, not for the use of the government, but for the benefit of the people; in other words, the industrious classes were robbed in order that industry might thrive.

Such, says Buckle, are some of the "benefits" which European trade owes to the paternal care of European legislation. Yet that European system which he depicts was a paradise of freedom in comparison with the innumerable and exasperating devices recently conceived by our federal government to harass and distress the American citizen in his person, and in his property, as well as in his trade. Nothing like our system of tariff "protection" has ever existed anywhere in the world. Regulation of wages, prices and profits, where the Europeans left off, has been a mere starting point with our government. We now are regulated as to hours of service, quality of goods, with arbitrary standards laid down for nearly every article of commerce, to be conformed to under severe penalties for disobedience. Trade is forbidden in any article of food or drink, in the wisdom of some administrative clerk, who has probably never made a living by private effort; and the right of property is confiscated or abolished in any species of property which Congress deems fit so to declare. Those hardy enough to remain in any business must constantly readapt themselves, their methods, plant and machinery, to some new rule or regulation, altering the established practices of production and trade. As to the excise men, the Fourth Amendment is no longer any protection to the privacies of life against him, while at our ports, we not only submit to the pillage of our trunks, but are intimidated into silence by insult.

There is yet a further comparison with the European system, as Buckle pictures it, which is quite as much in its favor:

> But worse still remains behind. For the economic evils, great as they were, have been far surpassed by the moral evils which this system produced. The first inevitable consequence was, that, in every part of Europe, there arose numerous and powerful gangs of armed smugglers, who lived by disobeying the laws which their ignorant rulers had imposed. These men, desperate from the fear of punishment, and accustomed to the commission of every crime, contaminated the surrounding population; introduced into peaceful villages vices formerly unknown; caused the ruin of entire families; spread wherever they came, drunkenness, theft and dissoluteness; and familiarized their associates with those coarse and swinish debaucheries, which were the natural habits of so vagrant and lawless a life. The innumerable crimes arising from this are directly chargeable upon European governments by whom they were provoked. The offenses were caused by the laws; and now that the laws are repealed, the offenses have disappeared.

We have an identical, though more desperate, condition of smuggling and violence, and attendant crimes and vices, in the United States today, provoked, as everyone knows, by the Prohibition amendment, and by other repressive federal laws.

Interference with commerce and industry in the United States radiates from a number of the ten so-called great executive departments and from hundreds of independent commissions seated at Washington. While their powers are supposed to be subject to review by the courts, while it is assumed that the citizen still possesses a right to go to court and defeat their arbitrary actions against him, in practice, it turns out that there is no review with respect to the facts, and that the administrative powers are final and conclusive. Thus in the case of Bates and Guild Co. v. Payne, decided in 1903, the Supreme Court, formulating a now settled rule, declared:

> Where the decision of questions of fact is committed by Congress to the judgment and discretion of the head of a department, his decision thereon is conclusive; and even upon mixed questions of law and fact, or just law alone, his action will carry with it strong presumption of its correctness, and the courts will not ordinarily review it.

Through such decisions as this, confirming judicial power in an administrative agent, the federal departments and bureaus have confounded in themselves the legislative, executive and judicial authority and have become irresistible.

The first formidable venture of the federal government into bureaucratic regulation of industry, was the act of 1887, establishing the Interstate Commerce Commission of five members, since increased to eleven. The declared objects were to secure just and reasonable railroad rates, to prevent discrimination, to prevent undue preference and to prohibit agreements in restraint of trade. Up to that time the carriers had operated under the general principles of the common law, that is to say, general laws enacted by Congress and the State legislatures, not laws enacted by an administrative body through an unconstitutional delegation by Congress of its legislative power. At the outset the Commission's powers were clearly limited to relations of the railroads which were of an interstate character; no attempt was made to usurp power over intrastate transportation, but that was to come.

Progressively the Commission's power has been extended until it became unlimited over rates, operations, profits, wages, equipment, financing, everything; it could even forbid the private stockholders, who own this $25,000,000,000 worth of private property, to elect an officer, if he is also the officer of another road.

Thus we read frequent news dispatches from Washington such as this one, under date of January 20, 1932:

> The Interstate Commerce Commission today authorized Harry M. Brown to become a vice-president of the Great Northern Railway. J. N. Haines was granted permission to become general manager of the Lehigh Valley Railroad and a director of five subsidiaries of the company.

Every detail as to service and equipment has been ordered by the Commission, even to the kind of ash pan for the locomotives.

The railroads could not issue a bond or a share of stock without a previous approval of the Commission; they must adopt such safety devices as the Commission prescribes; new lines may not be built or acquired, nor old ones abandoned without its approval. But it has compelled the railroads to buy equipment and extend their tracks. They must keep accounts according to prescribed methods, which are far from those in use by the federal Inland Waterways Corporation. They cannot keep their profits in excess of six per cent, if they are fortunate enough to earn them, which means they can retire no bonded debt. The hours of service of their employees is fixed by federal statute.

The financial burden placed upon the railroads by prescribed accounting and necessary legal services, mounts into hundreds of millions of dollars annually. They must maintain a costly array of lawyers in Washington, who must first be admitted to practice before the Commission. There are 4,351 so enrolled, who are spending their lives in the eleven story building in Washington, which houses the Commission, engaged in artificial problems of the Commission's own creation.

The exactions of the federal government are varied and persistent. The La Follette bill for the valuation of railroads alone has cost the railroads $150,000,000 — which means their stockholders — and it has cost federal taxpayers, through the Treasury, $60,000,000. Meantime the railroads are paying taxes, State and federal, annually of over $400,000,000, or at the rate of about $1,600 a mile of track. All of this must be reflected in rates and passed back to the public. This strangulation of the railroads works not only to destroy enterprise in a great private industry but it recoils upon labor in diminishing employment due to enforced economies. There are today engaged in railroad transportation about 4,000,000 persons of whom about 1,285,000 are the operating employees. The operating employees numbered 1,686,769 in 1929. The railroads disburse in taxes, wages, capital expenditures, interest and the like nearly $6,000,000,000 annually.

It is of interest to note here that, for the two year period following July, 1918, when the railroads were taken over by the federal government and the Interstate Commerce Commission's powers were suspended in favor of supreme authority in the U. S. Railroad Administration, although passenger rates were raised $33^{1/3}$ per cent and freight rates 25 per cent, there was a deficit of $2,000,000,000. The government played politics with the railroad employees at the expense of the stockholders and of federal taxpayers. On returning the railroads to their owners, rates were reduced but not to pre-war levels because of the greatly increased fixed costs that had been saddled on them.

The general principles of law were, and remain, wholly adequate to obtain from the railroads all, and more, than is now given in service and otherwise, while leaving to them a measure of freedom and initiative indispensable to their progressive development. These qualities are now annihilated. It is significant that railroad building ceased in this country with the coming of this commission. That is the blight that invariably follows upon all bureaucratic control.

The Interstate Commerce Commission was supposed to be an independent quasi-judicial body, free from the possibility of influence. Among its powers, under a recent act, was that to permit or refuse to permit consolidations of the railroads into a number of major systems. In January, 1931, President Hoover, after confidential conferences with certain railroad executives, announced from the White House a plan of consolidations, for which he had obtained their approval.

In this action we see that the Interstate Commerce Commission, the members of which are appointed by the President, were expected to do the President's bidding. It is not conceivable that they would refuse. If the President can indicate to the members of the Interstate Commerce Commission a certain course of action of which he approves, he can as well indicate his disapproval of other action. The illusion of the independent and disinterested character of the Commission thus vanishes, and we behold that it is the President who ultimately holds the power of life and death over the railroads. No such arbitrary power over private property should be in the hands of any man or group of men.

The status of the Interstate Commerce Commission was rendered somewhat precarious by an "emergency" act, of June 13, 1933, based on the assumption that while eleven dictators had destroyed the railroads a single dictator could restore them. It created such a dictator, styled a Federal Coordinator, with unlimited power over the financial and physical structures of the railroads. He will attempt to consolidate what remains of the systems, eliminating duplicative services and unnecessary trackage, while forbidding all economies based upon the discharge of unneeded union employees.

It remains to be seen whether the Coordinator's losses to the stockholders will equal the billion a year piled up by the U. S. Railroad Administrator, in 1918 and 1919, which was repaid by federal taxpayers.

Though the Interstate Commerce Commission appears thus to have been displaced by the single member who has been made railroad dictator, the fine salaries of the remaining ten Commissioners, and of the thousands of other jobs, have not been disturbed.

The same bureaucratic control that has been imposed upon the great railway industry is being extended to express companies and to telephone and telegraph companies. They, with wireless communication, will undergo the same rigid regulation and suffer the same loss of enterprise, which the public will feel in cost and in service. And this, in turn may lead to the more disastrous policy of so-called public-ownership, when all initiative has been killed by the bureaucrats.

Besides the Interstate Commerce Commission and Coordinator, now entrenched behind a most despotic authority, there are about, twenty other so-called independent federal administrative agencies, which are progressively enlarging their powers to place like restrictions and impediments upon other lines of private business activities. Among these, the Federal Trade Commission and the Federal Power Commission possess vast capacity for bedevilment. In fact, the Federal Trade Commission has already made its vexatious power felt in its pursuit of so-called "unfair competition.' This commission may require annual reports, special reports, answers to its letters of inquiry, the production of books and papers, from "any person, partnership or corporation", except banks and railroads, which are "engaged in commerce". Observe that no distinction is made in this act as to whether the commerce is interstate or intrastate. The design is to subject all commerce to inquisition by this federal board.

It may, on its own motion, summon whom it will to Washington, and "no person shall be excused from attending and testifying or from producing documentary evidence before the Commission on the ground or for the reason that the testimony or evidence, documentary or otherwise, required of him may tend to incriminate him". But no natural person shall be prosecuted for anything concerning which he has been compelled to testify.

Here is a tyrannical power to make all men's private business public, in defiance of the Fourth Amendment; to harass private business through arbitrary demands; to expose trade secrets.

In the provision seeking to compel one to testify, under heavy penalties for disobedience, the Fifth Amendment is likewise violated. The guarantee against compulsory self-incrimination embodied in this amendment is a guarantee against being compelled to testify at all, and is not satisfied by the mere waiving of prosecution.

The degree of intelligence displayed by these boards may be judged from the case of a "Cease and Desist" order, issued by the Federal Trade Commission in proceedings against the New Jersey Asbestos Co., when its alleged unfair competition consisted in nothing but "lavishly giving gratuities, such as liquor, cigars, meals, theatre tickets and entertainment" to the salesmen of their customers. In this order we may discern the influence of the Volstead Act. Such practices are universal and only a small-minded bureaucrat would take any cognizance of them.

This commission was created in 1914 to concern itself with "unfair competition", with the intended object of affording an expeditious recourse to small business unfairly competed with by big business and by unlawful trade groups. Hearings on all complaints were made mandatory. But the commission found this method too slow and in hundreds of cases it has investigated on its own motion, arrived at its own ex parte conviction and has advised its victims accordingly, demanding at the same time signature to its own form letter confession, termed a stipulation of facts. If the victim will sign he is informed that the matter will be kept secret; if not, that he will be prosecuted. Such is the prevailing bureaucratic conception of "due process of law."

Latterly, this commission has assumed the power of censorship over medical advertising, in which there is no element of competition or monopoly. True to all bureaucratic growth, it has simply found a new field of "usefulness", without any statutory authority for its actions.

By an act of May 27, 1933, Congress greatly enlarged the powers of the Federal Trade Commission, making of it a sort of dictator over the issuance and sale of securities. The act does permit appeal to the courts from the Commission's arbitrary orders, if filed within 60 days of the entry of such orders.

The Commission's power is practically that to prevent the raising of capital to finance the future industrial and commercial growth of the United States. This is in harmony, however, with a "planned national economy", under rigid control from Washington, which contemplates not growth, but an unchanging and wholly static condition, such as we see in the economy of the hive.

What this "planned economy" means may be seen in the so-called "Philadelphia Milk Agreement", under which the Secretary of Agriculture, in imposing regulations and fixing the prices of milk, has assumed to forbid anyone to start a dairy farm until he, the Secretary, has issued to the applicant a "Certificate of Necessity".

All that is sought through these acts can be better and much more safely accomplished by general statutes, with the courts open to any complainant. The power for evil, the power to reward or to ruin any particular person, partnership or corporation under this legislation, is too alarming to be confided to any administrative agency. As a potential instrument of corruption and favoritism it takes an important place in our federal bureaucracy. Honest men, no doubt, fill these positions of authority, but that will not always be so; not confidence in, but distrust of, governmental power is the only safe rule for any free people.

The Federal Power Commission has come upon the scene very recently. It will be within the authority of that body, not only to kill the initiative and check the growth of the great privately-owned power industry of the country, by infinite rules and regulations, such as now oppress the railroads, but, in the newly authorized federal irrigation projects it will find an entering wedge for enlarged direct public competition with them, and thus bring about speedier destruction. Ironically enough, the Federal Power Commission is justified under the federal policies of so-called Conservation.

The Federal Power Commission was authorized by Congress to concern itself with the "location, design, construction, maintenance and operation of power projects on navigable streams". With the characteristic urge for more power inherent in all such regulatory bodies, its very first official act was to assert that its authority extended to all streams flowing into navigable streams, thus invading the field of State jurisdiction.

Among the ten great and expensive federal departments each presided over by a secretary, clothed with the most arbitrary powers, none has pursued the policy of intermeddling with private trade and commerce more persistently, or is accomplishing more toward destroying the economic freedom of the country than the Department of Agriculture. It has become a ubiquitous meddler in every county and city in the United States.

Up to 1901 this department had accumulated patronage for only 3,388 job-holders; the number, in 1933 has been expanded to above 30,000, operating out of about twenty principal bureaus.

The Secretary of Agriculture, having finally subjected the great packing plants of the country to his control in 1918, through a reversal by the Supreme Court of its own opinion of a hundred years standing, that such powers of inspection are not inferable from the interstate commerce power, it was logical that the next step should be to control the stockyards. This he obtained in 1921, in legislation known as the Packers and Stockyards Act. These great stockyards in East St. Louis, Kansas City, Chicago, Omaha, St. Paul and at other points in the middle west, with their livestock exchanges, similar to grain exchanges, deal in hogs and cattle already arrived in the yards. The purchases and sales are begun and completed therein, and are as essentially a local and intrastate transaction as the purchase and sale of a necktie in a department store. There is no constitutional power in Congress to interfere with them, though it may regulate the shipment of cattle across State lines.

When the livestock dealers of the country realized the purpose of this act, they challenged it in a suit, which reached the Supreme Court in 1923. To the amazement of all who understood its significance the court upheld this new stretch of federal power as valid, with this remarkable declaration:

> Obviously, that power, (the interstate commerce power) if it is to exist, must include the authority to deal with obstructions to interstate commerce, and with a host of other acts, which, because of their relation to and influence upon interstate commerce, come within the power of Congress to regulate, although they are not interstate commerce in and of themselves.

Congress is thus given a free hand to usurp control over intrastate commerce on any pretext of removing an obstruction to interstate commerce. In consequence of this decision, every livestock dealer in the United States is now a creature of the Secretary of Agriculture, carrying on business by his license, and liable, at any time, to be ruined by the revocation of that license.

The destruction of the private character of the business of a livestock dealer in our stockyards, during the last eleven years, and his present condition of hog-tied subjection to federal bureaucratic control, is typical of what is going on in the harassment of all

184

private commerce and industry from Washington. The great stockyards of the country were built up by private enterprise. There were from time to time abuses, as in all human undertakings, which the Livestock Exchanges themselves did and could correct. But government saw an opportunity to intermeddle and, in 1921, Congress passed the Packers and Stockyards Act, giving to the Secretary of Agriculture despotic powers of control over all persons engaged in operating a stockyard and all engaged in receiving, buying, selling, marketing, even feeding and handling the livestock.

The Secretary was required to cause all to register with him — as licensees to do business; to put them under bond; he was empowered to fix their charges for any services and to issue any regulations he saw fit to make control complete. Any person disobeying a regulation was liable to a fine of $500 a day during its continuance, a fine heavy enough to intimidate those who might wish to challenge the lawfulness of his actions in the courts; and the violator of the regulation was further liable to suspension and forbidden to do business, after hearing before the Department of Agriculture's own judge, the appointee of the Secretary.

After vexatious years of daily inspection, investigation and repression on the part of federal regulators assigned to each stockyard, these dealers are now confronted with interloping groups of new dealers, known as cooperatives, launched in all the stockyards, supplied with taxpayers' money borrowed from the Farm Board at one and one-half per cent or less and encouraged by the Secretary of Agriculture to monopolize the livestock business of the country, in order to fix prices to the consumer. We shall hear more of them a little later.

A more ambitious reach for power was attempted in the same year by the Secretary of Agriculture, in what is known as the Future Trading Act of 1921. It was a design to carry over into peace the congenial arbitrary powers exercised during war. Particularly, it aimed at subjecting all of the great grain exchanges of the United States to an unlimited regulatory authority in the Secretary of Agriculture. It was sought to accomplish this by imposing a federal tax of 20 cents a bushel on all contracts for the sale of grain for future delivery, except sales on boards of trade willing to perpetuate wartime control voluntarily under the Secretary. It was not a taxing measure in any sense; that was a disguise. It was plainly a measure to coerce boards of trade to place themselves in the power of the Secretary of Agriculture, or be ruined by a discriminatory and excessive penalty, imposed in addition to other taxes.

Obviously, dealing in futures is a local transaction, between the parties thereto, in the exchange room. There is no element of interstate commerce in it. There is no authority, whatever, in Congress to meddle in these purely intrastate sales. Certain members of the Chicago Board of Trade challenged the Future Trading Act and took the case to the Supreme Court. The act was held unconstitutional. Unfortunately, Chief Justice Taft wrote the decision. While he held that sales for future delivery were "not in and of themselves interstate commerce", he laid down this remarkable doctrine for the guidance of Congress in curing the "defects" of the Future Trading Act:

> They cannot come within the regulatory power of Congress as such, unless they are regarded by Congress, from the evidence before it, as directly interfering with interstate commerce, so as to be an obstruction or burden thereon.

Again, in the decision, we observe the Supreme Court saying that Congress may regulate the internal commerce of the States, whenever, in its opinion, State regulation interferes with interstate commerce, "so as to be an obstruction or burden thereon." That, as has been said, is to sanction any usurping legislation.

Congress promptly took the Chief Justice's hint in this case and passed the new Future Trading Act of 1922, as "an act for the prevention and removal of obstructions and burdens upon interstate commerce in grain, by regulating transactions on grain future exchanges". And this act was declared constitutional by the Supreme Court in 1923.

Grain Exchanges that wish to operate what is known as a contract market, that is, deal in futures, are now helplessly under the power of the Secretary of Agriculture. They all operate under his license and they must conform to a complicated code of changing regulations or be put out of business. Supervisors and snoopers infest each exchange, requiring daily statements from each trader. The local federal supervisor himself has autocratic powers, and may even compel a trader to cease buying and to sell. It is not to be wondered at that one large Chicago grain operator has taken flight from this tyranny to Winnipeg, where government clerks have as yet no power over his freedom of contract.

And all of this oppression is practiced to the declared end of "preventing and removing obstructions and burdens upon the freedom of interstate commerce".

A new astounding stretch of power, that led up to the Agricultural Relief Act, of 1933, that is seeking to replace all private effort in agricultural production and commerce by government-financed and controlled socialized monopolistic groups, is found in the

Agricultural Marketing Act, of June 15, 1929. The preparatory step was taken under an act of July, 1926, authorizing the Secretary of Agriculture to establish a division of Cooperative Marketing in the Bureau of Agricultural Economics, and appropriating $225,000 for propagandizing and assisting in organizing farmers, planters, ranchmen, dairymen, nut growers, fruit growers, and others into cooperative associations under federal control, and with federal loans. The deliberate purpose behind the scheme was and is to destroy the independent middleman and dealer in every line of agricultural commerce and erect a monopoly in food products, on the supposition that the farmer will thereby reap the middleman's profit. This, of course, is open and shameless robbery.

The act attempts to force commerce out of its natural channels into new, artificial ones, incidentally ruining thousands of middlemen and dealers in produce, grain, nuts, fruit, livestock and other commodities for the declared purpose of conferring benefits upon a numerous class of rural voters. And the sum of $500,000,000 of taxpayers' money, partly taken from those same citizens who are to be destroyed, was appropriated to accomplish these objects.

The act created the Federal Farm Board, with eight jobs at $12,000 a year each to be filled by the President, the Secretary of Agriculture being an ex officio member. This board shall invite cooperative associations, to establish advisory commodity committees of seven members each, under regulations to be made by the Board. The Board shall call commodity committee meetings from time to time and may pay the visiting farmers $20 a day. Upon application of any cooperative association the board is authorized to make loans of taxpayers' money for any purpose in connection with the merchandizing of agricultural products, even to the building of cooperative canneries, grain elevators, stockyards, and the like, and other facilities, in the discretion of the politicians on the Farm Board. The loans are to bear interest at a rate equal to the lowest rate of any government obligation issued since April 6, 1917 — which at present is one and one-half per cent — and in no case more than four per cent. They may be repaid in twenty years.

When any cooperative association procures a loan from the Farm Board, it is compelled to sign an agreement whereby it invests this federal agency with total and absolute control over its business, its personnel, its trade policies, including the power to discharge every officer, which powers have been exercised by the Farm Board in specific cases. Such associations become themselves federal governmental instrumentalities in competition with every private dealer. It is pertinent to inquire, in view of these facts, whether these government controlled and financed cooperative groups are or not such instrumentalities of the federal government as to be beyond the taxing power of the States, under the doctrine laid down in McCulloch v. Maryland? Such a claim may not unreasonably be set up against the States and the federal government, making of them tax-supported but non-tax paying institutions.

How many loans, and in what amounts, the Farm Board has made to the various cooperative associations, appears not to be public information, yet the money is public money. No voluntary report has ever been made. Disclosure of "confidential information" is made penal by the act. Yet information as to the following loans was extracted from the Farm Board at a hearing before the Senate Committee on Agriculture November 24, 1931:

Cooperatives Dealing In	Loans	Repayments
Beans	$6,885,049	$71,859
Cotton	140,525,937	95,674,997
Dairy Products	13,291,662	4,235,354
Citrus Fruits	3,020,882	712,818
Other deciduous fruits	1,844,717	353,596
Miscellaneous fruits and vegetables	350,470	9,398
Grain	47,215,932	34,236,294
Honey	45,839	6,158
Livestock	4,829,704	1,661,559
Nuts	445,000	46,000
Poultry and eggs	531,000	139,500
Rice	988,538	198,529
Seeds	153,141	37,214
Tobacco	2,782,131	580,178
Wool and mohair	18,741,746	2,889,527
Totals	$255,866,458	$146,367,203
Cotton stabilization	133,460,038	58,509,156
Grain stabilization	272,972,604	112,823,842
Grand Totals	$662,299,100	$317,697,202

The $12,389,200 loan to the California wine brick makers was not included in the list.

But the Agricultural Marketing Act further provided that, upon application of the advisory commodity committee for any commodity, the Federal Farm Board may recognize a "stabilization corporation" for the commodity, and lend it sufficient taxpayers' money to buy up any surplus on the market, to be carried over, and thus peg the price. If a private individual did such a thing he would be running a pool, in violation of the laws against conspiracy and restraint of trade. It would further cause his suspension from any exchange. But these federal cooperatives are expressly exempted by the act from prosecution under the anti-trust laws. The word "stabilization", used in the act, is disingenuous; the accurate description is "price-fixing"; yet these corporations have only met with failure in their attempts thus far to fix prices.

If such practices are properly the concern of government and are economically sound, why should government restrict them to agricultural products? Why not extend them to the lagging markets of oil, copper, zinc, lead, iron, lumber, coal? That folly is now actually contemplated in spite of the costly failures of other governments in that field. Over production in agriculture will cease, when the law of supply and demand is left free to operate, when there is private responsibility and the necessity of learning by experience or perishing.

A typical example of how these price-fixing corporations really work may be seen in the great grain stabilization corporation, now operating on the Chicago Board of Trade. This is by far, the largest agency of its kind created by the Federal Farm Board, and as a means of federal patronage, it excites the envy of every federal official in Washington. Its general manager receives a salary of $50,000 a year, its vice-president, $32,500, its treasurer, $30,000 and there are numerous jobs that pay from $10,000 to $25,000.

On August 7, 1929, the political farmers on the Federal Farm Board advised the grain farmers to hold their wheat for a higher price than $1.34 per bushel, then obtaining. A little later the Board agreed to make loans on wheat at $1.18. Before the end of the winter wheat had dropped to $1.00. Then to keep up the price, the Board,

191

through the stabilization corporation bought 60,000,000 bushels. On September 19, 1930 the price of wheat went down to 81 cents. Six days later it touched $78^{3/8}$ cents. In December the Board adopted the plan of taking all wheat offered at 73 cents. In spite of this, before January 1, 1931, wheat had dropped to $64^{3/4}$ cents, and by September, 1931, to 36 cents; and, while everything is done secretly, while the public and taxpayers have no access to the information, it was elicited from the Farm Board by the Senate Committee on Agriculture, on November 24, 1931, that it had bought and was holding off the market 189,656,187 bushels of wheat and 2,073,178 bales of cotton, with a loss, on October 31, 1931, of $185,000,000 of taxpayers' money.

For five years prior to the appearance of the Farm Board the average price of wheat in Chicago had been $146^{1/2}$. All interferences of governments with the law of supply and demand have invariably turned out in this ruinous manner, whether the Brazilian government, in the matter of coffee, or the British government, in the matter of rubber. And the most serious aspect is that these practices destroy the market for all time by raising up new competitors elsewhere.

The 73rd Congress abolished the Farm Board in name, as an exploded experiment, but turned its powers, functions and jobs over to the Secretary of Agriculture for use in a new price-fixing experiment. Of the $500,000,000 received by the Farm Board, it lost about $420,000,000, not counting the millions of unpaid loans to cooperatives. Of the expected salvage of $80,000,000 so much as may be collected is to be added to a freshly-appropriated $40,000,000 for "Crop Production" loans, under the Farm Credit Administration, in about a dozen privileged States, in 1933-34.

While the Farm Credit Administration will thus seek to increase crop production, the agricultural dictator will be paying out the proceeds of his processing tax as rentals for farm lands withheld from cultivation, to the end of reducing crop production.

The Department of Agriculture is indulging in daily propaganda over the great radio systems of the country in an endeavor to persuade the 90 per cent of our self-reliant, independent farmers, who are not in cooperative organizations, to join in the federal cooperative scheme.

To what degree more direct forms of pressure are being exerted on the independent farmers and dealers is not known. One who is licensed by the federal government to earn his living discusses such things at his peril. Yet one interesting case has come to light, in a proceeding to revoke the licenses of certain independent livestock dealers at National Stockyards, Illinois, in 1931. The competing cooperative had — it became public for the first time in the hearing — borrowed $300,000 from the Farm Board and began underselling the market, thus suffering a continuous loss, amounting to $14,000 in a three months' period in 1930. The independents, about 50 in number, refused to deal with this cooperative and thus contribute to their own ruin, and filed a complaint of "unfair practices" against it with the Department of Agriculture, as required by the regulations under the Packers and Stockyards Act. To the surprise of the independent dealers, within ten days, they themselves had been cited by the Secretary of Agriculture, not to present their evidence in the case, but to show cause why their licenses should not be revoked for boycotting the cooperative in question. Yet under the Stockyards and Packers Act, it is mandatory upon the Department to hold a hearing on every complaint of "unfair practices" filed with it.

Not a word was heard from their previous complaints of "unfair practices" against the cooperative, yet such conduct warrants suspension and revocation of license. On the contrary, the independents submitted to hearing before a Department of Agriculture examiner and there, to their surprise, they found the cooperative was represented by a federal department attorney, who constantly objected to any evidence tending to establish the unfair methods of the cooperative and its losses of public money. The examiner refused to summon various witnesses whose presence was demanded by the accused independents, and plainly exhibited the subservient character of this so-called tribunal.

Following this hearing, on February 24, 1931, C. F. Marvin, head of the Weather Bureau, and then acting Secretary of Agriculture, in Secretary Hyde's absence, ordered the fifty independents to "cease and desist" from refraining to have business dealings with the cooperative in question, and further ordered them suspended from the Live Stock Exchange for ninety days. The independents obtained an injunction from the United States District Court for the Eastern District of Illinois, in which, as is now the practice, the Court refused to disturb the Secretary of Agriculture's findings, saying the proceedings were "not violative of the plaintiff's constitutional rights."

Obviously, as such complaints are made by the Secretary of Agriculture, who is an ex officio member of the Farm Board, his power ultimately to decide such cases is necessarily that of judge, jury and executioner, which has no place in our system of government. The examiner has the alternative of upholding every complaint or jeopardizing his own job.

The Agricultural Marketing Act and its successor, the Agricultural Relief Act, have superimposed upon the people of the United

States a monstrous machine that is seeking to destroy all initiative, all self-reliance, all enterprise, and to reduce all citizens, engaged in agricultural and related pursuits, to servitude under the federal government. It will, if permitted to continue, become a vast political engine, in which the shiftless and cunning will find an interest; it will be oppressive and promotive of violence, and it cannot escape becoming corrupt, with huge sums placed in the hands of politicians to dispense secretly, and under the widest discretion.

The acts contemplate the destruction of the system of marketing of our foodstuffs which has obtained since the foundation of our Republic, based upon equality of opportunity and competitive buying and selling in an open market, under the self-correcting law of supply and demand — the only system for a free people, rewarding initiative and enterprise — and the institution of a wholly artificial, non-competitive price-fixing governmental system.

Unless the courts of this country, including the Supreme Court, unless Cooley and Story and other authorities on constitutional law, have been in error since the Federal Constitution was adopted, the Agricultural Marketing Act and the Emergency Agricultural Relief Act are unconstitutional and void on the single ground alone — though there are others — that they attempt to appropriate public moneys and to tax for a private, as distinguished from a public, purpose. As Judge Walter Sanborn said for the United States Circuit Court, Eighth Circuit, as late as 1901, of an act of the Kansas legislature authorizing townships and cities to subscribe for stock in sugar factories:

> The legislative power of taxation and the power of eminent domain are alike limited to the exercise thereof for public objects, and they cannot be successfully prostituted for

private purposes. * * * A legislature cannot make a private purpose a public one by its mere fiat, and the determination of the question in any case, is a judicial and not a legislative function. * * * The true answer to the question seems to be plain and certain. Speaking generally a public purpose is a governmental purpose, one of the purposes for which governments are instituted and maintained among men, such as the maintenance of order, the prevention and punishment of crime, the care of highways, the relief of the destitute, the education of youth, the erection of buildings for the use of schools and the officers of government; while a private object is one which is ordinarily sought and attained by private individuals, such as cultivation of the soil, the manufacture of useful and attractive articles, the purchase and sale of merchandize, and the thousand and one purposes which enlist individual enterprise and energy in a complex and advancing civilization.

Yet, when we consider the dictum of the Supreme Court in the case of Massachusetts v. Mellon, the constitutionality of recent extraordinary acts may never be passed upon, since they, too, may be said to involve a "domestic political question", all which seem now to be excluded from review.

> *Power imposes; power receives everywhere respect by its own character. However illegally acquired, the great action of power obtains homage. The success of usurpers is in part founded upon this fact; so that usurpation itself becomes a new acquisition to farther usurpation.*

— Francis Lieber

Chapter 8 –
Can We Turn Back?

"The people of these United States are the rightful masters of both Congress and Courts, not to overthrow the Constitution, but to overthrow the men who pervert the Constitution." – Abraham Lincoln.

Our heritage of civil liberty, under the protection of the great guarantees, comes to us from our political ancestors, the Anglo-Saxons. Like all rights anywhere protected by law, it has been bought by the blood of thousands. It is well to recall that on not less than thirty-nine distinct occasions, within seven centuries, the Englishman has been compelled to make the choice of servitude or freedom, by submission to tyranny or rebellion — and he has chosen to rebel. On each occasion he forced his unwilling government to make solemn reconfirmation of his liberty and immunities, now enshrined in those thrilling Bills and Petitions of Rights, beginning with Magna Charta in 1215, which form the foundation stones of freedom wherever it exists.

In these times of the Americans, when a salutary distrust of power in our ancestors has been replaced by its apotheosis among us, when we attribute to government the wisdom and benignity of the deity, it is clarifying to our thinking to ponder this history of the relatively mildest and least despotic government of the old world, that of the English. It is an indictment of repeated perfidy and dishonor. It reveals the solemn oath of government to respect the rights of the citizen to be wholly worthless. This is not peculiar to governments presided over by Kings; Kings are but men possessed of power, whatever the official designation, with all the frailties and vices of other men. It has its perfectly rational explanation in the natural vanity of man. As Gouverneur Morris said in the Constitutional Convention in 1787:

> The mind of man is fond of power. Enlarge his prospects and you increase his desires.

While the great guarantees of civil liberty in our Bill of Rights are a heritage from the Englishman, our revolutionary ancestors gave to liberty yet another protecting device of inestimable value, in a written organic Constitution of government. Constitutional government, as the Americans gave it to the world, in 1789, was founded upon two basic principles, and these are, that it must be representative government, and that it must be limited government. All ultimate power resides in the people, the sovereign, who designate government as a mere agency to execute such powers as are confided in its commission. In such limited written Constitution lies the protection of the minority against what would otherwise be a majority wielding all power. In a constitutional system the people, the sovereign, cannot govern; it would be a contradiction in terms, since the powers of the sovereign are absolute and unlimited.

It results, in the theory of the American constitutional system, that no power of an unlimited character can be possessed by constitutional government without destroying the system and that protection which limitation of power seeks to achieve for the citizen. Such is the great contribution which our ancestors made to the elevation of man in political society, and which we, their posterity, have lightly permitted our government to trample under foot.

While the English people have their written guarantees of immunity against governmental power, in their Bills and Petitions of Rights, they have no constitutional government; that is to say, there are no limitations upon the power of the British Parliament. They have no device by which to reform the government peaceably, similar to that provision in our Constitution, embodied in Article V, by which it was intended by the framers that the American people might alter the powers of government, as the occasion required, in an orderly manner. The Englishman has no alternative but acquiescence or rebellion, in meeting oppression.

Well knowing, from the lessons of history, the innate and insatiable greed of governmental power, and its unsleeping purpose to break through the most solemnly-imposed limitations; and understanding the political truism, that as governmental power increases the liberty of the citizen must correspondingly diminish; seeing government clearly, as mere groups of men, like other men, who will violate the rights of other men, when there is a strong incentive, our forefathers founded this government as a constitutional one, of limited and enumerated powers, to insure the blessings of liberty to themselves, and to us, their posterity, and to those who shall come after us.

And there comes down to us from them an anxious warning that "a frequent recurrence to fundamental principles is absolutely necessary to preserve the blessings of liberty and keep a government free." There is nothing obscure in this. What Franklin and Jefferson meant by it was, simply, that if the people relied with confidence upon the limited government just established, if they failed to preserve a sense of distrust and frequently measure the acts of government by the limited powers conferred, and by the great principles of the Bill of Rights, their posterity would be enslaved to governmental power.

And that is precisely what has taken place. As we study the present-day acts of the federal government, and the approving pronouncements thereon by the Supreme Court, it becomes clear, that the federal government of limited and enumerated powers established in 1789, has been replaced by one that recognizes no limitations upon its power to despoil the citizen in his liberty and property.

The last recurrence of the American people to fundamental principles — which means the reestablishment of old and weakened limitations upon governmental power or the imposition of new ones — may be said to have been in the ratification of the Fourteenth and Fifteenth Amendments, in 1868 and 1870, respectively. These amendments forbade both the federal and State governments to reduce any person to slavery, and prohibited any State from depriving any person of life, liberty or property without due process of law, and from denying to any person the equal protection of the laws.

These two amendments were designed primarily to protect the black citizen in his new freedom. Today not only he, but his white American brothers, find themselves in a new bondage under unlimited federal power, which the great guarantees have been rendered impotent to prevent.

In the intervening sixty years or more of thoughtless confidence on the part of the people since their adoption, the federal government, through the progressive enlargement of precedent, and through amendments proposed by Congress and ratified, not by the people, but by the State legislatures — never more than 6,000 persons — has practically set aside the former limited system, and erected in its place a new one of irresistible and despotic character. If the energy and power of the federal government multiply during the next two or three decades, with the same rapidity and to the same degree that is evident in the last, in the ordering of the lives and habits of the people of the States, rebellion or servitude appears inevitable.

Article V, the amending clause of our Constitution, as has been said, was conceived as a unique device by which the American people might, upon any appearance of oppression, reform its government peaceably, by imposing new limits upon its field of action. Everywhere else in the world we observe that when oppression becomes unendurable, there is no alternative for the people but violence, which usually results in a mere change of oppressors. Jefferson wrote of the amending article of our Constitution:

> If this avenue be shut to the call of sufferance it will make itself felt through that of force, and we shall go on as other nations are doing, in an endless circle of rebellion, oppression, reformation; and oppression, rebellion, reformation, again; and so on forever.

Article V has not fulfilled the vital function it was designed to perform. It may be said that this avenue to the call of sufferance — the right of the people peaceably to throw off oppressions of the federal government and tame its spirit of arrogance into considerate conduct — has been shut, in the perversion of its use by Congress, in conjunction with the State legislatures, to remove the constitutional limits upon some of its most important powers. The article reads:

The Congress, whenever two-thirds of both Houses shall deem it necessary, shall propose amendments to this Constitution, or, on the application of the legislatures of two-thirds of the States, shall call a convention for proposing amendments, which, in either case, shall be valid to all intents and purposes, as part of this Constitution, when ratified by the legislatures of three-fourths of the several States, or by conventions in three-fourths thereof, as the one of the other mode of ratification may be proposed by the Congress.

While it is in the power of the legislatures of two-thirds of the States to require Congress to call a convention to propose amendments, which Congress may require to be submitted to the State legislatures or to conventions in the States, this method has never been used. Not a single amendment to the Constitution has ever been proposed to conventions of the people; in every case, Congress has proposed them to the legislatures of the States, which were in no true sense representative, for such purpose. And within the last twenty years the changes thus formally made have been fatal to any conception of limited or constitutional government.

Can we turn back? Is it possible for the American people peaceably to reform their now arrogant federal government, strip it of the dangerous and unlimited powers it has assumed and reestablish its powers within constitutional limits? Is the American citizen ever again to enjoy the protection of general law before his ordinary courts? Are the State governments ever to be reinvigorated, under a new sense of authority and responsibility, in the domestic concerns of the people? Or is local self-government forever displaced by an engulfing regulatory system, radiating from Washington into every village, directing every business activity and all personal conduct, under the watchful eye of the resident federal agent?

The path to reformation is plain, and that is, pressure in the States upon their legislatures to apply to Congress for the calling of a convention, which shall in turn submit its proposals to conventions of the people in the States. It is the people who are sovereign over government; it is they who delegate power to government and they who may take it away. Obviously, since no government ever willingly relinquished power, Congress would never initiate any proposal that contemplated its own reformation. No powerful and self-satisfied government ever has or ever will. Nor is it likely that the legislatures of two-thirds of the States could be induced to apply to Congress for the calling of a convention, without the most persistent and aroused demand on the part of the outraged people of the States. The federal power is now so deeply entrenched in the States that it would instantly meet the challenge with all of those instruments of bribery and intimidation which arbitrary government knows so well how to use.

The new federal bureaucracy is a numerous and powerful body, bent not only upon holding what it has, but upon gaining more. Nearly two millions of persons are in the pay of the federal government, in activities of some kind. When we consider the interested members of their families as voters, the number of partisans of the present order may reach five million or more. It has attached, through loans of public moneys, through education and entertainment, a very considerable body of citizens in our rural sections. Through the policy of "federal aid" and "cooperation" with the States, there are other thousands who are its financial beneficiaries. These constitute no small phalanx of defenders of the prevailing system, who may be counted on, when any occasion arises for the mobilization of influence against any serious agitation among the private citizens of the States to put an end to federal tyranny.

Congress, which has brought this oppressive bureaucratic system into being, by delegating to it its own legislative, and even judicial, power, must, of course, champion and defend its own creation. With purposes so pure, and aims so noble, in behalf of "the people", as appear in the titles and preambles of its volumes of recent legislative acts, Congress would no doubt denounce as base ingratitude, the conduct of any citizen bold enough to attempt to lead the way back to limited government and liberty.

Some of the socialistic programs of the new bureaucracy, with respect to motherhood and children, have made a powerful appeal to certain organized groups of women, and their influence has been capitalized by the directors of these programs, for use as it has been needed. History, precedent, experience, limited government, the Constitution, mean nothing against their sympathy and their zeal.

The States are fully able to meet and solve, each in its own way, all of the problems of local self-government that arise; they can do so more efficiently and more economically than can a distant government dependent upon agents; and it is their constitutional function. Their revenues would be more than ample, without heavy taxation, for the most exemplary services to the people, but for the excessive sums taken from their citizens by the federal government to finance its own unconstitutional duplication of services.

It is clear that the problem of restoring the Constitution of the United States as a limiting agency upon the powers of the federal government, and of rescuing civil and economic liberty, before they are completely overwhelmed, is no simple matter. Such a problem has never been a simple one with any people. As Von Jhering tells us in The Struggle for Law:

> A principle of law won without toil is on a level with the children brought by the stork; what the stork has brought the fox and vulture can take away again. But from the mother who gave it birth, neither the fox nor the vulture can take the child away; and just as little can a people be deprived of the laws and institutions which they have had to labor and to bleed for, in order to obtain.

The things necessary to be done by the American people are apparent — return to fundamental principles. Whether it can or will be done, is in the lap of the gods. Particularly:

There must be called by Congress, on application of the legislatures of two-thirds of the States, a national constitutional convention, which must propose to conventions of the people of the States, amendments accomplishing the following objects:

1. Repeal of the Sixteenth Amendment. In this amendment, ratified in 1913, Congress conferred upon itself, with the approval of the State legislatures — like bodies of politicians, all of whom hoped sometime to be elected to Congress — unlimited power to take from the income of any citizen, what it will and in any way that it sees fit; to take from one, and not from another, as it pleases; to take in different proportions from different citizens. This is not a power of constitutional taxation, for the term "constitutional" implies limits. This is the power of confiscation, which Congress has exercised, at various times, to take as much as 65 per cent of the income of certain classes of citizens. If it can take 65 per cent it can take 100 per cent. And the Supreme Court, reversing an opinion of Chief Justice Marshall, has recently said of this power,

that no one can plead due process of law against it; which means that total confiscation by Congress is valid.

Federal taxes are now levied upon the citizen on the basis of "ability to pay", with all of the implications and ruthlessness attaching to an indemnity imposed upon a vanquished enemy.

In this amendment, the citizen's right of property is gone. By narrowing these confiscations to less than two per cent of the citizens, and exempting more than 98 per cent, the federal government has created an overwhelming popular support for any and all irregular measures of extravagance undertaken for the supposed welfare of the people. And it is this artificial support, and not its constitutional powers, that sustains it in whatever course it wishes to pursue.

The framers of our Constitution deliberately prohibited to Congress the exercise of the power to levy direct taxes, save according to population in the States, as a necessary restraint upon the pillage of property. They well knew that no government of limited powers would remain a limited government, with its most important power, taxation, unlimited. And the whole course of arbitrary development in the federal government — its usurpation of State powers, its strangulation of trade and industry, its regulation of the habits of the people, its fantastic scheme for the destruction of all engaged in private agricultural commerce, its contempt for the immunities of the citizen, under the Bill of Rights — and universal corruption — all this, is directly the outcome of the Sixteenth Amendment. Unless this power is taken from Congress, and some limits imposed, the outlook for the American people is one of incalculable misery and calamity.

It must not be forgotten that by the same unlimited power of Congress to discriminate and take, on an ascending scale, from the rich, the Congress can, if it wishes, exempt the rich, and take all from the poor or middle classes. History gives us such examples. What is involved, is the vital principle of the protection of private property from public or private plundering, whether the possession of the humblest or the mightiest. Their rights stand or fall together.

2. The repeal of the Seventeenth Amendment. This amendment, ratified in 1913, along with the Sixteenth Amendment, made of the United States Senate a second popular branch of Congress, destroying the important principle theretofore recognized, since 1789, that the Senate represents the States, as political entities, two members from each State to be elected for six years by the legislatures thereof. It is significant that the steady progress of federal usurpation of the powers of the States has succeeded this far-reaching change, which put an end to the representation of the States, as such, in Congress; and it has greatly weakened the influence and inclination of the United States Senate to prevent abuses of power under the Sixteenth Amendment, when undertaken in the supposed interest of "the people." It is to be remarked, too, that there has been a noticeable decline in the abilities and character of popularly-elected Senators, who must now scramble in primaries and elections, compared with those chosen by the State legislatures before 1913.

If the vigor of the original dual system of government is to be restored, if the principle of local-self-government is to survive, the States, as such, must again have the protection of their representatives in the Senate.

3. Repeal of the Eighteenth Amendment. After twelve years of unspeakable tyranny practiced upon the people of the United States

under this vicious amendment and its crime-producing enforcement acts, repeal appears assured before the close of 1933, giving us a heartening example of what an aroused people can accomplish in the peaceable reform of its government.

4. An amendment forbidding the acquisition and government of colonies and dependencies and putting an end to our imperial policies and proconsular administrations beyond the United States, as incompatible with the purposes and powers of any limited government. Until we acquired the Philippines, the Supreme Court had consistently held, from the earliest days that, upon the acquisition of territory, the limitations imposed by the Constitution upon government, automatically applied to such territory. It is impossible to govern subject peoples if their rights are as complete as those who govern. The Supreme Court conveniently reversed this principle with respect to the Philippines and Porto Rico, and despotic government by proconsuls in those places has been the result.

The effect of the federal government exercising arbitrary and unlimited powers over subject peoples abroad could not fail to encourage it in the exercise of like power at home. Our safety requires that this cease, and that no territory acquired anywhere shall be governed outside the Constitution.

5. An amendment which shall clearly restate that the powers not delegated to the federal government nor prohibited to the States, in the Constitution are reserved to the people of the States; to the end that all of the costly and dangerous activities of the federal departments and bureaus in State concerns, including those dealing with agriculture, education and health, may cease.

6. An amendment which shall restate the power in Congress to regulate interstate commerce among the States, to be limited by the powers reserved to the States over their own internal commerce and manufactures; that Congress is not empowered to prohibit it or to impose impediments upon State or interstate commerce, and that such power as is given shall relate only to articles of commerce; that no police powers and no powers of local inspection or local regulation shall be inferred from it.

The Supreme Court has, in effect, construed the interstate commerce power to be unlimited. The dangers of consolidated despotism inherent in such a construction are real and ominous. It must again be so circumscribed as to bring it under constitutional law, if the States are to be rescued from impotency and annihilation.

7. An amendment forbidding Congress to delegate to any person, board, commission or department any authority of a legislative or of a judicial nature, and, particularly, any power to make rules and regulations with the force of law, and any power to sit in judgment in the execution of its own rules. The curse of commerce and industry in the United States today is this alien institution of an administrative agency, which is both law-maker and judge, summoning whom it pleases, when it pleases, to Washington, with his private books and papers, for a hearing, and, by the findings on the facts, concluding such person before the courts. It is wholly arbitrary and despotic.

8. An amendment which will alter Article V, the amending clause, so as to deny to Congress the authority to augment its own powers by submitting proposals to the State legislatures; and requiring every proposal to be submitted to conventions of the people in the States. The ultimate power over government is in the people and they are the only logical ones to resort to.

9. An amendment which will put an end to the reckless squandering of public moneys by Congress upon any object, by forbidding the appropriation of any moneys for other than strictly governmental purposes. This would effectually prevent the ruinous waste of taxes in subsidies for private groups and in other costly and highly socialistic federal enterprises, and permit a host of pampered favorites of government to learn again the lessons of self-reliance, self-support and self-respect.

10. An amendment to the judiciary article requiring the Supreme Court to assume jurisdiction in any suit brought by a taxpayer to determine the constitutionality of any act of Congress appropriating public moneys; and reestablishing beyond the power of Congress to alter, the right of any litigant to appeal from the lower courts, as it originally existed.

It is shocking that a taxpayer is not now permitted by the Supreme Court to be heard in so important a matter as an appropriation of his own money to fasten upon the country an unconstitutional policy. And there is certainly no free system of justice in a policy which leaves with the Supreme Court the arbitrary power to hear or not hear a case on appeal, which involves a constitutional question.

It is further desirable that the Supreme Court be directed to take jurisdiction in all cases challenging the constitutionality of treaties, under a declaration that no treaty shall deprive any State of its reserved powers. In the Migratory Bird case the court declared a treaty could swallow up the powers of the States. As there are no settled limits to which this process may be carried, the safest course is to forbid it in any degree.

11. When we reflect upon the extent to which the efficacy of the great guarantees of our Bill of Rights to protect our immunities

against governmental oppression, has been whittled down by the Supreme Court's recent interpretations of their scope, we perceive an urgent need to restate these in their full vigor. We need, particularly, to declare:

(a) That the Constitution is a limitation upon the powers of government in times of war as in times of peace, and that none of its provisions is to be violated on any pretext of necessity.

(b) That Congress shall pass no law abridging the freedom of speech or of press, such as espionage and sedition acts, to restrain criticism of the government or its acts, by any citizen of the United States.

(c) That the President of the United States shall have no power to call the Militia of the States into the service of the United States for use beyond its borders, nor may the citizen be conscripted.

(d) That the right of the people to be secure in their persons, houses, papers and effects, is a right to be free from search, except upon a warrant, issued upon probable cause, supported by oath or affirmation, particularly describing the place to be searched and the person or things to be seized; that evidence obtained by anyone by search without a warrant, by espionage or by entrapment, shall not be admissible in any court of the United States or of any of the States.

(e) That Congress shall have no power to pass a law to deprive any citizen of his citizenship.

(f) That Congress shall have no power to pass a law denying the right of trial by jury in respect of any offense committed against the United States.

(g) That Congress shall have no power to pass a law authorizing the use of the equity processes of injunction and contempt in relation to any prosecution of a criminal character.

(h) That Congress shall have no power to authorize the trial and punishment of any person who has previously been tried upon the same facts in any court.

In view of the recent ambition of the House and Senate to become legislative tribunals and to embark upon legislative trial by hue and cry, it would be timely, finally to declare that, the judicial power, having been confided by the Constitution to the courts, neither House shall have any authority to compel anyone to give testimony before it, beyond what he chooses to do voluntarily. The Supreme Court enunciated this principle very clearly in 1880, but has recently reversed itself.

And, finally, to restore to the people the power freely to change the officers of government at elections, an amendment which will deny to federal officeholders any right to vote so long as they are on the public payroll. Through the vast patronage of the federal government it is possible for an administration to hold the balance of power against the electorate and perpetuate its tenure indefinitely.

This is an extensive program, and perhaps not complete, but it will go a long way toward undoing the augmentation of oppressive power that has gone on, largely through usurpation, during a half century of lethargy on the part of the confident citizen.

It is consonant with the truism that the most beneficial legislation which has ever been enacted is that which repeals prior legislation and restores that condition of freedom which has meantime been unnaturally repressed. If it were possible to achieve the objects here indicated we should probably remain a free people for another half century before a new occasion arose for a heroic assertion of the power of self-protection. Can it be done?

The Union is dependent on the will of the State governments for its chief magistrate and for its Senate. A blow aimed at the members must give a fatal wound to the head, and the destruction of the States must be at once a political suicide. Can the national government be guilty of such madness?

— Alexander Hamilton

To support with vigor a single government over the whole extent of the United States would demand a system of the most unqualified and the most unremitted despotism.

— James Wilson

What is a Dollar Worth?

In 1933, $1.00 has a relative value equivalent to $16.60 in 2009. This is roughly based on the Consumer Price Index; however, there are numerous other ways to determine relative value from year to year, depending on what type of value you are interested in understanding.

Throughout The Federal Octopus we read about the costs of various programs, projects, federal budgets, amounts of taxation, salaries, gains, losses and wastes.

To help put into perspective what these dollar values mean to us today we can use a relative value calculator. For our research we used several calculators, with our preference being the one from the www.measuringworth.com web site, which introduces the concept this way:

> Determining the *relative* value of an amount of money in one year compared to another is more complicated than it seems at first. There is no single "correct" measure, and economic historians use one or more different indicators depending on the context of the question.
>
> ...
>
> Presented [on the www.measuringworth.com web site] are seven indicators for making such comparisons in U. S. dollars between any two years from 1774 to the present.

They are the CPI, the GDP Deflator, the Consumer Bundle, the Unskilled Wage, the Production Worker Compensation, the GDP Per Capita, and the Relative Share of GDP.

There are a number of ways to measure relative worth.

To determine what the value of a dollar was in 1933, there is no single correct answer. A price or an income from 1933 is valued in different ways in 1933 by different people and under different contexts. That must be taken into account when looking at the numbers presented in this book.

Some examples of different types of expenditures and suggestions concerning which measure to use are provided below. All examples are based on using 2009 values for "today", and 2008 for the Consumer Bundle Index.

A Commodity. If you are asking about the "present worth" of buying a loaf of bread or buying a gallon of milk in 1933, are you thinking in terms of the amount of money you are spending today on such things? If so, use the price index of the average household called the CPI. On the other hand, if you are wondering how "affordable" this would be to the average person, use the GDP Per Capita Index, or a wage or average earnings index.

In 1933, the average price of a gallon of milk in the U.S. was 48 cents. Compared to other things that the average consumer bought that year, this would be comparable to $7.95 using the CPI Index for 2009. As to how "affordable" the gallon of milk is for the average person, 48 cents in 1933 would correspond to spending $49.60 out of an average income by using the GDP Per Capita Index.

A Wage or Income. If you are asking about the current equivalence of what someone earned in the past, and you are thinking in terms of the household items that person might buy, then use the CPI. If you are thinking about how this income would compare in terms of affording to run that average household today, then use the Consumer Bundle. A third possibility is that you want to know how that person ranked in status compared to what others earned so it would be best to use GDP Per Capita Index. Lastly, you may want to know how economically "powerful" that person was within the context of the overall economy; to do so, you should use the Relative Share of GDP Index.

In 1933, an accountant in the U.S. would be earning about $2,340, an amount that would represent a comparative purchasing power of $38,700 in current dollars. However, this salary is more than what the average household spent in those days and using the Value of Consumer Bundle this accountant's income corresponds to $101,000 today in earnings "status" (the Consumer Bundle compares through 2008).

You may want to know how very rich people compare. Recently it was reported that Bill Gates is the richest person in the world and is worth $53 billion today. When John D. Rockefeller died in 1937 he was worth $1.4 billion. Who is richer in their time? Either man could buy anything they want. But the question of how economically powerful they are can be best measured by how big their wealth is compared to the economy they live in. This is measured by using the Relative Share of GDP and for Rockefeller, that number is $217 billion, or nearly four times greater than Bill Gates at $53 billion.

A "Project". If the amount you are asking about is the construction of a church, the cost of a war, or a new highway, again the context is important. If the question is how much it cost compared to the present cost of materials or labor, you would use the GDP Deflator and / or the Wage or Earning Index. However, you may be more interested in how important this project was to the community or the country. In the past there were lesser amounts of materials and labor available for all projects. So the Share of GDP Index measures the importance of a project (shows how it compares to other projects).

In 1931, the Empire State building, a giant of a structure in its day, was built at a cost of $41 million. This may seem inexpensive in today's terms when we compare its cost using the GDP Deflator Index and determine a contemporary cost of $491 million. As a share of the economy, using the Share of GDP Index, an amount of $7.64 billion in 2009 dollars shows how important this building was in its day.

The various Indexes show us the relative worth of a dollar.

In 2009, $1.00 from 1933 is worth:

$16.60   using the Consumer Price Index

$13.90   using the GDP Deflator Index

$48.20   using the Unskilled Wage Index

$43.10   using the Consumer Bundle Index (2008)

$59.30   using the Production Worker Compensation Index

$103.00   using the Nominal GDP Per Capita Index

$253.00   using the Relative Share of GDP Index

For our consumer price comparisons in the next chapter, we use reference and primary source data for a product price and use the Consumer Price Index for the relative value comparison. So, for our basic dollar to dollar comparisons, $1.00 in 1933 is roughly equivalent to $16.60. We also use the GDP Per Capita Index to provide an indication of how affordable a certain commodity or product was in 1933.

For salaries we use the CPI to show the relative purchasing availability of money for buying products, and we use the GDP Per Capita Index to show the status or rank based on the annual salary.

For larger projects, such as the Boulder Dam and the TVA project, we use the cost value cited by the author and then two relative value comparisons; first the GDP Deflator Index to understand the relative cost of the project, and second, the Share of GDP Index to understand the importance of the project relative to the overall economy.

Source: www.measuringworth.com

Historical Prices

Listed below are general, everyday items showing a comparison in price from 1933 to 2009 / 2010. This comparison is very general in nature, and is not scientific. Also, keep in mind that quality, brand, size and volume of product content affects prices as much today as it did in the early 1900's. As such, listed costs are approximate, and are derived from numerous sources, including periodicals and source material from the early 1930's. Sterling Edmunds frequently references costs and expenditures, primarily to support his argument that government spending (of taxpayer dollars) results in a questionable return to the taxpayer. The historical costs below are provided in order to present a realistic and understandable context.

> For consumer price comparisons we use the Consumer Price Index for the relative value comparison, and we use the GDP Per Capita Index to provide an indication of the affordability of the commodity or product.

Item	1933 Price Approximate	Current Equivalent	Equivalent Affordability
Food			
Chicken	22 ¢ a pound	$3.64	$22.70
Butter	50 ¢ a pound	8.28	51.70
Eggs	29 ¢ a dozen	4.80	30.00
Milk	48 ¢ a gallon	7.95	49.60

Historical Prices

Item	1933 Price Approximate	Current Equivalent	Equivalent Affordability
Bread	7 ¢ a loaf	1.16	7.23
Cornflakes	8 ¢ a box	1.32	8.27
Oranges	30 ¢ a dozen	4.97	31.00
Potatoes	3 ¢ a pound	.50	3.10
Candy Bar	5 ¢ each	.83	5.17
Water	5 ¢ a gallon	.83	5.17

Personal

Men's Hair Cut	20 ¢	3.31	20.70
Women's Perm	30 ¢	4.97	31.00
Hand Soap	4 ¢ a bar	.66	4.13
Toilet Paper	5 ¢ a roll	.83	5.17
Tooth Powder	30 ¢ a can	4.97	31.00
Tooth Brush	50 ¢	8.28	51.70
Shaving Kit (razor and 50 blades)	$5.00	82.80	517.00
Razor Blade (10 pack)	$1.00	16.60	103.00
Shaving Cream	25 ¢	4.14	25.80
Cigarettes (pack of 20)	15 ¢	2.48	15.50

Medical

Physician Visit (each call)	$1.00	16.60	103.00
Hospital Bed (open unit day rate)	$4.00	66.20	413.00
Hospital, Private Room (daily)	$6.50	108.00	672.00

Historical Prices

Item	1933 Price Approximate	Current Equivalent	Equivalent Affordability
Child Birth	$100.00	1,660.00	10,300.00
Eyeglasses, Prescription (each)	$10.00	166.00	1,030.00
Thermometer	79 ¢	13.10	81.60
Milk of Magnesia (200 tablets)	$1.00	16.60	103.00
Absorbine Jr.	$1.75	29.00	181.00
Heating Pad, electric	$1.00	16.60	103.00

Reading Material

Saturday Evening Post	5 ¢ copy	83 ¢	5.17
	$2.00 for 52 issues	33.10	207.00
Parents Magazine	25 ¢ an issue	4.14	25.80
Good Housekeeping	25 ¢	4.14	25.80
Women's World	10 ¢	1.66	10.30
Ladies Home Journal	$1.00 one year	16.60	103.00
Comic Book	10 ¢	1.66	10.30

Household

Room Heater, electric	$5.95 small	98.50	615.00
	$7.95 large	132.00	822.00
Slip Covers, Chair	$3.95	65.40	408.00
Paper Towel (two 300 sheet rolls)	25 ¢	4.14	25.80
Washing Machine	$65.00	1,080.00	6,720.00
Electric Stove	$50.00	828.00	5,170.00

Historical Prices

Item	1933 Price Approximate	Current Equivalent	Equivalent Affordability
Toaster	$1.00	16.60	103.00
Radio (in two tone cabinet)	$20.00	331.00	2,070.00
Coffee Pot	50 ¢	8.28	51.70
Dinner Plates (for one dozen)	84 ¢	13.90	86.80
Flatware, silver plated (26 pieces)	$28.00	464.00	2,890.00

Automotive

	1933 Price Approximate	Current Equivalent	Equivalent Affordability
Pontiac 4-door, straight 8	$585 base	9,680.00	60,500.00
Anti-freeze	$2.95 a gallon	48.00	305.00
Gasoline	15 ¢ a gallon	2.48	15.50

Clothing

	1933 Price Approximate	Current Equivalent	Equivalent Affordability
Homburg Hat, felt	$7.00	116.00	723.00
Men's Shoes, leather	$8.75	145.00	904.00
Women's Dress, long sleeve	$5.95	98.50	615.00
Women's Dress, suit	$8.95	148.00	925.00
Women's Coat, full length	$19.95	330.00	2,060.00

For salaries we use the CPI to show the relative purchasing availability of money for buying products, and we use the GDP Per Capita Index to show the status or rank based on the annual salary.

Historical Prices

	1933 Approximate	Current Equivalent	Equivalent Earning Status
Salaries			
Health Aide	$810 a year	$13,400.00	$83,700.00
Public School Teacher	$1,300 a year	21,500.00	134,000.00
Farm Laborer	$259 a year	4,290.00	26,800.00
Accountant ($45 a week)	$2,340 a year	38,700.00	242,000.00
Cook ($15 a week)	$780 a year	12,900.00	80,600.00
Dress Maker ($5 a week)	$260 a year	4,300.00	26,900.00
Federal Worker (low range)	$1,260 a year	20,900.00	130,000.00
(high range)	$3,400 a year	56,300.00	351,000.00
Office Assistant ($15 a week)	$780 a year	12,900.00	80,600.00
Painter ($2.50 a day)	$650 a year	10,800.00	67,200.00

The following salaries are taken from references in The Federal Octopus.

	1933 Approximate	Current Equivalent	Equivalent Earning Status
Bureau of Fisheries (Hawes Act appropriation)			
Chief	$6,400 a year	$106,000.00	$661,000.00
Asst Chief	$5,400 a year	89,400.00	558,000.00
Enforcement Officer	$2,600 a year	43,000.00	269,000.00
Stenographer	$1,800 a year	29,800.00	186,000.00

	1933 Approximate	Current Equivalent	Equivalent Earning Status

Civilian Conservation Corps

CCC Worker (annual low range) .... $360 .... 5,960.00 .... 37,200.00

(annual high range) .... $540 .... 8,940.00 .... 55,800.00

Widow of CCC Worker (free clothing, room, board, laundry and medical)

(annual pension) .... $540 .... 8,940.00 .... 55,800.00

U.S. Army

Widow of Brigadier General

(annual pension) .... $180 .... 2,980.00 .... 18,600.00

Enlisted Service Member (Includes laundry, room, board and medical)

$221.40 a year .... 3,670.00 .... 22,900.00

For public works or building projects, we use the GDP Deflator Index to understand its relative value compared to current costs of labor and materials, and we use the Share of GDP Index to show the importance of the within the overall economy.

	1933 Cost Approximate	Current Equivalent	Equivalent Economic

Public Projects

Empire State Building (1931)

$41 million ..... $491 million .. $7.64 billion

	1933 Cost Approximate	Current Equivalent	Equivalent Economic
Boulder Dam Project	$165 million	2.3 billion	41.7 billion
Public Road Work	$400 million	5.58 billion	101 billion
Cove Creek Dam (TVA)	$6 million	83 million	1.52 billion
Columbia River Basin project	$400 million	5.58 billion	101 billion
Department of Commerce Building (D.C.)	$17 million	237 million	4.3 billion

Senate Salaries Since 1789

Year	Annual
1789-1815	$6.00 per diem
1815-1817	$1,500
1817-1855	$8.00 per diem
1855-1865	$3,000
1865-1871	$5,000
1871-1873	$7,500
1873-1907	$5,000
1907-1925	$7,500
1925-1932	$10,000
1932-1933	$9,000
1933-1935	$8,500
1935-1947	$10,000
1947-1955	$12,500
1955-1965	$22,500
1965-1969	$30,000
1969-1975	$42,500
1975-1977	$44,600
1977-1978	$57,500
1979-1983	$60,662
1983	$69,800
1984	$72,600
1985 -1986	$75,100
1987 (Jan 1 – Feb 3)	$77,400
1987 (Feb 4)	$89,500

Senate Salaries Since 1789

Year	Annual
1990 (Feb 1)	$98,400
1991	$101,900
1991 (Aug 15)	$125,100
1992	$129,500
1993	$133,600
1994	$133,600
1995	$133,600
1996	$133,600
1997	$133,600
1998	$136,700
1999	$136,700
2000	$141,300
2001	$145,100
2002	$150,000
2003	$154,700
2004	$158,100
2005	$162,100
2006	$165,200
2007	$165,200
2008	$169,300
2009	$174,000
2010	$174,000

Note: Since the early 1980s, Senate leaders -- majority and minority leaders, and the president pro tempore -- have received higher salaries than other members. Currently, leaders earn $193,400 per year.

Source: http://www.senate.gov

Collier's Editorial:
Roosevelt's Revolution

This editorial, from Collier's, September 23, 1933, is shared as an example from the contemporary press in 1933, in which the very "federal autocracy" Sterling Edmunds cautions us about, is praised. In the opening to this Third Edition, Mr. Edmunds writes: "All governments reach out to seize power; no government ever voluntarily relinquished it."

We have passed through an economic and social revolution since March 4th. Vastly important changes have been brought about within these six months. Nothing more far-reaching in its consequence has ever happened before in this country.

President Roosevelt's revolution has been so orderly and good-tempered and hopeful that it has been hard to realize the depth of the changes made.

We have seen none of the pageantry which history associates with revolutions. Trumpets have not been sounded. So we underrate the meaning of what is happening before our eyes.

The great change recorded in the Roosevelt revolution is the final abandonment of the rule of laissez faire, the let-alone policy of competition and of drift.

During a hundred and fifty years we had been taught that the least government was the best. Government was merely police power. The police would arrest those who violated the law. That is all.

The government, however, had little to do with business and still less with the conditions under which men and women worked and lived and reared children. The important affairs of normal life were all private. The laissez-faire principle said that out of private struggle and personal competition public good would emerge.

Of course that was not so. Out of laissez-faireism slums arose, and premature child labor and the pitiless employment of women in factories. Economic competition and political irresponsibility allowed unemployment to continue.

Long ago the old rule of governmental non-interference was outlived. During two generations at the least it has been perfectly obvious that the government of every great industrial nation must take notice of the conditions under which men live and work and must control those conditions in the national interest.

Year after year, however, we refused to make the increasingly necessary decision. When times were good we said it was dangerous to interfere. When times were lean we said it was also dangerous to interfere.

All this nonsense was forgotten the day Franklin D. Roosevelt was inaugurated. Lustily the new President accepted responsibility for improving conditions then so unsatisfactory to everybody.

Rapidly a great series of revolutionary measures were proposed and as swiftly adopted by Congress. Each law was specifically proposed to deal with some phase of the emergency we confronted. Taken together, these emergency statutes embodied a new philosophy of government. Laissez-faireism was abandoned. Intelligent control was established.

Not enough time has elapsed to sum up the gains and losses of this new national policy. We expect and hope that improvement will be steady and well founded. Regardless of the progress made within the next few months, however, there will be no turning back.

The old policy of drift and non-interference, of individual competition and of governmental irresponsibility, was a product of the simple agricultural life of the eighteenth century.

When steam engines, electricity and gasoline came, the very foundations of our life were remade. We tried pathetically to stretch the old ideas to meet our new needs. It was impossible. Government had to be reorganized to fit modern conditions.

It is a fortunate circumstance that the opportunity should have come to a man so well disposed and so widely liked as Franklin D. Roosevelt. In the hands of a less considerate leader, or of one in whom the masses had less confidence, these changes would have been difficult.

Consider the broad outlines of the measures which have been undertaken. Their fundamental meaning is clear.

Take first the farmer. In all the new laws adopted one clear principle is obvious: the power of the government is being utilized to increase the incomes and to improve the economic position of farmers.

In the old laissez-faire system farmers did not share equitably in the fruits of our industrial civilization. So the government is taxing consumers, controlling agricultural production, lending money and doing numerous other things to increase the share the farmers may have of our national income. This is a new development, an agricultural revolution of the first magnitude.

Under the recovery act the government is attempting to render similar assistance to industrial workers. Factories and shops must now be conducted so that the largest number may be employed and the most generous wages practicable be paid.

In finance the same principle has emerged. In the old days financial stability was supposed to be attained as the blind result of the efforts of bankers and investors to earn profits on their capital. The scheme did not work so well and so now the government has taken command.

Behind all the laws controlling banks and security houses, behind all the talk about gold and inflation and the other monetary reforms, is the principle that in financial matters the public interest must be supreme.

Quietly, peacefully, in good temper we have been led. We have had our revolution and we like it.

> "... understanding the innate and insatiable greed of governmental power ... and understanding that as governmental power increases the liberty of the citizen must correspondingly diminish ... our forefathers founded this government as a constitutional one, of limited and enumerated powers, to insure the blessings of liberty to themselves, and to us, their posterity, and to those who shall come after us."
>
> – Sterling E. Edmunds

The Declaration of Independence

Drafted by Thomas Jefferson between June 11 and June 28, 1776, the Continental Congress adopted the Declaration of Independence on July 4, 1776. It was engrossed on parchment and on August 2, 1776, delegates began signing it.

IN CONGRESS, July 4, 1776.

The unanimous Declaration of the thirteen united States of America,

When in the Course of human events, it becomes necessary for one people to dissolve the political bands which have connected them with another, and to assume among the powers of the earth, the separate and equal station to which the Laws of Nature and of Nature's God entitle them, a decent respect to the opinions of mankind requires that they should declare the causes which impel them to the separation.

We hold these truths to be self-evident, that all men are created equal, that they are endowed by their Creator with certain unalienable Rights, that among these are Life, Liberty and the pursuit of Happiness. --That to secure these rights, Governments are instituted among Men, deriving their just powers from the consent of the governed, --That whenever any Form of Government becomes destructive of these ends, it is the Right of the People to alter or to abolish it, and to institute new Government, laying its foundation on such principles and organizing its powers in such form, as to them shall seem most likely to effect their Safety and Happiness. Prudence, indeed, will dictate that Governments long established should not be changed for light and transient causes; and accordingly all experience hath shewn, that mankind are more disposed to suffer, while evils are sufferable, than to right themselves by abolishing the forms to which they are accustomed. But when a long train of abuses and usurpations, pursuing invariably the same Object evinces a design to reduce them under absolute Despotism, it is their right, it is their duty, to throw off such Government, and to provide new Guards for their future security. --Such has been the patient sufferance of these Colonies; and such is now the necessity which constrains them to alter their former Systems of Government. The history of the present King of Great Britain is a history of repeated injuries and usurpations, all having in direct object the establishment of an absolute Tyranny over these States. To prove this, let Facts be submitted to a candid world.

He has refused his Assent to Laws, the most wholesome and necessary for the public good.

He has forbidden his Governors to pass Laws of immediate and pressing importance, unless suspended in their operation till his Assent should be obtained; and when so suspended, he has utterly neglected to attend to them.

He has refused to pass other Laws for the accommodation of large districts of people, unless those people would relinquish the right of Representation in the Legislature, a right inestimable to them and formidable to tyrants only.

He has called together legislative bodies at places unusual, uncomfortable, and distant from the depository of their public Records, for the sole purpose of fatiguing them into compliance with his measures.

He has dissolved Representative Houses repeatedly, for opposing with manly firmness his invasions on the rights of the people.

He has refused for a long time, after such dissolutions, to cause others to be elected; whereby the Legislative powers, incapable of Annihilation, have returned to the People at large for their exercise; the State remaining in the mean time exposed to all the dangers of invasion from without, and convulsions within.

He has endeavoured to prevent the population of these States; for that purpose obstructing the Laws for Naturalization of Foreigners;

refusing to pass others to encourage their migrations hither, and raising the conditions of new Appropriations of Lands.

He has obstructed the Administration of Justice, by refusing his Assent to Laws for establishing Judiciary powers.

He has made Judges dependent on his Will alone, for the tenure of their offices, and the amount and payment of their salaries.

He has erected a multitude of New Offices, and sent hither swarms of Officers to harrass our people, and eat out their substance.

He has kept among us, in times of peace, Standing Armies without the Consent of our legislatures.

He has affected to render the Military independent of and superior to the Civil power.

He has combined with others to subject us to a jurisdiction foreign to our constitution, and unacknowledged by our laws; giving his Assent to their Acts of pretended Legislation: For Quartering large bodies of armed troops among us: For protecting them, by a mock Trial, from punishment for any Murders which they should commit on the Inhabitants of these States: For cutting off our Trade with all parts of the world: For imposing Taxes on us without our Consent: For depriving us in many cases, of the benefits of Trial by Jury: For transporting us beyond Seas to be tried for pretended offences.

For abolishing the free System of English Laws in a neighbouring Province, establishing therein an Arbitrary government, and enlarging its Boundaries so as to render it at once an example and fit instrument for introducing the same absolute rule into these Colonies: For taking away our Charters, abolishing our most valuable Laws, and altering fundamentally the Forms of our Governments: For suspending our own Legislatures, and declaring themselves invested with power to legislate for us in all cases whatsoever.

He has abdicated Government here, by declaring us out of his Protection and waging War against us.

He has plundered our seas, ravaged our Coasts, burnt our towns, and destroyed the lives of our people.

He is at this time transporting large Armies of foreign Mercenaries to compleat the works of death, desolation and tyranny, already begun with circumstances of Cruelty & perfidy scarcely paralleled in the most barbarous ages, and totally unworthy the Head of a civilized nation.

He has constrained our fellow Citizens taken Captive on the high Seas to bear Arms against their Country, to become the executioners of their friends and Brethren, or to fall themselves by their Hands.

He has excited domestic insurrections amongst us, and has endeavoured to bring on the inhabitants of our frontiers, the merciless Indian Savages, whose known rule of warfare, is an undistinguished destruction of all ages, sexes and conditions.

In every stage of these Oppressions We have Petitioned for Redress in the most humble terms: Our repeated Petitions have been answered only by repeated injury. A Prince whose character is thus marked by every act which may define a Tyrant, is unfit to be the ruler of a free people.

Nor have We been wanting in attentions to our Brittish brethren. We have warned them from time to time of attempts by their legislature to extend an unwarrantable jurisdiction over us. We have reminded them of the circumstances of our emigration and settlement here. We have appealed to their native justice and magnanimity, and we have conjured them by the ties of our common kindred to disavow these usurpations, which, would inevitably interrupt our connections and correspondence. They too have been deaf to the voice of justice and of consanguinity. We must, therefore, acquiesce in the necessity, which denounces our Separation, and hold them, as we hold the rest of mankind, Enemies in War, in Peace Friends.

We, therefore, the Representatives of the united States of America, in General Congress, Assembled, appealing to the Supreme Judge of the world for the rectitude of our intentions, do, in the Name, and by Authority of the good People of these Colonies, solemnly publish and declare, That these United Colonies are, and of Right ought to be Free and Independent States; that they are Absolved from all Allegiance to the British Crown, and that all political connection between them and the State of Great Britain, is and ought to be totally dissolved; and that as Free and Independent States, they have full Power to levy War, conclude Peace, contract Alliances, establish Commerce, and to do all other Acts and Things which Independent States may of right do. And for the support of this Declaration, with a firm reliance on the protection of divine Providence, we mutually pledge to each other our Lives, our Fortunes and our sacred Honor.

Signed by:

Georgia: Button Gwinnett; Lyman Hall; George Walton

North Carolina: William Hooper; Joseph Hewes; John Penn

South Carolina: Edward Rutledge; Thomas Heyward; Jr.; Thomas Lynch, Jr.; Arthur Middleton

Massachusetts: John Hancock

Maryland: Samuel Chase; William Paca; Thomas Stone; Charles Carroll of Carrollton

Virginia: George Wythe; Richard Henry Lee; Thomas Jefferson; Benjamin Harrison; Thomas Nelson, Jr.; Francis Lightfoot Lee; Carter Braxton

Pennsylvania: Robert Morris; Benjamin Rush; Benjamin Franklin; John Morton; George Clymer; James Smith; George Taylor; James Wilson; George Ross

Delaware: Caesar Rodney; George Read; Thomas McKean

The Declaration of Independence

New York: William Floyd; Philip Livingston; Francis Lewis; Lewis Morris

New Jersey: Richard Stockton; John Witherspoon; Francis Hopkinson; John Hart; Abraham Clark

New Hampshire: Josiah Bartlett; William Whipple

Massachusetts: Samuel Adams; John Adams; Robert Treat Paine; Elbridge Gerry

Rhode Island: Stephen Hopkins; William Ellery

Connecticut: Roger Sherman; Samuel Huntington; William Williams; Oliver Wolcott

New Hampshire: Matthew Thornton

The Constitution of the United States

Note: The following text is a transcription of the Constitution in its original form. Items that are italicized have since been amended or superseded.

Drafted in secret by delegates to the Constitutional Convention during the summer of 1787, this four-page document, signed on September 17, 1787, established the government of the United States.

We the People of the United States, in Order to form a more perfect Union, establish Justice, insure domestic Tranquility, provide for the common defence, promote the general Welfare, and secure the Blessings of Liberty to ourselves and our Posterity, do ordain and establish this Constitution for the United States of America.

Article. I.

Section. 1.

All legislative Powers herein granted shall be vested in a Congress of the United States, which shall consist of a Senate and House of Representatives.

Section. 2.

The House of Representatives shall be composed of Members chosen every second Year by the People of the several States, and the Electors in each State shall have the Qualifications requisite for Electors of the most numerous Branch of the State Legislature.

No Person shall be a Representative who shall not have attained to the Age of twenty five Years, and been seven Years a Citizen of the United States, and who shall not, when elected, be an Inhabitant of that State in which he shall be chosen.

Representatives and direct Taxes shall be apportioned among the several States which may be included within this Union, according to their respective Numbers, which shall be determined by adding to the whole Number of free Persons, including those bound to Service for a Term of Years, and excluding Indians not taxed, three fifths of all other Persons. The actual Enumeration shall be made within three Years after the first Meeting of the Congress of the United States, and within every subsequent Term of ten Years, in such Manner as they shall by Law direct. The Number of Representatives shall not exceed one for every thirty Thousand, but each State shall have at Least one Representative; and until such enumeration shall be made, the State of New Hampshire shall be entitled to chuse three, Massachusetts eight, Rhode-Island and Providence Plantations one, Connecticut five, New-York six, New Jersey four, Pennsylvania eight, Delaware one, Maryland six, Virginia ten, North Carolina five, South Carolina five, and Georgia three.

When vacancies happen in the Representation from any State, the Executive Authority thereof shall issue Writs of Election to fill such Vacancies.

The House of Representatives shall chuse their Speaker and other Officers; and shall have the sole Power of Impeachment.

Section. 3.

The Senate of the United States shall be composed of two Senators from each State, *chosen by the Legislature* thereof for six Years; and each Senator shall have one Vote.

Immediately after they shall be assembled in Consequence of the first Election, they shall be divided as equally as may be into three Classes. The Seats of the Senators of the first Class shall be vacated at the Expiration of the second Year, of the second Class at the Expiration of the fourth Year, and of the third Class at the Expiration of the sixth Year, so that one third may be chosen every second Year; *and if Vacancies happen by Resignation, or otherwise, during the Recess of the Legislature of any State, the Executive thereof may make temporary Appointments until the next Meeting of the Legislature, which shall then fill such Vacancies.*

No Person shall be a Senator who shall not have attained to the Age of thirty Years, and been nine Years a Citizen of the United States, and who shall not, when elected, be an Inhabitant of that State for which he shall be chosen.

The Vice President of the United States shall be President of the Senate, but shall have no Vote, unless they be equally divided.

The Senate shall chuse their other Officers, and also a President pro tempore, in the Absence of the Vice President, or when he shall exercise the Office of President of the United States.

The Senate shall have the sole Power to try all Impeachments. When sitting for that Purpose, they shall be on Oath or Affirmation. When the President of the United States is tried, the Chief Justice shall preside: And no Person shall be convicted without the Concurrence of two thirds of the Members present.

Judgment in Cases of Impeachment shall not extend further than to removal from Office, and disqualification to hold and enjoy any Office of honor, Trust or Profit under the United States: but the Party convicted shall nevertheless be liable and subject to Indictment, Trial, Judgment and Punishment, according to Law.

Section. 4.

The Times, Places and Manner of holding Elections for Senators and Representatives, shall be prescribed in each State by the Legislature thereof; but the Congress may at any time by Law make or alter such Regulations, except as to the Places of chusing Senators.

The Congress shall assemble at least once in every Year, and such Meeting shall *be on the first Monday in December*, unless they shall by Law appoint a different Day.

Section. 5.

Each House shall be the Judge of the Elections, Returns and Qualifications of its own Members, and a Majority of each shall constitute a Quorum to do Business; but a smaller Number may adjourn from day to day, and may be authorized to compel the Attendance of absent Members, in such Manner, and under such Penalties as each House may provide.

Each House may determine the Rules of its Proceedings, punish its Members for disorderly Behaviour, and, with the Concurrence of two thirds, expel a Member.

Each House shall keep a Journal of its Proceedings, and from time to time publish the same, excepting such Parts as may in their Judgment require Secrecy; and the Yeas and Nays of the Members of either House on any question shall, at the Desire of one fifth of those Present, be entered on the Journal.

Neither House, during the Session of Congress, shall, without the Consent of the other, adjourn for more than three days, nor to any other Place than that in which the two Houses shall be sitting.

Section. 6.

The Senators and Representatives shall receive a Compensation for their Services, to be ascertained by Law, and paid out of the Treasury of the United States. They shall in all Cases, except Treason, Felony and Breach of the Peace, be privileged from Arrest during their Attendance at the Session of their respective Houses, and in going to and returning from the same; and for any Speech or Debate in either House, they shall not be questioned in any other Place.

No Senator or Representative shall, during the Time for which he was elected, be appointed to any civil Office under the Authority of the United States, which shall have been created, or the Emoluments whereof shall have been encreased during such time; and no Person holding any Office under the United States, shall be a Member of either House during his Continuance in Office.

Section. 7.

All Bills for raising Revenue shall originate in the House of Representatives; but the Senate may propose or concur with Amendments as on other Bills.

Every Bill which shall have passed the House of Representatives and the Senate, shall, before it become a Law, be presented to the President of the United States: If he approve he shall sign it, but if not he shall return it, with his Objections to that House in which it shall have originated, who shall enter the Objections at large on their Journal, and proceed to reconsider it. If after such Reconsideration two thirds of that House shall agree to pass the Bill, it shall be sent, together with the Objections, to the other House, by which it shall likewise be reconsidered, and if approved by two thirds of that House, it shall become a Law. But in all such Cases the Votes of both Houses shall be determined by yeas and Nays, and the Names of the Persons voting for and against the Bill shall be entered on the Journal of each House respectively. If any Bill shall not be returned by the President within ten Days (Sundays excepted) after it shall have been presented to him, the Same shall be a Law, in like Manner as if he had signed it, unless the Congress by their Adjournment prevent its Return, in which Case it shall not be a Law.

Every Order, Resolution, or Vote to which the Concurrence of the Senate and House of Representatives may be necessary (except on a question of Adjournment) shall be presented to the President of the United States; and before the Same shall take Effect, shall be approved by him, or being disapproved by him, shall be repassed by two thirds of the Senate and House of Representatives, according to the Rules and Limitations prescribed in the Case of a Bill.

Section. 8.

The Congress shall have Power To lay and collect Taxes, Duties, Imposts and Excises, to pay the Debts and provide for the common Defence and general Welfare of the United States; but all Duties, Imposts and Excises shall be uniform throughout the United States;

To borrow Money on the credit of the United States;

To regulate Commerce with foreign Nations, and among the several States, and with the Indian Tribes;

To establish an uniform Rule of Naturalization, and uniform Laws on the subject of Bankruptcies throughout the United States;

To coin Money, regulate the Value thereof, and of foreign Coin, and fix the Standard of Weights and Measures;

To provide for the Punishment of counterfeiting the Securities and current Coin of the United States;

To establish Post Offices and post Roads;

To promote the Progress of Science and useful Arts, by securing for limited Times to Authors and Inventors the exclusive Right to their respective Writings and Discoveries;

To constitute Tribunals inferior to the supreme Court;

To define and punish Piracies and Felonies committed on the high Seas, and Offences against the Law of Nations;

To declare War, grant Letters of Marque and Reprisal, and make Rules concerning Captures on Land and Water;

To raise and support Armies, but no Appropriation of Money to that Use shall be for a longer Term than two Years;

To provide and maintain a Navy;

To make Rules for the Government and Regulation of the land and naval Forces;

To provide for calling forth the Militia to execute the Laws of the Union, suppress Insurrections and repel Invasions;

To provide for organizing, arming, and disciplining, the Militia, and for governing such Part of them as may be employed in the Service of the United States, reserving to the States respectively, the Appointment of the Officers, and the Authority of training the Militia according to the discipline prescribed by Congress;

To exercise exclusive Legislation in all Cases whatsoever, over such District (not exceeding ten Miles square) as may, by Cession of particular States, and the Acceptance of Congress, become the Seat of the Government of the United States, and to exercise like Authority over all Places purchased by the Consent of the Legislature of the State in which the Same shall be, for the Erection of Forts, Magazines, Arsenals, dock-Yards, and other needful Buildings; --And

To make all Laws which shall be necessary and proper for carrying into Execution the foregoing Powers, and all other Powers vested by this Constitution in the Government of the United States, or in any Department or Officer thereof.

Section. 9.

The Migration or Importation of such Persons as any of the States now existing shall think proper to admit, shall not be prohibited by the Congress prior to the Year one thousand eight hundred and eight, but a Tax or duty may be imposed on such Importation, not exceeding ten dollars for each Person.

The Privilege of the Writ of Habeas Corpus shall not be suspended, unless when in Cases of Rebellion or Invasion the public Safety may require it.

No Bill of Attainder or ex post facto Law shall be passed.

No Capitation, or other direct, Tax shall be laid, *unless in Proportion to the Census or enumeration herein before directed to be taken.*

No Tax or Duty shall be laid on Articles exported from any State.

No Preference shall be given by any Regulation of Commerce or Revenue to the Ports of one State over those of another; nor shall Vessels bound to, or from, one State, be obliged to enter, clear, or pay Duties in another.

No Money shall be drawn from the Treasury, but in Consequence of Appropriations made by Law; and a regular Statement and Account of the Receipts and Expenditures of all public Money shall be published from time to time.

No Title of Nobility shall be granted by the United States: And no Person holding any Office of Profit or Trust under them, shall, without the Consent of the Congress, accept of any present, Emolument, Office, or Title, of any kind whatever, from any King, Prince, or foreign State.

Section. 10.

No State shall enter into any Treaty, Alliance, or Confederation; grant Letters of Marque and Reprisal; coin Money; emit Bills of Credit; make any Thing but gold and silver Coin a Tender in Payment of Debts; pass any Bill of Attainder, ex post facto Law, or Law impairing the Obligation of Contracts, or grant any Title of Nobility.

No State shall, without the Consent of the Congress, lay any Imposts or Duties on Imports or Exports, except what may be absolutely necessary for executing it's inspection Laws: and the net Produce of all Duties and Imposts, laid by any State on Imports or Exports, shall be for the Use of the Treasury of the United States; and all such Laws shall be subject to the Revision and Controul of the Congress.

No State shall, without the Consent of Congress, lay any Duty of Tonnage, keep Troops, or Ships of War in time of Peace, enter into any Agreement or Compact with another State, or with a foreign Power, or engage in War, unless actually invaded, or in such imminent Danger as will not admit of delay.

Article. II.

Section. 1.

The executive Power shall be vested in a President of the United States of America. He shall hold his Office during the Term of four Years, and, together with the Vice President, chosen for the same Term, be elected, as follows:

Each State shall appoint, in such Manner as the Legislature thereof may direct, a Number of Electors, equal to the whole Number of Senators and Representatives to which the State may be entitled in the Congress: but no Senator or Representative, or Person holding an Office of Trust or Profit under the United States, shall be appointed an Elector.

The Electors shall meet in their respective States, and vote by Ballot for two Persons, of whom one at least shall not be an Inhabitant of the same State with themselves. And they shall make a List of all the Persons voted for, and of the Number of Votes for each; which List they shall sign and certify, and transmit sealed to the Seat of the Government of the United States, directed to the President of the Senate. The President of the Senate shall, in the Presence of the Senate and House of Representatives, open all the Certificates, and the Votes shall then be counted. The Person having the greatest Number of Votes shall be the President, if such Number be a Majority of the whole Number of Electors appointed; and if there be more than one who have such Majority, and have an equal Number of Votes, then the House of Representatives shall immediately chuse by Ballot one of them for President; and if no Person have a Majority, then from the five highest on the List the said House shall in like Manner chuse the President. But in chusing the President, the Votes shall be taken by States, the Representation from each State having one Vote; A quorum for this purpose shall consist of a Member or Members from two thirds of the States, and a Majority of all the States shall be necessary to a Choice. In every Case, after the Choice of the President, the Person having the greatest Number of Votes of the Electors shall be the Vice President. But if there should remain two or more who have equal Votes, the Senate shall chuse from them by Ballot the Vice President.

The Congress may determine the Time of chusing the Electors, and the Day on which they shall give their Votes; which Day shall be the same throughout the United States.

No Person except a natural born Citizen, or a Citizen of the United States, at the time of the Adoption of this Constitution, shall be eligible to the Office of President; neither shall any Person be eligible to that Office who shall not have attained to the Age of thirty five Years, and been fourteen Years a Resident within the United States.

In Case of the Removal of the President from Office, or of his Death, Resignation, or Inability to discharge the Powers and Duties of the said Office, the Same shall devolve on the Vice President, and the Congress may by Law provide for the Case of Removal, Death, Resignation or Inability, both of the President and Vice President, declaring what Officer shall then act as President, and such Officer shall act accordingly, until the Disability be removed, or a President shall be elected.

The President shall, at stated Times, receive for his Services, a Compensation, which shall neither be increased nor diminished during the Period for which he shall have been elected, and he shall not receive within that Period any other Emolument from the United States, or any of them.

Before he enter on the Execution of his Office, he shall take the following Oath or Affirmation: --"I do solemnly swear (or affirm) that I will faithfully execute the Office of President of the United States, and will to the best of my Ability, preserve, protect and defend the Constitution of the United States."

Section. 2.

The President shall be Commander in Chief of the Army and Navy of the United States, and of the Militia of the several States, when called into the actual Service of the United States; he may require the Opinion, in writing, of the principal Officer in each of the executive Departments, upon any Subject relating to the Duties of their respective Offices, and he shall have Power to grant Reprieves and Pardons for Offences against the United States, except in Cases of Impeachment.

He shall have Power, by and with the Advice and Consent of the Senate, to make Treaties, provided two thirds of the Senators present concur; and he shall nominate, and by and with the Advice and Consent of the Senate, shall appoint Ambassadors, other public Ministers and Consuls, Judges of the supreme Court, and all other Officers of the United States, whose Appointments are not herein otherwise provided for, and which shall be established by Law: but the Congress may by Law vest the Appointment of such inferior Officers, as they think proper, in the President alone, in the Courts of Law, or in the Heads of Departments.

The President shall have Power to fill up all Vacancies that may happen during the Recess of the Senate, by granting Commissions which shall expire at the End of their next Session.

Section. 3.

He shall from time to time give to the Congress Information of the State of the Union, and recommend to their Consideration such Measures as he shall judge necessary and expedient; he may, on extraordinary Occasions, convene both Houses, or either of them, and in Case of Disagreement between them, with Respect to the Time of Adjournment, he may adjourn them to such Time as he shall think proper; he shall receive Ambassadors and other public Ministers; he shall take Care that the Laws be faithfully executed, and shall Commission all the Officers of the United States.

Section. 4.

The President, Vice President and all civil Officers of the United States, shall be removed from Office on Impeachment for, and Conviction of, Treason, Bribery, or other high Crimes and Misdemeanors.

Article III.

Section. 1.

The judicial Power of the United States shall be vested in one supreme Court, and in such inferior Courts as the Congress may from time to time ordain and establish. The Judges, both of the supreme and inferior Courts, shall hold their Offices during good Behaviour, and shall, at stated Times, receive for their Services a Compensation, which shall not be diminished during their Continuance in Office.

Section. 2.

The judicial Power shall extend to all Cases, in Law and Equity, arising under this Constitution, the Laws of the United States, and Treaties made, or which shall be made, under their Authority; --to all Cases affecting Ambassadors, other public Ministers and Consuls; --to all Cases of admiralty and maritime Jurisdiction; --to Controversies to which the United States shall be a Party; --to Controversies between two or more States; --*between a State and Citizens of another State*, --between Citizens of different States, --between Citizens of the same State claiming Lands under Grants of different States, and between a State, or the Citizens thereof, and foreign States, Citizens or Subjects.

In all Cases affecting Ambassadors, other public Ministers and Consuls, and those in which a State shall be Party, the supreme Court shall have original Jurisdiction. In all the other Cases before mentioned, the supreme Court shall have appellate Jurisdiction, both as to Law and Fact, with such Exceptions, and under such Regulations as the Congress shall make.

The Trial of all Crimes, except in Cases of Impeachment, shall be by Jury; and such Trial shall be held in the State where the said Crimes shall have been committed; but when not committed within any State, the Trial shall be at such Place or Places as the Congress may by Law have directed.

Section. 3.

Treason against the United States, shall consist only in levying War against them, or in adhering to their Enemies, giving them Aid and Comfort. No Person shall be convicted of Treason unless on the Testimony of two Witnesses to the same overt Act, or on Confession in open Court.

The Congress shall have Power to declare the Punishment of Treason, but no Attainder of Treason shall work Corruption of Blood, or Forfeiture except during the Life of the Person attainted.

Article. IV.

Section. 1.

Full Faith and Credit shall be given in each State to the public Acts, Records, and judicial Proceedings of every other State. And the Congress may by general Laws prescribe the Manner in which such Acts, Records and Proceedings shall be proved, and the Effect thereof.

Section. 2.

The Citizens of each State shall be entitled to all Privileges and Immunities of Citizens in the several States.

A Person charged in any State with Treason, Felony, or other Crime, who shall flee from Justice, and be found in another State, shall on

Demand of the executive Authority of the State from which he fled, be delivered up, to be removed to the State having Jurisdiction of the Crime.

No Person held to Service or Labour in one State, under the Laws thereof, escaping into another, shall, in Consequence of any Law or Regulation therein, be discharged from such Service or Labour, but shall be delivered up on Claim of the Party to whom such Service or Labour may be due.

Section. 3.

New States may be admitted by the Congress into this Union; but no new State shall be formed or erected within the Jurisdiction of any other State; nor any State be formed by the Junction of two or more States, or Parts of States, without the Consent of the Legislatures of the States concerned as well as of the Congress.

The Congress shall have Power to dispose of and make all needful Rules and Regulations respecting the Territory or other Property belonging to the United States; and nothing in this Constitution shall be so construed as to Prejudice any Claims of the United States, or of any particular State.

Section. 4.

The United States shall guarantee to every State in this Union a Republican Form of Government, and shall protect each of them against Invasion; and on Application of the Legislature, or of the Executive (when the Legislature cannot be convened), against domestic Violence.

Article. V.

The Congress, whenever two thirds of both Houses shall deem it necessary, shall propose Amendments to this Constitution, or, on the Application of the Legislatures of two thirds of the several States, shall call a Convention for proposing Amendments, which, in either Case, shall be valid to all Intents and Purposes, as Part of this Constitution, when ratified by the Legislatures of three fourths of the several States, or by Conventions in three fourths thereof, as the one or the other Mode of Ratification may be proposed by the

Congress; Provided that no Amendment which may be made prior to the Year One thousand eight hundred and eight shall in any Manner affect the first and fourth Clauses in the Ninth Section of the first Article; and that no State, without its Consent, shall be deprived of its equal Suffrage in the Senate.

Article. VI.

All Debts contracted and Engagements entered into, before the Adoption of this Constitution, shall be as valid against the United States under this Constitution, as under the Confederation.

This Constitution, and the Laws of the United States which shall be made in Pursuance thereof; and all Treaties made, or which shall be made, under the Authority of the United States, shall be the supreme Law of the Land; and the Judges in every State shall be bound thereby, any Thing in the Constitution or Laws of any State to the Contrary notwithstanding.

The Senators and Representatives before mentioned, and the Members of the several State Legislatures, and all executive and judicial Officers, both of the United States and of the several States, shall be bound by Oath or Affirmation, to support this Constitution; but no religious Test shall ever be required as a Qualification to any Office or public Trust under the United States.

Article. VII.

The Ratification of the Conventions of nine States, shall be sufficient for the Establishment of this Constitution between the States so ratifying the Same.

The Word, "the," being interlined between the seventh and eighth Lines of the first Page, the Word "Thirty" being partly written on an Erazure in the fifteenth Line of the first Page, The Words "is tried" being interlined between the thirty second and thirty third Lines of the first Page and the Word "the" being interlined between the forty third and forty fourth Lines of the second Page.

Attest William Jackson Secretary

done in Convention by the Unanimous Consent of the States present the Seventeenth Day of September in the Year of our Lord one thousand seven hundred and Eighty seven and of the Independence of the United States of America the Twelfth In witness whereof We have hereunto subscribed our Names,

G. Washington, Presidt and deputy from Virginia

Delaware: Geo: Read; Gunning Bedford; John Dickinson; Richard Bassett; Jaco: Broom

Maryland: James McHenry; Dan of St Thos. Jenifer; Danl. Carroll

Virginia: John Blair; James Madison Jr.

North Carolina: Wm. Blount; Richd. Dobbs Spaight; Hu Williamson

South Carolina: J. Rutledge; Charles Cotesworth Pinckney; Charles Pinckney; Pierce Butler

Georgia: William Few; Abr Baldwin

New Hampshire: John Langdon; Nicholas Gilman

Massachusetts: Nathaniel Gorham; Rufus King

Connecticut: Wm. Saml. Johnson; Roger Sherman

New York: Alexander Hamilton

New Jersey: Wil. Livingston; David Brearley; Wm. Paterson; Jona. Dayton

Pennsylvania:
B Franklin; Thomas Mifflin; Robt. Morris; Geo. Clymer; Thos. FitzSimons; Jared Ingersoll; James Wilson; Gouv. Morris

The Bill of Rights

Although 12 amendments were originally proposed, the 10 that were ratified became the Bill of Rights in 1791. They defined citizens' rights in relation to the newly established government under the Constitution.

The Preamble to The Bill of Rights

Congress of the United States begun and held at the City of New-York, on Wednesday the fourth of March, one thousand seven hundred and eighty nine.

THE Conventions of a number of the States, having at the time of their adopting the Constitution, expressed a desire, in order to prevent misconstruction or abuse of its powers, that further declaratory and restrictive clauses should be added: And as extending the ground of public confidence in the Government, will best ensure the beneficent ends of its institution.

RESOLVED by the Senate and House of Representatives of the United States of America, in Congress assembled, two thirds of both Houses concurring, that the following Articles be proposed to the Legislatures of the several States, as amendments to the Constitution of the United States, all, or any of which Articles, when ratified by three fourths of the said Legislatures, to be valid to all intents and purposes, as part of the said Constitution; viz.

ARTICLES in addition to, and Amendment of the Constitution of the United States of America, proposed by Congress, and ratified by the Legislatures of the several States, pursuant to the fifth Article of the original Constitution.

Note: The following text is a transcription of the first ten amendments to the Constitution in their original form. These amendments were ratified December 15, 1791, and form what is known as the "Bill of Rights."

The Bill of Rights

Amendment I

Congress shall make no law respecting an establishment of religion, or prohibiting the free exercise thereof; or abridging the freedom of speech, or of the press; or the right of the people peaceably to assemble, and to petition the Government for a redress of grievances.

Amendment II

A well regulated Militia, being necessary to the security of a free State, the right of the people to keep and bear Arms, shall not be infringed.

Amendment III

No Soldier shall, in time of peace be quartered in any house, without the consent of the Owner, nor in time of war, but in a manner to be prescribed by law.

Amendment IV

The right of the people to be secure in their persons, houses, papers, and effects, against unreasonable searches and seizures, shall not be violated, and no Warrants shall issue, but upon probable cause, supported by Oath or affirmation, and particularly describing the place to be searched, and the persons or things to be seized.

Amendment V

No person shall be held to answer for a capital, or otherwise infamous crime, unless on a presentment or indictment of a Grand Jury, except in cases arising in the land or naval forces, or in the Militia, when in actual service in time of War or public danger; nor shall any person be subject for the same offence to be twice put in jeopardy of life or limb; nor shall be compelled in any criminal case to be a witness against himself, nor be deprived of life, liberty, or property, without due process of law; nor shall private property be taken for public use, without just compensation.

Amendment VI

In all criminal prosecutions, the accused shall enjoy the right to a speedy and public trial, by an impartial jury of the State and district wherein the crime shall have been committed, which district shall have been previously ascertained by law, and to be informed of the nature and cause of the accusation; to be confronted with the witnesses against him; to have compulsory process for obtaining witnesses in his favor, and to have the Assistance of Counsel for his defence.

Amendment VII

In Suits at common law, where the value in controversy shall exceed twenty dollars, the right of trial by jury shall be preserved, and no fact tried by a jury, shall be otherwise re-examined in any Court of the United States, than according to the rules of the common law.

Amendment VIII

Excessive bail shall not be required, nor excessive fines imposed, nor cruel and unusual punishments inflicted.

Amendment IX

The enumeration in the Constitution, of certain rights, shall not be construed to deny or disparage others retained by the people.

Amendment X

The powers not delegated to the United States by the Constitution, nor prohibited by it to the States, are reserved to the States respectively, or to the people.

Amendments 11-27 to the Constitution

Constitutional Amendments 1-10 make up what is known as The Bill of Rights; Amendments 11-27 are listed below.

AMENDMENT XI

Passed by Congress March 4, 1794. Ratified February 7, 1795.

Note: Article III, section 2, of the Constitution was modified by amendment 11.

The Judicial power of the United States shall not be construed to extend to any suit in law or equity, commenced or prosecuted against one of the United States by Citizens of another State, or by Citizens or Subjects of any Foreign State.

AMENDMENT XII

Passed by Congress December 9, 1803. Ratified June 15, 1804.

Note: A portion of Article II, section 1 of the Constitution was superseded by the 12th amendment.

The Electors shall meet in their respective states and vote by ballot for President and Vice-President, one of whom, at least, shall not be an inhabitant of the same state with themselves; they shall name in their ballots the person voted for as President, and in distinct ballots the person voted for as Vice-President, and they shall make distinct lists of all persons voted for as President, and of all persons voted for as Vice-President, and of the number of votes for each, which lists they shall sign and certify, and transmit sealed to the seat of the government of the United States, directed to the President of the Senate; -- the President of the Senate shall, in the presence of the Senate and House of Representatives, open all the certificates and the votes shall then be counted; --The person having the greatest number of votes for President, shall be the President, if such number be a majority of the whole number of Electors appointed; and if no person have such majority, then from the persons having the highest numbers not exceeding three on the list of those voted for as President, the House of Representatives shall choose immediately, by ballot, the President. But in choosing the President, the votes shall be taken by states, the representation from each state having one vote; a quorum for this purpose shall consist of a member or members from two-thirds of the states, and a majority of all the states shall be necessary to a choice. [And if the House of Representatives shall not choose a President whenever the right of choice shall devolve upon them, before the fourth day of March next following, then the Vice-President shall act as President, as in case of the death or other constitutional disability of the President. --]* The person having the greatest number of votes as Vice-President, shall be the Vice-President, if such number be a majority of the whole number of Electors appointed, and if no person have a majority, then from the two highest numbers on the list, the Senate shall choose the Vice-President; a quorum for the purpose shall consist of two-thirds of the whole number of Senators, and a majority of the whole number shall be necessary to a choice. But no person constitutionally ineligible to the office of President shall be eligible to that of Vice-President of the United States.

*Superseded by section 3 of the 20th amendment.

AMENDMENT XIII

Passed by Congress January 31, 1865. Ratified December 6, 1865.

Note: A portion of Article IV, section 2, of the Constitution was superseded by the 13th amendment.

Section 1. Neither slavery nor involuntary servitude, except as a punishment for crime whereof the party shall have been duly convicted, shall exist within the United States, or any place subject to their jurisdiction.

Section 2. Congress shall have power to enforce this article by appropriate legislation.

AMENDMENT XIV

Passed by Congress June 13, 1866. Ratified July 9, 1868.

Note: Article I, section 2, of the Constitution was modified by section 2 of the 14th amendment.

Section 1. All persons born or naturalized in the United States, and subject to the jurisdiction thereof, are citizens of the United States and of the State wherein they reside. No State shall make or enforce any law which shall abridge the privileges or immunities of citizens of the United States; nor shall any State deprive any person of life, liberty, or property, without due process of law; nor deny to any person within its jurisdiction the equal protection of the laws.

Section 2. Representatives shall be apportioned among the several States according to their respective numbers, counting the whole number of persons in each State, excluding Indians not taxed. But when the right to vote at any election for the choice of electors for President and Vice-President of the United States, Representatives in Congress, the Executive and Judicial officers of a State, or the members of the Legislature thereof, is denied to any of the male inhabitants of such State, being twenty-one years of age,* and citizens of the United States, or in any way abridged, except for participation in rebellion, or other crime, the basis of representation therein shall be reduced in the proportion which the number of such male citizens shall bear to the whole number of male citizens twenty-one years of age in such State.

Section 3. No person shall be a Senator or Representative in Congress, or elector of President and Vice-President, or hold any office, civil or military, under the United States, or under any State, who, having previously taken an oath, as a member of Congress, or as an officer of the United States, or as a member of any State legislature, or as an executive or judicial officer of any State, to support the Constitution of the United States, shall have engaged in insurrection or rebellion against the same, or given aid or comfort to the enemies thereof. But Congress may by a vote of two-thirds of each House, remove such disability.

Section 4. The validity of the public debt of the United States, authorized by law, including debts incurred for payment of pensions and bounties for services in suppressing insurrection or rebellion, shall not be questioned. But neither the United States nor any State shall assume or pay any debt or obligation incurred in aid of insurrection or rebellion against the United States, or any claim for the loss or emancipation of any slave; but all such debts, obligations and claims shall be held illegal and void.

Section 5. The Congress shall have the power to enforce, by appropriate legislation, the provisions of this article.

Changed by section 1 of the 26th amendment.

AMENDMENT XV

Passed by Congress February 26, 1869. Ratified February 3, 1870.

Section 1. The right of citizens of the United States to vote shall not be denied or abridged by the United States or by any State on account of race, color, or previous condition of servitude --

Section 2. The Congress shall have the power to enforce this article by appropriate legislation.

AMENDMENT XVI

Passed by Congress July 2, 1909. Ratified February 3, 1913.

Note: Article I, section 9, of the Constitution was modified by amendment 16.

The Congress shall have power to lay and collect taxes on incomes, from whatever source derived, without apportionment among the several States, and without regard to any census or enumeration.

AMENDMENT XVII

Passed by Congress May 13, 1912. Ratified April 8, 1913.

Note: Article I, section 3, of the Constitution was modified by the 17th amendment.

The Senate of the United States shall be composed of two Senators from each State, elected by the people thereof, for six years; and each Senator shall have one vote. The electors in each State shall have the qualifications requisite for electors of the most numerous branch of the State legislatures.

When vacancies happen in the representation of any State in the Senate, the executive authority of such State shall issue writs of election to fill such vacancies: Provided, That the legislature of any State may empower the executive thereof to make temporary appointments until the people fill the vacancies by election as the legislature may direct.

This amendment shall not be so construed as to affect the election or term of any Senator chosen before it becomes valid as part of the Constitution.

AMENDMENT XVIII

Passed by Congress December 18, 1917. Ratified January 16, 1919. Repealed by amendment 21.

Section 1. After one year from the ratification of this article the manufacture, sale, or transportation of intoxicating liquors within, the importation thereof into, or the exportation thereof from the United States and all territory subject to the jurisdiction thereof for beverage purposes is hereby prohibited.

Section 2. The Congress and the several States shall have concurrent power to enforce this article by appropriate legislation.

Section 3. This article shall be inoperative unless it shall have been ratified as an amendment to the Constitution by the legislatures of the several States, as provided in the Constitution, within seven years from the date of the submission hereof to the States by the Congress.

AMENDMENT XIX

Passed by Congress June 4, 1919. Ratified August 18, 1920.

The right of citizens of the United States to vote shall not be denied or abridged by the United States or by any State on account of sex.

Congress shall have power to enforce this article by appropriate legislation.

AMENDMENT XX

Passed by Congress March 2, 1932. Ratified January 23, 1933.

Note: Article I, section 4, of the Constitution was modified by section 2 of this amendment. In addition, a portion of the 12th amendment was superseded by section 3.

Section 1. The terms of the President and the Vice President shall end at noon on the 20th day of January, and the terms of Senators and Representatives at noon on the 3d day of January, of the years in which such terms would have ended if this article had not been ratified; and the terms of their successors shall then begin.

Section 2. The Congress shall assemble at least once in every year, and such meeting shall begin at noon on the 3d day of January, unless they shall by law appoint a different day.

Section 3. If, at the time fixed for the beginning of the term of the President, the President elect shall have died, the Vice President elect shall become President. If a President shall not have been chosen before the time fixed for the beginning of his term, or if the President elect shall have failed to qualify, then the Vice President elect shall act as President until a President shall have qualified; and the Congress may by law provide for the case wherein neither a President elect nor a Vice President shall have qualified, declaring who shall then act as President, or the manner in which one who is to act shall be selected, and such person shall act accordingly until a President or Vice President shall have qualified.

Section 4. The Congress may by law provide for the case of the death of any of the persons from whom the House of Representatives may choose a President whenever the right of choice shall have devolved upon them, and for the case of the death of any of the persons from whom the Senate may choose a Vice President whenever the right of choice shall have devolved upon them.

Section 5. Sections 1 and 2 shall take effect on the 15th day of October following the ratification of this article.

Section 6. This article shall be inoperative unless it shall have been ratified as an amendment to the Constitution by the legislatures of three-fourths of the several States within seven years from the date of its submission.

AMENDMENT XXI

Passed by Congress February 20, 1933. Ratified December 5, 1933.

Section 1. The eighteenth article of amendment to the Constitution of the United States is hereby repealed.

Section 2. The transportation or importation into any State, Territory, or Possession of the United States for delivery or use therein of intoxicating liquors, in violation of the laws thereof, is hereby prohibited.

Section 3. This article shall be inoperative unless it shall have been ratified as an amendment to the Constitution by conventions in the several States, as provided in the Constitution, within seven years from the date of the submission hereof to the States by the Congress.

AMENDMENT XXII

Passed by Congress March 21, 1947. Ratified February 27, 1951.

Section 1. No person shall be elected to the office of the President more than twice, and no person who has held the office of President, or acted as President, for more than two years of a term to which some other person was elected President shall be elected to the office of President more than once. But this Article shall not apply to any person holding the office of President when this Article was proposed by Congress, and shall not prevent any person who may be holding the office of President, or acting as President, during the term within which this Article becomes operative from holding the office of President or acting as President during the remainder of such term.

Section 2. This article shall be inoperative unless it shall have been ratified as an amendment to the Constitution by the legislatures of three-fourths of the several States within seven years from the date of its submission to the States by the Congress.

AMENDMENT XXIII

Passed by Congress June 16, 1960. Ratified March 29, 1961.

Section 1. The District constituting the seat of Government of the United States shall appoint in such manner as Congress may direct:

A number of electors of President and Vice President equal to the whole number of Senators and Representatives in Congress to which the District would be entitled if it were a State, but in no event more than the least populous State; they shall be in addition to those appointed by the States, but they shall be considered, for the purposes of the election of President and Vice President, to be electors appointed by a State; and they shall meet in the District and perform such duties as provided by the twelfth article of amendment.

Section 2. The Congress shall have power to enforce this article by appropriate legislation.

AMENDMENT XXIV

Passed by Congress August 27, 1962. Ratified January 23, 1964.

Section 1. The right of citizens of the United States to vote in any primary or other election for President or Vice President, for electors for President or Vice President, or for Senator or Representative in Congress, shall not be denied or abridged by the United States or any State by reason of failure to pay poll tax or other tax.

Section 2. The Congress shall have power to enforce this article by appropriate legislation.

AMENDMENT XXV

Passed by Congress July 6, 1965. Ratified February 10, 1967.

Note: Article II, section 1, of the Constitution was affected by the 25th amendment.

Section 1. In case of the removal of the President from office or of his death or resignation, the Vice President shall become President.

Section 2. Whenever there is a vacancy in the office of the Vice President, the President shall nominate a Vice President who shall take office upon confirmation by a majority vote of both Houses of Congress.

Section 3. Whenever the President transmits to the President pro tempore of the Senate and the Speaker of the House of Representatives his written declaration that he is unable to discharge the powers and duties of his office, and until he transmits to them a written declaration to the contrary, such powers and duties shall be discharged by the Vice President as Acting President.

Section 4. Whenever the Vice President and a majority of either the principal officers of the executive departments or of such other body as Congress may by law provide, transmit to the President pro tempore of the Senate and the Speaker of the House of Representatives their written declaration that the President is unable to discharge the powers and duties of his office, the Vice President shall immediately assume the powers and duties of the office as Acting President.

Thereafter, when the President transmits to the President pro tempore of the Senate and the Speaker of the House of Representatives his written declaration that no inability exists, he shall resume the powers and duties of his office unless the Vice President and a majority of either the principal officers of the executive department or of such other body as Congress may by law provide, transmit within four days to the President pro tempore of the Senate and the Speaker of the House of Representatives their written declaration that the President is unable to discharge the powers and duties of his office. Thereupon Congress shall decide the issue, assembling within forty-eight hours for that purpose if not in session. If the Congress, within twenty-one days after receipt of the latter written declaration, or, if Congress is not in session, within twenty-one days after Congress is required to assemble, determines by two-thirds vote of both Houses that the President is unable to discharge the powers and duties of his office, the Vice President shall continue to discharge the same as Acting President; otherwise, the President shall resume the powers and duties of his office.

AMENDMENT XXVI

Passed by Congress March 23, 1971. Ratified July 1, 1971.

Note: Amendment 14, section 2, of the Constitution was modified by section 1 of the 26th amendment.

Section 1. The right of citizens of the United States, who are eighteen years of age or older, to vote shall not be denied or abridged by the United States or by any State on account of age.

Section 2. The Congress shall have power to enforce this article by appropriate legislation.

AMENDMENT XXVII

Originally proposed Sept. 25, 1789. Ratified May 7, 1992.

No law, varying the compensation for the services of the Senators and Representatives, shall take effect, until an election of representatives shall have intervened.

Bibliography

Board of Governors Federal Reserve System. *The Federal Reserve System: Purposes and Functions.* 2005.

Colebaugh, Charles, Managing Editor, William L. Chenery Editor, and Thomas H. Beck, Editorial Director. "Roosevelt's Revolution." *Collier's, The National Weekly* 23 Sept. 1933: 58.

"Consumer Price Index (CPI)." *U.S. Bureau of Labor Statistics.* U.S. Bureau of Labor Statistics, Division of Consumer Prices and Price Indexes, Web. 25 Mar. 2010. <http://www.bls.gov/cpi/>.

Edmunds, Sterling E. *The Roosevelt Coup d'Etat 1933-1940.* 1940.

The Federal Reserve. *History of Central Banking: From 1791 to the 21st Century.* (2009).

Hanes, Sharon M., and Richard C. Hanes. *Great Depression and New Deal: Primary Sources Edition 1. (U-X-L Great Depression and New Deal Reference Library).* 1st ed. Boston: U·X·L, 2002.

Kessler-Harris, Alice. "A Century of Struggle." *Monthly Labor Review* 110.8 (1987): 33-54.

Leuchtenburg, William E. *The Life History of The United States; Volume II 1933-1945.* New York: Time Incorporated, 1964.

"Product Advertisements." *The Literary Digest* 25 Mar. 1933: various pages.

"Product Advertisements." *The Saturday Evening Post* 2 Dec. 1933.

Bibliography

"Product Advertisements." *Women's World* Oct. 1933.

"Product Advertisements." *Collier's, The National Weekly* Sep. 1933.

"Product Advertisements." *Good Housekeeping* Feb. 1935.

"Product advertisements." *Parents Magazine* June 1933.

Reagan, Ronald. *Farewell Address*. 11 Jan. 1989.
<http://www.reaganlibrary.com/.>

Scott, Derks. *The Value of a Dollar: Prices and Incomes in the United States, 1860-2004 (Value of a Dollar) (Value of a Dollar)*. 3 ed., Lakeville: Grey House Publishing, 2004.

"Seven Ways to Compute the Relative Value of a U.S. Dollar Amount, 1774 to Present." *Measuring Worth - Home*. Economic History Association, Web. 10 Apr. 2010.
<http://www.measuringworth.com/uscompare/>.

Unser, Mike, Editor. "Inflation Calculator: Money's Real Worth Over Time" *Coin News for Collectors, Numismatic Articles, Coin Collecting, Price Guides and Collector Tools - Coin News*. CoinNews Media Group, LLC, Web. 18 Feb. 2010.
<http://www.coinnews.net/tools/cpi-inflation-calculator/>.

"What is a dollar worth? The Federal Reserve Bank of Minneapolis." *The Federal Reserve Bank of Minneapolis*. Web. 23 May 2010.
<http://www.minneapolisfed.org/community_education/teacher/calc/>.

Williamson, Samuel H., and Lawrence H. Officer. "Measuring Worth - Home." *Measuring Worth - Home*. Web. 10 Apr. 2010.
<http://www.measuringworth.com/>.

Bibliography

Williamson, Samuel H., and Lawrence H. Officer. "Measuring Worth - Relative Value of US Dollars." *Measuring Worth - Home.* Web. 10 Apr. 2010. <http://www.measuringworth.com/uscompare/>.

Young, William H., and Nancy K. Young. *American Popular Culture Throughout History: The 1930s.* New York: Greenwood Press, 2002.

Index

Index

Index

Index

About the Authors

Sterling Edwin Edmunds (1880-1944), attorney and member of the St. Louis Bar, authored numerous books dealing with international law, the U.S. Constitution, and other legal and political matters related to our Constitutional form of government.

A former newspaper man, in 1933 Mr. Edmunds wrote the third edition of "The Federal Octopus," which assailed the growing power of the federal government.

He was a reporter on the St. Louis Post Dispatch at the turn of the century, later he joined the St. Louis Chronicle, and ultimately became its editor-in-chief.

Mr. Edmunds was born in St. Louis, a son of Sterling Edwin and Mollie Garnhart Edmunds. He attended public schools in Louisville, KY; Benton College of Law, St. Louis, and the University of Virginia, where he received an LL.B. St. Louis University conferred on him an Honorary Degree of Doctor of Laws.

He was admitted to the Missouri bar in 1906, and in 1918 became a special assistant in the United States Department of State. From 1909 to 1926 he lectured on international law at St. Louis University Law School. He was organizer and director of the National

Committee for the Protection of Child, Family, School and Church, a former vice president of the United States Golf Association and a member of the American and St. Louis Bar Associations.

Among his many other books, well known titles include "International Law Applied to the Treaty of Peace," (1919); "The Lawless Law of Nations" (1925) and "The Roosevelt Coup d'Etat of 1933-40."

A. Philip Espinosa (Alvaro Felipe Espinosa), the great-grandson of Sterling E. Edmunds, has a Master's degree from Central Michigan University and a Bachelor's degree from the University of Colorado. Prior to a career spent in health care leadership, where he worked with employee and management teams to support the delivery of quality health care, he served in the U.S. Army, worked at the Pentagon, worked for a White House agency during the term of President Ronald Reagan and at The Library of Congress. He took a break from his health care executive role to work on some personal projects, such as this book. He currently lives with his family in the mountains west of Boulder, Colorado.

Mindi M. Espinosa, began her career in health care and then chose to dedicate herself to raising a family. She is engaged with various community and church groups. Today she works with her husband on a range of projects, providing research and editorial assistance. She lives with her family in the mountains west of Boulder, Colorado.

You can learn more about this and other related projects at www.thefederaloctopus.com.